THE MONGOL WARLORDS

GENGHIS KHAN · KUBLAI KHAN · HÜLEGÜ · TAMERLANE

DAVID NICOLLE
Plates by RICHARD HOOK

BROCKHAMPTON PRESS

LONDON

First published in the United Kingdom in 1990 by Firebird Books
P.O. Box 327, Poole, Dorset BH15 2RG

Copyright © 1990 Firebird Books Ltd
Text copyright © 1990 David Nicolle

This edition published 1998 by Brockhampton Press.
a member of Hodder Headline PLC Group

British Library Cataloguing in Publication Data

Nicolle, David 1944–
    The Mongol warlords: Genghis Khan, Kublai Khan, Hulegu, Tamerlane.
    1. Mongol Empire. Warlords
    I. Title
    950'.2'0922
ISBN 1 86019 4079

Designed by Kathryn S.A. Booth
Line illustrations and maps by David Nicolle
Colour plates by Richard Hook
Typeset by Inforum Typesetting, Portsmouth
Monochrome origination by Castle Graphics, Frome
Colour separations by Kingfisher Facsimile
Colour printed by Barwell Colour Print Ltd. (Midsomer Norton)
Printed at Oriental Press, Dubai, U.A.E.

Contents

GENGHIS KHAN
MONGOL WORLD CONQUEROR

Genghis Khan in old age, one of a series of idealised paintings of the Mongol rulers and their successors which was in the Chinese Imperial Portrait Gallery. The aged conqueror wears his hair in a pair of typical Mongol looped plaits, coiled behind his ears, and his coat has the double-breasted front designed to withstand Central Asia's ferocious climate (National Palace Museum, Taiwan).

The great Mongol conquests resulted in the creation of an exotic mixed civilization in much of Asia and the Middle East. By the start of the 15th century, when this miniature from the Fatih Album *was painted, the Mongol ruling elite could draw upon the traditions of China and the Muslim world, as well as those of Central Asia. All are reflected in this rider's costume, weapons and horse harness (Topkapi Museum, Ms. Haz.2153, f.6v, Istanbul).*

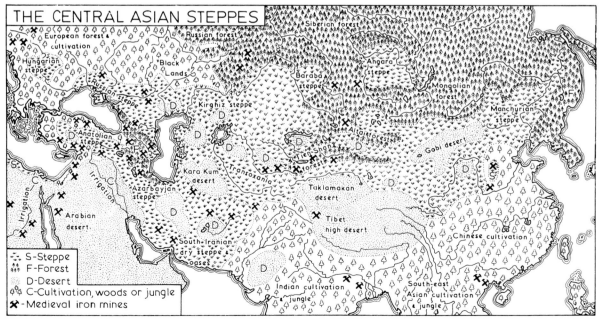

THE CENTRAL ASIAN STEPPES

European forest & cultivation
Hungarian steppe
Russian forest
Black Lands
Siberian forest
Angara steppe
Baraba steppe
Mongolian forest
Manchurian steppe
Anatolian steppe
Kirghiz steppe
Altai forest
Tien Shan forest
Gobi desert
Kara Kum desert
Transoxania
Taklamakan desert
Azarbayjan steppe
Arabian desert
Irrigation
South-Iranian dry steppe oasis
Tibet high desert
Chinese cultivation
Indian cultivation & jungle
South-east Asian cultivation & jungle

S-Steppe
F-Forest
D-Desert
C-Cultivation, woods or jungle
Medieval iron mines

6

Under the reign of Genghis Khan, all the country between Iran and the land of the Turks enjoyed such peace . . .

(Abu'l Ghazi)

In the Muslim countries devastated by Genghis Khan, not one in a thousand inhabitants survived . . .

(al Juvayni)

The Greatest Conqueror

Genghis Khan the Mongol is the most famous conqueror in history, perhaps even eclipsing Attila the Hun. Both these warrior leaders came from a similar background, the Eurasian steppes, that vast belt of open grassland stretching from the Carpathian mountains in eastern Europe to the Pacific Ocean. Both led Asiatic tribal hordes of Turkish or Turco-Mongol origin and both carved out immense empires. But whereas Attila's empire collapsed on his death, Genghis Khan's state and its still huge successors endured for many years. Attila was the first 'Turkish' conqueror to sweep into eastern Europe, his followers largely being of Altaic or Turco–Mongol origin. Many such peoples followed in his steps, periodically overrunning their more civilized neighbours to the south and west. Last of all came Genghis and his Mongols. The steppes would throw up later leaders and conquerors but none was able to pose a mortal threat to settled civilization. The world was changing, and Genghis Khan represented the steppe's final and greatest challenge to the urban cultures of China and the Middle East.

History is not always written by the winning side and the steppe nomads were seen by their victims – the settled peoples of China, the Muslim world and Russia – as the worst of barbarians. Mongol history was largely written by such foes, who almost invariably portrayed the Turco-Mongol nomads as the destroyers of cities, the ruin of agriculture and the exterminators of entire peoples. Even today, when the settled world has not only defeated the nomad threat but seems bent on destroying all vestiges of the nomadic way of life, few people see Genghis Khan and the society he stood for as anything but barbaric. The Mongols may sometimes be portrayed as free, unconstrained by law and modern morality, and even as romantic savages, but they remain the archetypal enemies of civilization and progress. Only dedicated students of nomadic culture seem able to strip the Mongol Hordes of their appalling reputation and to see them as they really were – ordinary human beings reacting to the world around them in a manner determined by their cultural heritage. Even so, such scholars are often warped by their own national prejudices, coming, as so many of them do, from countries whose memory of the Mongols is far from happy.

For millennia the Eurasian steppes poured forth periodic waves of nomadic invaders. Some were thrown back by their settled neighbours, others were rapidly absorbed and a few established wide empires that lasted for several generations. For the last two thousand years such waves consisted of Altaic or Turco-Mongol peoples and the cultural background that produced such amazingly successful horse warriors was remarkably consistent. Of course there was 'progress', cultural, political and technological change within the steppes, forests and mountains of central Asia. The area had its own, albeit poorly recorded, history even when it was not threatening its more literate neighbours. Nor was its population uniform. Most steppe tribes were now Turkish with a few Indo-European peoples surviving from earlier ages. But at the eastern end of the Eurasian steppes was a smaller group of tribes who spoke Mongol and Tatar tongues. They were, in general, more primitive and certainly poorer than their Turkish neighbours. Even more backward peoples inhabited the dense forests of Siberia to the north but, being concerned solely to survive in their inhospitable homeland, these hunter-gatherers had virtually no impact on their neighbours.

Genghis the Man

Not surprisingly the life and character of a man who made such an impact on history was later overlaid with legend. Some idealize the

The Central Asian composite bow eventually spread from China to Morocco and Spain. Though highly resistant to heat and cold, it could be badly affected by damp or humid climates, limiting its use in Western Europe or South Asia. This fully developed form shows how much further the composite bow could be drawn back, compared to the simple European bow. Its construction also gave a more regular release and thus a much greater power-to-weight ratio than, for example, the English longbow. The so-called Mongolian release, in which the bowstring was held by the thumb locked behind the first two fingers, also enabled the string to be pulled back to a more acute angle than was possible with the so-called Mediterranean release used throughout Christian Europe.

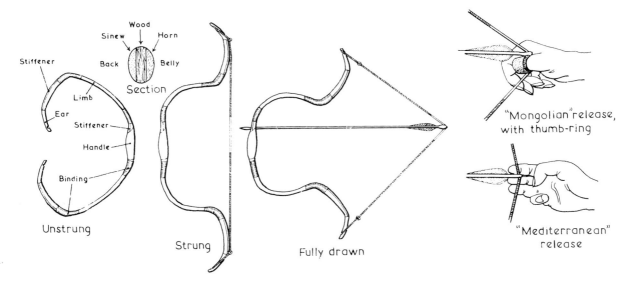

individual while others portray him as a sub-human monster. Fortunately one document survives that does not stem from one-time foes or 'civilized' successors. This is the *Secret History of the Mongols*, which, although it describes the life of a 'hero', also includes personal details less flattering to its subject. As a child Genghis Khan was, for example, afraid of dogs and he murdered his own half-brother Bekter. In later life the Khan took additional wives, though apparently remaining devoted to his now aged companion Börte. Other biographers record further details that shed light on Genghis Khan's character. The Muslim historian Rashid al Din quotes him as saying, in typical nomad manner, that the greatest pleasure in life was:

to cut my enemies to pieces, drive them before me, seize their possessions, witness the tears of those who are dear to them and to embrace their wives and daughters.

A Chinese philosopher who visited the Mongol court recorded the Khan's view of himself:

Heaven is weary of the luxury of China. I shall remain in the wilderness of the north. I shall return to simplicity and moderation once again. As for the clothes I wear and the food I eat, I shall have the same as cowherds and grooms and I shall treat my soldiers as brothers. In a hundred battles I have been at the forefront and within seven years I have performed a great work, for in the six directions of space all things are subject to one ruler.

Lake Baikal, in the Buryat autonomous republic of the USSR, is one of the world's deepest, clearest and coldest lakes. The Buryats are themselves a Mongol people and the modern Soviet frontier with Mongolia lies only a hundred kilometres to the south. In medieval times Lake Baikal was surrounded by various nomadic or forest-dwelling peoples of whom the Mongols were only one (Novosti Press).

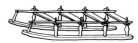

Behind such rhetoric some things remain clear. Not only was Genghis Khan obviously a natural leader and a fine general, but he was willing to learn even from his enemies. Nor was he entirely deaf to the voice of civilization and by the end of his life he had adopted a veneer of Chinese culture. Like so many men, he doubted the ability of his successors to carry on where he had left off and was also haunted by the consequences of his own death. He clearly feared for the future, once saying:

After us the people of our race will wear garments of gold, eat sweet greasy food, ride decorated horses, hold the loveliest of women, and will forget the things they owe to us.

There can be little doubt that Genghis Khan believed in his mission to unify the world, but realized that even he could not do such a thing in a single lifetime. So he toyed with notions – and potions – of immortality. This, however, was the one victory that eluded him.

The Mongols

Though hundreds of pagan Central Asian warrior graves have been excavated, relatively few helmets have been found, presumably indicating the value and scarcity of such pieces of armour. These two examples are variations on the framed and segmented construction. (upper) 13th century Mongol from southern Russia (ex-Pletnyeva); (lower) 13th–14th century Mongol from the upper reaches of the Yenesi river (Regional Museum, Abakan, USSR).

The Mongol tribes – Naimans, Keraits, Uirats, Merkits and Jalair – inhabited both slopes of the mineral-rich Altai mountains, northwards to Lake Baikal and south-eastwards into Manchuria. Their way of life was harsh but no more warlike than that of other central Asian nomads or even of the medieval European aristocracy. Little is known of these peoples before the twelfth century. To their east lived the Tatars who, more powerful than the Mongol tribes, enjoyed the support of the Chin or Jurchid kingdom of northern China. These Tatars were, however, hereditary foes of the Mongols. There also seems to have been a decline of settled civilization and an extension of nomadism in the Mongol area from the tenth to twelfth centuries.

Because they lived on the northern frontier of the steppes, on the edge of the vast Siberian forest, the Mongols were split into the groups – the sheep-herding pastoralists of the grasslands and the even poorer hunting-fishing clans of the forest fringe. The groups were not clear cut and a clan could move from one to the other depending on its circumstances – Genghis Khan's family did just this during his early life. The Mongol people were also divided into units such as the *ulus* (tribe), *oboq* (clan) and *yasun* (sub-clan or family). Though they had no towns, the steppe Mongols sometimes lived in huge, circular-tent cities. Those within reach of wooded areas used a round, felt-covered but wood-framed tent called a *ger* (wrongly referred to in Europe as a *yurt*). Though relatively easy to dismantle, the *ger* could also be transported intact on great wheeled wagons. Mongol clans living on the treeless steppe or close to the Gobi desert used wide, low, woollen tents called *maikhan*, which had more in common with those of the Arab bedouin.

Life, for the pastoral steppe-dwelling tribes, revolved around flocks of sheep, herds of horses and, to a lesser extent, two-humped Bactrian camels. Clans moved from pasture to pasture along well-established and generally agreed routes, according to the time of year. Only when such pastures failed would competition for somebody else's grassland lead to savage warfare, either within the tribe or against outsiders. Mutton, milk and cheese formed a basic diet, *qumiss* or fermented mare's milk being the nomad's most potent beverage. In fact, a remarkably high proportion of the Mongol nobility died young from over-drinking. Among these pastoralists a hereditary aristocracy was also highly developed. While such aristocrats hunted with hawks, all Mongols were hunters of one kind or another. They used bows, lassos and, in the forest, various kinds of trap. Yet it was the bow, used from horseback, that remained the nomad's primary weapon in both hunting and warfare. Archery was basic to Mongol military prowess and the fact that all able-bodied males – not to mention many women – were fully trained horse-archers gave the Mongols a considerable advantage over their settled neighbours. Men fought as a unit under their clan or tribal leader and, since women and children were capable of looking after the herds, all adult males were available for combat.

Relations between the Mongol and settled peoples were not always unfriendly. The nomads needed metals for their weapons, grain for bread and luxuries like tea and textiles for their aristocracy. These they generally obtained through trade, and while the settled civilizations welcomed nomad products like sheepmeat wool and horses, there can be little doubt that the nomads needed their agricultural neighbours more than the other way around. Despite this, however, the Mongols never appreciated settled life, though they did admire the things that it could provide. Such a paradox led to horrific results during Genghis Khan's career of conquest.

Whether any of the Mongol aristocratic élite fought as fully armoured cavalry before the days of Genghis Khan is far from clear. Lamellar armour for both men and horses had been known in central Asia for centuries and was, of course, common in China and the Muslim lands. It had also been used by some of the richer peoples of the steppes as well as by the settled oasis-dwelling peoples of the desert that lay between China or Islam and by the nomadic peoples of the steppe. During times of prosperity and conquest such sophisticated and expensive military equipment had appeared among nomadic peoples like the Kirghiz.

While Mongol society had its ruling clans and military élite, the tribes were in realilty very fragmented. Political bonds were complicated and, by the twelfth century, already changing. A system had emerged whereby a talented but relatively obscure warrior could build up his own following while at the same time attaching himself to a more powerful man as his *nöker* or 'comrade'. Genghis Khan was to use this almost

Most of the best examples of Central Asian art date from well before Genghis Khan's lifetime, for there had been a definite cultural decline prior to the rise of the Mongol World Empire. But the type of armour shown in 9th century art, like this stucco statuette from Karashar (Mingoi), changed very little over the next three centuries. This warrior has a segmented helmet, a full cuirass of lamellar construction, a spear and a round shield (British Museum).

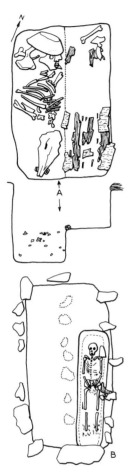

Graves containing both men and horses are common on the medieval Central Asian steppes. These 11th–14th century Turkish examples from the Elovsky burial mounds near the upper reaches of the Siberian Ob river include one example (A) containing a man and his horse. The man's bones have apparently been disturbed while the animal's were laid at a lower depth along with a very large cooking pot. A 13th–14th century example (B) only contains a man's bones which are laid on one side of a grave surrounded by a number of large stones (ex-Pletnyeva).

feudal system during his early years. Khans existed solely for the convenience of those they ruled. Chiefs were proclaimed when they were needed as war leaders or to settle serious disputes. Most came from aristocratic families, as did Genghis himself, but incompetence meant instant disqualification – an unsuccessful chief would simply not be obeyed. This 'political' freedom was in marked contrast to the iron discipline within Mongol armies once an effective leader had been accepted. Success was self-perpetuating as clans and tribes flocked to the standard of a victorious chief. In time of peace, however, the people merely agreed not to go against their khan's interests, but would equally resist interference in their own everyday lives. Genghis Khan's achievement was to create a government that not only governed but whose wide-ranging activities were accepted by those he ruled – or at least by those who wielded political and military clout.

Meanwhile, outside powers like China tried to keep the Mongols divided by balancing one leader against another so that none became too strong. When nomad leaders did rise to prominence they almost invariably raided the wealth of China. Some even made themselves masters of northern China before losing touch with their steppe origins and being absorbed within Chinese civilization. These earlier efforts to unify the Mongols are mostly shrouded in legend, though the last seems to have taken place in the middle of the twelfth century. It was foiled by the Chin rulers of northern China, who were themselves of nomad ancestry, aided by the Tatars, blood enemies of the Mongols. Genghis claimed to be descended from these earlier Mongol rulers and certainly followed in their footsteps.

The Mongols were thus backward but not totally barbaric. While many of their nomadic neighbours had been influenced by, or converted to, Buddhism, Manichaeism, Islam and Christianity, the Mongols remained largely Shamanist. Few details are known about their animist beliefs, which seem to have revolved around a multitude of spirits. They recognized a supreme god identified as the 'Everlasting Blue Sky', beneath whom was Itügen, goddess of fertility and the earth. Nevertheless the Mongols were impressed by the power – and magical potential – of more sophisticated faiths and their attitudes could often be summed up as seeking as much religious insurance as they could find. Their spiritual leaders, the shamans, were travelling seers who communicated with the spirit world through trances and were highly respected, not to say feared. They generally wore white, rode white horses and carried a drum and staff as their insignia. As well as officiating at blessings of one kind or another and supervising sacrifices and funeral celebrations, they prophesied by examining the cracks on a sheep's scorched shoulder blade. Their pronouncements often had a powerful impact on tribal politics. Like so many ancient religions, Mongol shamanism also involved prayer and ritual on high places, rocks, hills and mountains.

The Naiman were slightly more advanced than other Mongol tribes and may, in fact, have been half Turk – their territory lay closer to the urbanized Turkish Uighurs. Like the Uighurs, too, there were many at least nominal Christians among them. Nestorian Christian missionaries from Iraq and Iran had been active in central Asia for many centuries and a whole chain of bishoprics extended along the caravan routes from the Middle East to northern China. The Kerait tribespeople were in a similar situation. They too might have been half Turkish and had been nominally Christian since around the year 1000 A.D., at which time the Nestorian church probably had several million adherents. Many Kerait aristocrats still bore Christian names, and wildly exaggerated rumours of their existence as a mighty power in central Asia fuelled the legend of Prester John in far-away Christian Europe.

A Mongol ger or tent of a type popularly known in Europe as a yurt. In fact, the word yurt refers to a stretch of grazing land. Such tents consist of a wooden frame covered with sheets of felt and having a wooden door-frame. They could either be dismantled or transported intact aboard large carts (Historical Museum, Bern).

The Mongols' Neighbours

Between the Mongols and the teeming urban civilizations of China and Islam lay a series of smaller tribes and states. Some were nomadic, like the Mongols themselves. Others were partly settled or were essentially merchant communities inhabiting the chain of oases along ancient caravan routes between China and the Middle East – the so-called Silk Road. Most of these peoples could boast a higher material culture than the Mongols, though some Turkish tribes, such as the Kirghiz who lived north of the Naiman, remained primitive pagan nomads.

Of greater importance to the Mongols were the Chin or Jurshid rulers of Peking and northern China. They originally came from Manchuria, but by the early thirteenth century seem to have abandoned the steppes and forests to anyone who could control them. Instead, the Chin concentrated on their rivalry with the original Sung dynasty that still ruled southern China. Meanwhile, western China was ruled by yet another dynasty, the Hsi–Hsia, who were of Tibetan origin.

West of China itself were the Uighurs, an ancient Turkish people whose small but highly civilized oasis kingdoms were part Buddhist and part Christian. They had their own art, alphabet, literature and fully developed system of administration, while much of their peasant population was of Iranian origin. The Uighurs were themselves technically dependent on the Kara Khitai, whose ramshackle empire spread both sides of the Tien Shan mountains. These Kara Khitai were in turn descended from another nomadic Mongol people that had once ruled northern China. After being expelled by the Chin they carved out an ephemeral empire that now included a large segment of Islamic territory. Kara Khitai exploits had further fed the European legend of Prester John. While most of the population were Muslim Turks, plus Buddhist, Manichaean and Christian minorities, the Kara Khitai themselves retained a veneer of Chinese civilization and a tradition of imperial

Another, now lost, religion that flourished for several centuries in Central Asia was Manicheanism. Founded in 3rd century AD in Iran by Mani, who was known to his followers as 'The Apostle of Light', it attempted to integrate Persian Zoroastrianism, Buddhism and Christianity into a universal faith. Manicheanism may have influenced medieval European heresies such as the Albigensian Cathars. This fragment of a Manichean book shows 'The Feast of Bema' and comes from Khocho. Once again a warrior-hero at the top-left wears lamellar armour in alternate rows of blue and gold (West Berlin State Museums).

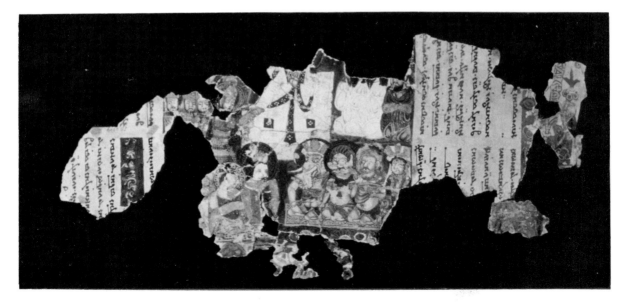

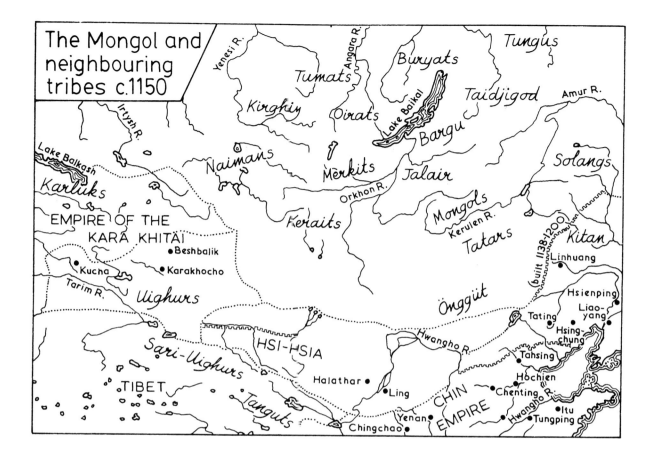

The Mongol and neighbouring tribes c.1150

grandeur. But the Kara Khitai state was now in great confusion, having been comprehensively defeated by its western neighbour, the Muslim Khwarazmshah of Transoxania. A Naiman Mongol prince also managed to seize the Kara Khitai throne in 1211. Brought up as a Christian but then converting to Buddhism, he now persecuted the Muslims who formed the bulk of his subjects. They in turn would soon welcome Genghis Khan as a liberator!

Beyond the Pamir mountains lay Transoxania, one of the richest provinces in the Muslim world, with its great cities such as Samarkand and Bukhara. This had been Islamic territory since the eighth century and, like China, was the seat of a flourishing, highly developed agricultural and urban civilization. Since 1215, when Ala al Din Muhammad conquered most of what is now Afghanistan almost the entire area had been ruled by the Khwarazmshahs. This short-lived but warlike dynasty sprang from Khwarazm, a fertile irrigated region south of the Aral sea. On the surface the Khwarazmshahs appeared very powerful. They, like their subjects, were Muslim. They had an enormous army, which included thousands of heavily armoured cavalry riding fully armoured horses. Unfortunately this largely consisted of unpopular Kipchak and Qangli Turkish tribal mercenaries, who quarrelled with the local Turco-Iranian troops. Unlike the armies of longer-established dynasties, which were generally built around a corps of dedicated *mamluks* of slave origin, Khwarazmshah forces consisted of mercenaries of dubious loyalty. Their empire was also a very new creation; it had grown with extraordinary speed and was not yet accepted by many of its subjects. Furthermore, the Khwarazmshah had quarrelled with the Abbasid Caliph in Baghdad, thus alienating a large section of his own religious establishment.

On the other hand, Transoxania and eastern Iran possessed large and strongly walled cities, many with citadels dating back to pre-Islamic times, while some had smaller fortified encampments dotted around them. For almost two hundred years, since the Seljuk Turkish invasion, most warfare in this area had been between competing Muslim dynasties rather than against a nomad threat from the steppes. Armies had aimed to seize cities and centres of government, while the countryside remained largely peaceful. Rural areas like Khwarazm might have been dotted with the small castles of a local aristocracy, but their defences were more ornamental than businesslike. The numerous fortified caravanserais, the 'motels' of the medieval Muslim world, were also designed to keep out brigands rather than armies.

North of the Muslim world the great Eurasian steppes stretched across what is now southern Russia and the Ukraine. The peoples of this area were again nomads of Turkish stock. Since the eleventh century the Kipchak tribes had dominated the region, while their predecessors, such as the Pechenegs, had been pushed into the forest fringe of Russia, into the Hungarian-ruled Carpathian mountains or across the Danube into Byzantine territory. Russia and Byzantium both had long experience of dealing with such nomads, often recruiting them as a vital element in their armies. The *Chernye Klobuky*, or 'Black Caps', who helped defend Russia's border principalities against the Kipchaks were, in fact, the still-nomadic descendants of Turkish tribes that had previously been ousted by the Kipchaks. Not, however, until the coming of the Mongols did a nomad people of the steppes seriously threaten the very existence and independence of medieval Russia.

East of Moscow, far from the steppes but on the fringe of the forests and the fertile agricultural 'Black Land' of what is now southern Russia, there existed a strange and isolated Muslim state – that of the Volga Bulgars. It was a flourishing and rich Turkish khanate deriving considerable wealth from trade up and down the mighty Volga river. Since the early twelfth century, however, these Volga Bulgars had faced pressure from the Russian principality of Vladimir. Other culturally isolated peoples survived on the southern edge of the steppes. They included the once-nomadic but now settled and Christian Alans, a warlike people

Genghis Khan (Temüchin) and his younger brother Qasar murder their half-brother Bekter in a quarrel over one fish and a small bird that they had caught while hunting.

of Iranian origin who inhabited the northern slopes of the Caucasus mountains. In the mountains of the Crimean peninsula there were still people of Germanic origin known as Saxi or Gothi. Partly descended from those Goths who passed through southern Russia during the fourth and fifth century Age of Migrations, they may also have included the offspring of Anglo-Saxon refugees who had sought service in the Byzantine army after the Norman conquest of England.

The abandoned temples of Chinese Central Asia have yielded many treasures of Buddhist art, including fragments of painted fabric, manuscripts and wall-paintings. This painted fabric from Khocho shows Vaishravana and, though the original subject was Indian, the style of painting and the armour are essentially Turco-Chinese. Here the figure wears a flexible armour with flap-like sleeves, basically similar to those perhaps felt or buff leather 'soft armours' worn by Mongol warriors in late 13th and 14th century Islamic art (West Berlin State Museums).

The Young Temüchin

The birth and early life of the man later to be known as Genghis Khan are shrouded in legend. He was born somewhere between 1155 and 1167 and was given the name Temüchin after a Tatar whom his father, a minor Mongol chief of the Borjigin clan, had recently slain. Temüchin, as the eldest son, took charge of the family when his father was in turn killed by the Tatars. Temüchin was, at this time, only about twelve or thirteen years old and his father's followers refused to serve a mere boy so he, his mother and brothers were forced to eke out a living as best they could.

These were hard times and the little family had to abandon the steppes in favour of the forested Kentai mountains. There they could hunt and fish and avoid their foes, who now included not only the Tatars but also rival Mongol families who had seized leadership of the Borjigin clan. Yet Temüchin already showed considerable powers of leadership, as well as ruthlessness. Later biographers described him as tall for a Mongol, strongly built and with 'cat's eyes'. He could endure extremes of heat or cold even better than most Mongols and was apparently indifferent to wounds. Temüchin's early life made him, in fact, a man of iron. Early adventures included skirmishing with rivals or robbers, losing and then recovering eight of the nine horses that were all his family owned, being captured, escaping and finally claiming the hand of Börte, daughter of a chieftain and the girl who had been promised to Temüchin since childhood.

But that lay in the future. For the present Temüchin and his brothers simply had to survive. The grimness of their way of life is betrayed in the episode in which Temüchin and his younger brother Qasar, the finest archer in the little group, ambushed and murdered their own half-brother Bekter. This was in revenge merely for his stealing a fish and a small bird that Temüchin had trapped. Though Bekter had been the son of another wife, their mother raged at them:

One of you was born clutching a clot of black blood! The other is like the savage Qasar dog after which he is named! . . . Except for your shadows you have no companions, except for your horses' tails you have no whips.

High in the Kentai mountains, Genghis Khan prayed to Tängri, God of the Eternal Blue Sky, after his wife Börte had been captured during an enemy raid.

Most Central Asian art from the centuries before Genghis Khan's rise to power shows religious subjects, reflecting the many faiths that vied for the souls of Turks and Mongols. This wall-painting in a basically Chinese style, though with strong Indian and Turkish elements, is a fine example of Buddhist art from Kumtara made at the height of Turkish Uighur civilization (West Berlin State Museums).

Yet, she accused, the brothers could not even win back leadership of their father's own clan. Temüchin would later do much more than retrieve his father's heritage, but in the meantime he slowly gathered a small following of warriors through his skill as a raider and by his loyalty to his own men. He would, they said, take the coat off his back and give it away.

The story of Temüchin's wife Börte adds a welcome touch of romance to an otherwise savage story. The two finally succeeded in getting wed at around the same time that Temüchin allied himself with the powerful Kerait tribe. Only a short while later the little band was ambushed by a party of raiders from the Merkit tribe, Börte being captured. Temüchin escaped though the speed of his horse and because one of his mother's servants, Qu'aqchin, had heard the drumming hoofbeats of their enemy. He fled back to the Kentai mountains where, climbing the highest peak, he threw his cap upon the ground and put his belt around his neck in sign of supplication. Then he prayed to Tängri, the Eternal Blue Sky:

Thanks to the weasel's ear and fox's eye of old Qu'aqchin I have escaped with my life. I have been able to slip with my horse along the paths of deer and elk.

So saying, Temüchin bowed nine times and made an offering of fermented mare's milk. (He seems to have had a special reverence for Tängri and would pray to the Eternal Blue Sky at all crucial moments in his life.) A sudden raid on the Merkit camp soon rescued Börte and few cared openly to express doubts about the fatherhood of the son she bore nine months after her capture. Suffice to say that Jöchi, though the eldest of Genghis Khan's sons, was never permitted to play a leading role in Mongol affairs.

One of Temüchin's first moves had been to take his warrior companions and less nobly born *nöker* followers into an alliance with a leading anti-Tatar chieftain, Togrul Khan of the Kerait tribe. Temüchin was, of course, still a minor player in the tangled and bloody politics of Mongolia, but he soon proved his worth to the Kerait. At the same time he was careful not to alienate Togrul, despite his own rapidly increasing prestige. Instead, the young Mongol warrior concentrated on destroying his family's hereditary foes, the Tatars. In this he was helped by the Chin rulers of northern China, who were growing concerned about Tatar power. In 1199, with Chin support and encouragement, the Keraits and their ally Temüchin inflicted a serious defeat on the overweening Tatars. In gratitude the Chin declared Togrul to be *wang*, or king, of areas north of China. It might have been around this time that Temüchin adopted the title of Genghis (more accurately Chingiz or 'Oceanic') Khan of the purely Mongol tribes.

Genghis's next few campaigns were theoretically fought on behalf of the Kerait. The Naiman were defeated and Togrul became the most powerful ruler in Mongolia. His realm was, in fact, to be the foundation upon which Genghis Khan built his own empire. But there was still much hard fighting. Genghis was himself once struck in the neck by an arrow that cut an artery, whereupon Jelme, one of his earliest companions, took him from the battlefield and sucked the clotted blood until the wound closed. Did Jelme know the damage that a blood clot could cause to his leader's unconscious brain, or was this another example of traditional medicine saving a life without anyone quite knowing how the treatment worked? Jelme's own story is an interesting one. He would later become a leading Mongol general, but his father had been a humble smith who arrived in Temüchin's camp 'with his bellows on his shoulders'. This man came from an area that had, for centuries, been famous for its sword-makers and his rôle may hint at the vital part the armourers of the mountains played in Genghis Khan's rise to power.

Genghis won another loyal follower at around this time when, after defeating a rival tribe and having massacred a suitable percentage of its captive warriors, the Mongol leader came across a young bowman who had once brought down the Khan's own horse. When the young warrior proudly admitted this fact, Genghis pardoned him, renamed him Jebe, 'the arrow', and thus earned the unswerving loyalty of a man who would eventually become the most illustrious of Mongol military commanders. When the Tatars were finally overthrown, their fate was less generous. The entire people was virtually wiped out, with only a few survivors being gradually absorbed by the Mongol tribes. It is, therefore, ironic that the Tatar name lived on, to be given by many of the Mongols' foes to the Mongols themselves. In Europe the name was corrupted to Tartar, perhaps implying that these savage and unknown eastern conquerors had sprung from Tartarus, an ancient name for Hell.

The almost inevitable break with the Keraits came in 1203. It was a decisive moment in Genghis Khan's career. A Kerait ambush was betrayed and a furious battle was subsequently fought near the headwaters of the Khalka river. Genghis Khan's outnumbered army got the worst of this fight and he had to retreat north, towards Siberia and into the inhospitable wastes of northern Manchuria. Only a few followers now remained with him, but their loyalty was eventually to be repaid a hundred-fold. For the present they simply had to survive until the Kerait coalition of allied tribes quarrelled and fell apart. As soon as this happened, Genghis returned to the offensive and crushed the Kerait. Their leader, Togrul, fled to Naiman territory, where he was accidentally killed by a man who failed to recognize him. Perhaps seeing in this the hand of Providence, the Kerait people accepted the fact of Genghis Khan's leadership and thereafter served him loyally. The Khan himself was not quite so confident and had the Kerait clans distributed among the Mongol tribes, but at least there was no massacre.

Genghis Khan's next move was to attack the Naiman, the only people now in a position to challenge his domination of Mongolia. This he did before they could act as a focus for the many scattered remnants of

The 'Demon with a Lamp' in this Uighur wall-painting from a Buddhist cave temple at Bezeklik is more Turkish in style. Such painting would have an influence on Islamic Middle Eastern art following the Turkish and Mongol conquests (West Berlin State Museums).

peoples whom the Mongols had already destroyed. The defeat of the Naiman had all the elements of a heroic tragedy. Overwhelmed in a furious battle, the mortally wounded Naiman chieftain retreated to a hill, where he asked his companions who were the four warriors who now pursued him like wolves. A one-time comrade of Genghis Khan who now fought for the Naiman replied that they were the four hunting dogs of Temüchin:

fed on human flesh and leashed with iron chains; their skulls are of brass, their teeth hewn from rock, their tongues like swords.

Asking the identity of the man who followed them, the Naiman chief was told, 'that is my blood-brother Temüchin, wearing a coat of iron'. As the Naiman lay dying, the last of his followers charged down the hill upon the victorious Mongols. Genghis, admiring their courage and loyalty, wanted to spare them, but they spurned his offer and fought till all were slain.

Unification of Central Asia

With the submission of the Naiman, Genghis Khan became effective ruler of all Mongolia. In 1206 he summoned a great *quriltai*, or assembly of the leaders of the people, near the source of the Onon river. Here he was proclaimed supreme Khan of all Turkish and Mongol tribes 'who lived in felt tents' in eastern Asia. A famous shaman named Kökchü declared that Genghis was Khan 'by the strength of the Eternal Heaven'. Thus fortified with divine approval, the new ruler selected a wise judge to reward those who had remained faithful and punish those who had betrayed him. Such judgements were then noted down in 'Blue Books', which later became the foundation of Genghis Khan's legal code.

It had been a great achievement, but it also posed Genghis Khan with the problem that faced all those nomad leaders who managed to unify the warlike and predatory tribes of Central Asia. What should he do now? Ready at his command stood a magnificent military machine, but one that would quarrel and start falling apart if it was not soon used. The obvious answer was to direct the tribesmen's warlike energies outwards. Thus Genghis was set, almost inevitably, on a career of conquest. So the only real question was whom to attack first. Meanwhile the shaman Kökchü continued to proclaim the Khan's Divine Mission but also started meddling in his family affairs. At last, Genghis Khan, despite his fear of the shaman's magical powers, heeded the warnings of his mother and his wife Börte. Kökchü had to be removed but, perhaps through fear of the shaman's powers, this was done by breaking the magician's back and thus shedding no blood.

At first the concept of Divine Mission referred only to the unification of the Mongols. Other nomadic peoples of central Asia were soon drawn into the grand design, but only later did a seemingly endless succession of victories lead to the idea of a Universal Empire – to the theory, in fact, of World Conquest. Meanwhile Genghis Khan had to mop up the neighbouring Turkish tribes. This he did between 1207 and 1209. The wild Kirghiz of the north submitted, as did some of the civilized Uigurs to the south. While other central Asian leaders ducked and weaved, or resisted and were destroyed, the Uighur king Barchuq, realizing that these were epoch-making changes, sent a fulsome message to Genghis Khan:

It is with great joy that I learned of the glory of my lord Genghis Khan. The clouds have made way for the sun, the river is freed from ice. Grant me your favour and I will dedicate my strength to you, I shall be as a fifth son to you.

By this means the Uighurs not only survived the conquest but flourished and become the Mongols' teachers in government and the arts. They may even have had much advice to offer in the techniques of siege warfare, because they were students of Chinese as well as Islamic military science.

Genghis Khan's troops also raided the rich but peaceful Hsi-Hsia kingdom of western China, which lay on the far side of the Gobi desert. Here the Mongol armies had their first clash with a settled agricultural and urban state. They learned much by the experience and forced the Hsi-Hsia king to recognize the overlordship of Genghis Khan. A much tougher proposition was the Chin state of northern China, which had its capital at Peking.

Genghis Khan's career sometimes reads like a catalogue of unbroken victories, but this was not really the case. His first attacks on the Chinese heartland were not very effective. The countryside was raided, but the Mongols could not take fortified towns. When they withdrew, the Chin army returned to repair the damage, resupply its garrisons and strengthen their fortifications. Nor could the Mongol tactic of massacring or dispersing a defeated foe work among the teeming millions of China; there were simply too many people to kill! Nor could the bulk of the unwarlike Chinese peasantry be enlisted in the Mongol army. Meanwhile the Chin themselves, though now a settled ruling dynasty, retained the martial vigour of their nomad ancestors and fought hard, aided by Chinese science and Chinese military engineers. (Contrary to popular opinion, though, recent archaeological research has shown that the Great Wall of China – at least in its present form – did not exist in Genghis Khan's day.) Even the month-long sack of Peking in 1215, after numerous attacks, did not mark the end of Chin resistance. In fact Mongol assaults on northern China continued almost unabated until Genghis Khan's death. Only under his successors was the invasion brought to a successful conclusion.

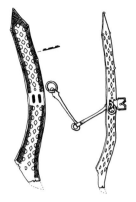

A few items such as this iron bit with silver inlay decoration show the splendour of a Turco-Mongol chieftain's military equipment. It dates from the 13th or 14th century and comes from a grave on the upper reaches of the Yenesi river (Regional Museum, inv. 6074, Minusinsk, USSR).

Mongol victories were more dramatic to the west. The realm of the Kara Khitai fell, with hardly a struggle, to Genghis Khan's loyal general, Jebe, in 1218. This also brought the remaining Uighur lands under Genghis Khan's control. Meanwhile Jebe showed himself to be a statesman, or at least politician, as well as a fine general. He ended the persecution of Islam that had characterized the last independent Kara Khitai ruler and was thus welcomed as a liberator by the Turkish Muslims of what is now the westernmost province of the Chinese People's Republic. This success meant that the Mongols' frontier had reached the Islamic world. On the far side of the towering Pamir mountains lay the rich and populous Muslim province of Transoxania and beyond that Iran. Here, however, the Mongols would not be so welcome.

Invasion of Islam

Genghis Khan's unification of Mongolia and eastern Turkestan involved considerable bloodshed but relatively little material damage. His raids on China had caused destruction but nothing out of the ordinary for a nomad invasion of the Celestial Empire. But his march west, across the Pamir mountains into the Muslim heartland, was to be something quite different. It was these campaigns that gave Genghis Khan his unenviable reputation of being one of the greatest destroyers of all time.

The appalling havoc wrought by Genghis Khan's armies across this part of the Middle East sometimes makes it seem as if the Mongol leader had a particularly vindictive attitude towards Islamic civilization. Yet his kindly treatment of Muslims in the old Kara Khitai realm, and the fact that Muslim Turks were counted among his soldiers, show that Genghis Khan had no particular hatred of Islam. The carnage resulted from political and military considerations, not from cultural ones.

After overthrowing the last Kara Khitai ruler, Genghis Khan found himself facing a man as warlike as himself, the Khwarazmshah Ala al Din Muhammad, ruler of a state that had appeared on the scene almost as suddenly as had Genghis Khan's own realm. Whether the clash between these two would-be rulers of central Asia resulted from the Khwarazmian massacre of one of Genghis Khan's merchant caravans and the murder of his ambassador, or was engineered by Genghis Khan, can never be known. What is certain is that in 1218 Genghis Khan sent a letter implying that the Khwarazmshah was his vassal. Ala al Din sent a non-committal and restrained reply. Then came the episode of the caravan, whose members probably did include spies, as the Khwarazmians claimed. The Khwarazmian ruler refused to punish those who had committed the outrage and, having recently defeated not only the Kara

Khitai in Transoxania but also his rivals in Afghanistan, he confidently prepared for war.

Perhaps the Khwarazmshah thought that the Mongols had their hands full in China. If so, he was wrong. Genghis Khan led an army up into the Irtysh valley where, during the summer of 1219, they fattened up their horses. In response, Ala al Din distributed his army among the strongly walled cities of Transoxania. Presumably he expected the Mongol attack to take the form of a short-lived raid and so decided not to oppose it in open battle. Late in 1219 the Mongols advanced on three fronts. Genghis Khan's eldest son, Jöchi, headed for the city of Jend. His other sons, Jagatai and Ogödäi, marched on Utrar. A third column rode towards Khojend. In February of the following year Genghis himself moved with his main force straight for the great city of Bukhara. Here the Khwarazmian garrison tried to cut its way out – but was butchered to a man. This first defeat seems to have shattered Ala al Din's confidence. His army still outnumbered that of the invaders, but it remained tied down in a series of

This very damaged Buddhist manuscript fragment comes from pre-Mongol Murtuq. It shows a lokapala, perhaps Virudhaka, with an apparently straight sword, a cuirass that opens down the front and is also held by buckled shoulder straps, and a very raised collar. Some lamellar armour can also be seen on his right shoulder (West Berlin State Museums).

garrisons while its morale was further undermined by its ruler's inaction.

In each city the Khwarazmian garrison found itself outnumbered by the fast-moving Mongol army. One by one the cities fell. Almost everywhere the defenders were slaughtered, even if they surrendered, and civic and religious leaders put to the sword. Their cities were burned, either intentionally or while being sacked. If resistance was prolonged, the entire population, including non-combatants, women and children, was methodically butchered. In general the skilled artisans were spared, either to be transported back to Mongolia or to be employed in the next siege. Each defeat further undermined morale so that, in many cases, the scattered garrisons begged to join the Mongol forces, though they were rarely permitted to do so.

Amid the chaos and defeat, some Khwarazmian troops still fought hard. At Khojend, in the mineral-rich, armour-producing valley of Ferghana, a famous Turkish warrior named Timur Melik (Iron King) withdrew to a fortress in the middle of the broad Syr Darya river. There he and a thousand picked followers defied up to twenty thousand Mongols, who used fifty thousand slave labourers to dam and divert the river. On his side Timur Melik had twelve large river boats manned by archers who daily harassed the shore-bound Mongols. When at last all was lost, Timur and his men took to these ships, bursting through a chain with which the Mongols had hoped to block the Syr Darya. Before reaching a pontoon bridge that would certainly had barred their escape, they landed and disappeared into the desert fastness of the Qyzil Qum (Red Sands).

The destruction that the Mongols wrought as they swept into Afghanistan and eastern Iran grew even more savage. Paralysed by their ruler's moral collapse, the Khwarazmian garrisons were unable to put up any effective resistance. Ala al Din Muhammad himself fled, first to Balkh, then to Nishapur, Qazwin, and finally to a tiny island in the Caspian sea, pursued all the way by a detachment of Mongol horsemen. These Mongols, under Jebe and Sübötäi, either sacked or simply by-passed the terror-stricken cities in their path. At last, in December 1220, Ala al Din died of exhaustion and despair on his little island. Meanwhile Genghis Khan had been spreading chaos across the eastern parts of the Khwarazmian realm. In the very month that Ala al Din died, the city of Urganj, the first seat of Khwarazmian power, fell after seven days of bitter fighting in which the entire population, women and children included, took part. Not only were the few survivors wiped out, but the Mongols diverted the very course of the Syr Darya river so that, for some years, it flowed through the crumbling ruins. Bukhara and Samarkand had already fallen. Merv, Nishapur and Balkh followed by the spring of 1221. Genghis Khan even destroyed the tombs of those who had once made this area rich and powerful. At Merv the mausoleum of the great Turkish Sultan Sinjar was burned and his grave emptied.

The Kalyan minaret, built in 1127 AD in Bukhara, is one of relatively few monuments from Islamic Transoxania which survived Genghis Khan's invasion intact. It is over forty-six metres high and is built of brick (Novosti Press).

25

Near Tus the Mongols obliterated the tomb of Harun al Rashid, the Caliph celebrated in the *Arabian Nights*, who had ruled the golden age of Arab-Iranian civilization in the eighth century. At Bamyan in Afghanistan, beneath the gaze of towering rock-hewn statues of Buddha, even the animals were slaughtered in revenge for the death of Genghis Khan's favourite grandson, killed in the fighting.

There had already been quarrels between Genghis Khan's sons, Jöchi and Jagatai, during the siege of Urganj, though Genghis solved this problem by depriving both of their commands and placing his third son, Ögotäi, in overall command. Jagatai made peace with his father but Jöchi took his men away north of the Aral sea. He was still refusing to bring them back under his father's command when, even as Genghis prepared to march against him, he suddenly died.

At last, the Muslims seemed to pull themselves together and managed to inflict a serious defeat upon the marauding Mongols. Ala al Din's son Jalal al Din had taken over leadership of the resistance after escaping from Urganj to Ghazna in Afghanistan. There many of the remaining Khwarazmian forces rallied to his standard and at Parwan, in an epic two-day battle, Jalal al Din defeated a large Mongol army – the first victory since the invasion had begun. Yet even so, this was not Genghis Khan's main force. The Mongol leader now turned upon Jalal al Din, forcing him back to the banks of the mighty Indus in Pakistan. There, on 24th November 1221, the Muslim forces were trapped with their backs against the river. A desperate fight ensued, but the Mongols had overwhelmingly superior numbers and the outcome was rarely in doubt. No one shot at Jalal himself, for Genghis Khan wanted him alive. Around midday Jalal al Din led a final charge, forcing the Mongols back. Realizing that his men could not break out of the trap, the Khwarazmian leader wheeled them around and galloped for the river. His horse leapt from the twenty-foot-high bank and, with Jalal still clutching his shield and banner, swam to the far shore. The Mongols wanted to follow, but Genghis restrained them. Instead he pointed to Jalal and told his sons, who were at his side, that there went a hero upon whom they could model themselves. Those of Jalal's soldiers who failed to escape were, of course, killed on the spot.

Genghis Khan went on to ravage a good part of Muslim northern India before returning, in the spring of 1222, to the cooler mountains of Khurasan. Jalal's gallant but futile resistance now brought a horrible vengeance down upon the people of Herat. Thinking that the tide had finally turned, they rose against their Mongol conquerors. Genghis never forgave any form of rebellion and so, knowing that they could expect no mercy, the citizens of Herat resisted for six terrible months. When the city finally fell it was said that one million six hundred thousand people were massacred. Yet at least one Muslim defender survived, through what must have seemed a miracle. He was a fully

armoured volunteer soldier who, missing his footing while walking along the ramparts, fell from the city wall and rolled down the hill into the Mongol lines. Not only did he survive this horrendous plunge, but the superstitious Mongols, amazed by the fact that he rose to his feet unscathed, took him prisoner and eventually set him free.

The large 'Battle Plate' in the Freer Gallery has recently been recognized as illustrating an event in the brief Islamic counter-attack against Genghis Khan's invasion of eastern Iran. Probably made to celebrate Jalal al Din's short-lived reconquest of Iran in 1223–9 AD, it shows the men who vainly stood up to the Mongol assault (Freer Gallery, Washington).

The Mongol Army

The army was basic to the structure, organization and character of the Mongol Empire. All fit adult males in Mongol society were warriors and remained so until the age of sixty. Everyone learned to ride in childhood and at an early age they were also expected to fight with bow, spear or sword, depending on their wealth or status. Thus, a Mongol ruler could, at least in theory, summon a huge and well trained citizen army. On the other hand, it should be remembered that this was more a tribal militia than a professional force. Archery skills were very advanced, since the bow was also a hunting weapon, but other military skills may have been inferior to those of many of the Mongols' foes. The standard of horsemanship was also high, although central Asian ponies were by no means as strong or fast as the heavier stall-fed chargers of professional cavalry armies. Outside the aristocratic Mongol military élite, individual skills with the sword and spear are unlikely to have been great. When it came to manoeuvring as a cohesive unit, responding to orders and maintaining discipline in adverse circumstances, even Mongol cavalry techniques were probably inferior to those of, for example, the slave-recruited *ghulam* and *mamluk* warriors of the Muslim world.

For the bulk of the Mongol army, military training revolved around hunting. The most important hunt was the annual *nerge*, a massive expedition in search of game to provide meat for the long Mongolian winter. In the *nerge* a huge ring of horsemen gradually drew together, forcing trapped animals into a small space where, after the leader had loosed his first arrow, the killing would begin. Such a hunt needed discipline as well as skill. The tactics of the *nerge* were applied to Mongol warfare, though here the quarry was men.

As Genghis Khan's empire grew, his army became decreasingly Mongol in any ethnic sense. Even in the early days it had been drawn from a confederation of Turco–Mongol (or Ural–Altaic) tribes to which Uighurs, Kirghiz and others were gradually added. By the time the Khan died in 1227, Turkish warriors greatly outnumbered real Mongols whose role was now that of a leading élite. At the summit of the military and social pyramid was Genghis Khan's own family, which became known as the *altan uruk* or Golden Clan. Beneath them was a tribal aristocracy of *ba'atut* (nobles), *noyan* (chiefs), *nökud* (free-warrior retainers), *arad* and *qarachu* (commoners), and non-Mongol *unaghan boghul* (serfs). This was echoed in the structure of the army, where men held personal allegiance to their leaders – *arban* (captains of ten), *jagun* (of hundreds), *mingghan* (of thousands) and *tumen* (of ten thousands). In reality these units are unlikely to have consisted of such exact round numbers. In many cases they would not have been up to strength and it also seems that, when the need arose, units could be enlarged above their official size. While the army theoretically consisted only of free men, its semi-professional backbone came from the *tarkhan* minor nobility. Senior officers were drawn from the aristocratic *noyan*.

A small part of the Mongol army was, of course, fully professional. This was the Khan's own ten-thousand-strong guard, which was divided into day and night guards, plus a separate unit of bowmen. Not only did a common guardsman rank above a captain of one thousand from the ordinary army, but Genghis Khan's generals were almost always drawn from his guard. Another feature that impressed foreign observers was the obedience of the Mongol army. Military disobedience

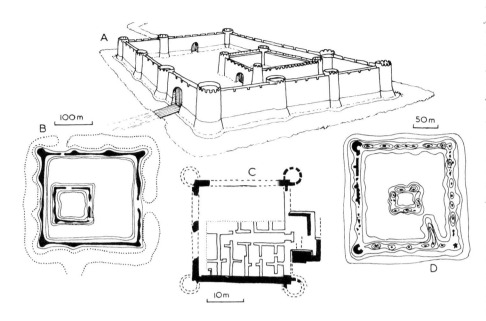

A

B

C

D

The Mongols are often said to have lacked skill in siege warfare, but this is probably greatly exaggerated. While the Mongol tribes of Genghis Khan's youth may rarely have attempted to attack fortified places, the Uighur and other Turkish peoples who soon formed the bulk of Genghis Khan's conquering armies had their own long heritage of fortification. This drew upon Chinese and Islamic traditions as well as local knowledge. (A–B) Reconstruction and unexcavated site plan of an Uighur fortress near the upper Yenesi river in the Tuva ASSR of the USSR, 10th century (after Pletnyeva). Such large castles were basically in the Chinese style. (C) Plan of the partially excavated Castle number 28 in the Berkut-Kalineski Oasis of Khwarazm, south of the Aral Sea, 12th–13th century (after Tolstov). Turco-Islamic Central Asia, particularly the frontier province of Khwarazm, was dotted with hundreds of fortifications, from small local castles such as this to enormous defended cities. Their design drew upon Central Asian, Chinese, ancient Iranian, Islamic and even Romano-Byzantine tradition – all of which became available to the Mongols. (D) Unexcavated site plan of Kumiyan fortress near Utrar, 12th–13th century (after Akhishev). This area was the furthest frontier of the Muslim world, north of Tashkent and within striking distance of Lake Balkash. Though built shortly before Genghis Khan's conquest, the fortresses of Utrar later served as Mongol bases and played a vital role in Tamerlane's eastern campaigns.

or lying to a superior were serious crimes, and this was enshrined in Genghis Khan's famous *yasaq* or code of laws. This supposedly dated from the *quriltai* of 1206, though in reality the laws were not fully codified until after the Khan's death. During Genghis Khan's day the Mongol soldier received no pay, other than his share of any booty, as warfare was seen as part of everyday life rather than a special job that needed payment. On the contrary, Mongol troops paid their commanders a small sum called *gübchür* as a sort of national insurance to help disabled or poverty-stricken old soldiers.

The tactical organization of the Mongol army reflected age-old Turco–Mongol steppe tradition. Overall it was divided into three divisions facing China to the east (the left wing), Turkestan and the Muslim world to the south-west (the centre), and the western steppes and Russia to the west (the right wing). This clearly shows the orientation of steppe policy and the Mongols' intended targets – the settled peoples to their south rather than the primitive folk of the Siberian forests to their north. On Genghis Khan's death over sixty thousand troops faced east, nearly forty thousand faced west, with the remainder either in the centre or in reserve.

The whole question of the size of Mongol armies has yet to be satisfactorily answered. According to their foes these armies were enormous, yet it is also clear that many of the territories that they invaded could not have supported the number of horses needed by such armies – Mongol ponies lived off available pasture and each warrior

The armour worn by the praying warrior on the left of this Buddhist temple wall-painting from Tumsuk, in what is now Chinese Central Asia, is virtually identical to that on the statuette from Karashar. The alternate rows of lamellae on the cuirass are painted grey and green, almost certainly indicating iron and bronze, just as has been found in a fragmentary 8th century Iranian cuirass. The same convention is seen in 12th and 13th century Islamic art and was continued well into the Mongol period. The figure on the right wears a form of perhaps less realistic quilted armour based on earlier Indian art (West Berlin State Museums).

went to war with a string of around four extra mounts. The inflated size of Mongol armies in the eyes of their enemies could result from their terrifying mobility, which was far greater than that of their non-nomadic foes, and on the natural tendency of defeated enemies to exaggerate the numbers of those who beat them. The Mongols also sometimes turned their spare horses to advantage by mounting straw dummies on their backs, hoping thus to overawe their enemy by numbers alone. The best available estimates put Genghis Khan's army at a little over one hundred thousand in 1206, and almost one hundred and thirty thousand at his death. Thus Islamic estimates of seven to eight hundred thousand men invading Transoxania alone are wildly improbable.

The Mongol ability to fight in all seasons also gave Genghis Khan a distinct advantage. His assault up the frozen rivers of Russia is the only recorded successful winter invasion of that country. The Mongols' possession of a rudimentary military staff system also gave them an edge, at least over their less-sophisticated steppe and east–European foes. Chinese and Islamic armies had even more highly developed military administrations, though these still failed to save them from the Mongol fury. The Mongols' sense of proper administration never seems to have left them, even when they were organizing the slaughter of thousands of people. In some cases they carefully attempted to wipe out four-fifths of a rural population, leaving the remaining fifth to recover under the guidance of a Mongol or loyal local official.

Genghis Khan's 'general staff' also administered the army, the battle layout of which may be reflected in a plan preserved in a thirteenth century Indo-Persian manuscript. This purports to portray 'The Battle Layout of the Turks when their Khaqan is present'. Though it may have more to do with the Kara Khitai than their Mongol successors, it obviously describes an army that, divided into nine sections and including a good number of infantry, was essentially organized for steppe horse-archery tactics. Cavalry and their 'corresponding infantry' were stationed on the left and right wings, the left flank and left rear. A lack of infantry on the right flank and right rear, and the identification of the right-flank cavalry's rôle as 'outflanking the foe', indicated that the task of the infantry concentrated on the left side was to resist similar outflanking by the enemy. The commander was stationed in front in the centre, where he also had the armoury under his direct control. Behind him were his household, together with technical troops (who presumably included any siege engineers), and herds of animals to provide food on the hoof. At the rear of the army were, on the left, spare horses guarded by infantry and cavalry, and, on the right side, the sick or injured, plus common prisoners with a cavalry escort. At the centre of the rear rode important hostages, also with a cavalry escort, and such fodder as a nomad force carried. At the head of such an army one might imagine the

white standard with its nine 'flames' or horse-tails that Genghis Khan had adopted as his imperial banner.

In addition to field armies, large or small, the Mongols organized special regional forces known as *tamma*. These were originally stationed near the edge of the steppe, close enough to newly conquered territory to maintain order and, when opportunity arose, to extend the Khan's domains. Such *tamma* later developed into the permanent armies of local governors and, after the breakup of the Empire, of regional Khanates.

Even before Genghis Khan died, non-Mongol non-Turkish troops were being enlisted. At first they served only in their own regions and tended to supply those infantry, siege-warfare or technical skills that the Mongols lacked, though of course Genghis Khan already had the technically sophisticated Uighurs at his command. The rôle of prisoners as sappers, miners and mere cannon-fodder driven ahead of Mongol ranks to absorb enemy fire cannot fairly be regarded as enlisting native troops. Chinese soldiers were, however recruited in large numbers almost from the time of the first Mongol invasion. Many deserted the Chin in favour of what they correctly judged to be the winning side. They proved invaluable against the strongly walled cities of their native land and when campaigning in intensively cultivated rice-growing regions criss-crossed by numerous waterways. When Genghis Khan attacked Muslim Transoxania, he left only 23000 Mongol troops under Muqali to carry on the fight against the Chin. But Muqali could also call upon an equal number of Chinese auxiliaries and with this relatively small army he continued to expand Genghis Khan's territory in northern China.

This 9th century Central Asian cave painting, from a temple at Kumtara, shows a civilian in Chinese costume being seized by two soldiers. Though their armour is simplified it is obviously of lamellar construction, as is the horse-armour on the left. All such equipment, even including the horseman's straight sword, continued to be used by Mongol and Turkish Central Asian warriors into and even beyond the 13th century (West Berlin State Museums).

The use of Persian troops as static garrisons and to guard mountain passes does not seem to have become common until after Genghis Khan's death. There were, however, Muslims in his army as early as 1219. These were Turks of the partly settled, partly nomadic Qarluq tribe who, inhabiting the region just south of lake Balkash, had formed part of the Kara Khitai state. As Muslims they had felt liberated by Genghis Khan's overthrow of the last Buddhist Kara Khitai ruler and thereafter served the conqueror loyally.

Mongol Warfare

Though Mongol tactics relied upon horse-archery and were fully within the ancient military traditions of the Eurasian steppes, there is no doubt that the Mongols used them to more devastating effect than any of their predecessors since Attila the Hun.

The bulk of Mongol tribesmen could fight only as lightly armoured or even unarmoured horse-archers, so a smaller élite of close-combat troopers was also needed. Such men often rode armoured horses and fought with sword, spear or mace. Their task was to crush a foe once the latter had been dispersed, disorganized, decimated and demoralized by the constant harassment of Mongol horse-archers. Their role was, in fact, a traditionally aristocratic one found in almost all cavalry armies; namely to finish off the foe. In open battle the Mongols normally tried to encircle their enemy, as they would animals during their annual *nerge* hunt. Full use was made of feigned flight, ambushes and surprise attacks from unexpected directions, all of which demanded greater man-oeuverability than that of the enemy, plus first-class communications between widespread units. And of course, there was the moral effect of simple terrorism. According to one tradition, Genghis Khan's advice to his warriors was: 'In daylight watch with the vigilance of an old wolf, at night with the eyes of a raven, and in battle fall upon the enemy like a falcon.'

Mongol scouts had the benefit of hunting experience and excellent fieldcraft. Once battle was joined, Mongol armies pressed home their attacks only when reasonably certain of victory, or on the rare occasions when they were themselves trapped. Light horse-archers attacked and wheeled away, one unit replacing another so that the enemy endured a constant barrage of arrows. When the foe was considered ripe for slaughter, the heavy cavalry was sent in. Orders mostly seem to have been communicated silently, by means of flags. The Mongols' use of drums was largely for moral effect, to terrify the enemy while building up Mongol courage for a final assault, which was carried out amid

The loyal Jelme saved the life of his friend Genghis Khan by sucking clotted blood from a neck artery severed whilst fighting early battles on behalf of the Naiman tribe.

shrieks, yells and war cries in stark contrast to the warriors' previous silence.

Quite why these age-old tactics should have suddenly become so effective is hard to understand. The Mongols may have improved them, but such changes would have been marginal. The answer almost certainly lies in the wider strategy used by Genghis Khan, the greater discipline and unity he managed to achieve over his warlike followers and, perhaps most important of all, in the disarray seen among most of his enemies. Whether Genghis Khan actually followed a grand strategy can never be known. According to this theory, he first built a confederation of nomad tribes, then neutralized the threat from China but refrained from outright conquest, then mopped up any remaining resistance among the Turco–Mongol peoples of the steppes, before returning to the conquest of China. Such a master plan seems unlikely, yet it remains a fascinating possibility. In this supposed grand strategy the attack on Transoxania, Iran and Afghanistan, and the virtual obliteration of their thriving Islamic civilization, is reduced to a mere sideshow to secure the Mongols' western flank.

Genghis Khan's poor showing against the fortified cities of China taught him the need to learn the techniques of siege warfare and ambitious tactics were soon being attempted. In 1209 the Mongols unsuccessfully tried to divert the huge Yellow River during their siege of the Hsi-Hsia capital of Ningsia. Quite why Genghis Khan's armies were more successful against the fortified cities of eastern Islam is unclear. Perhaps their initial success and slaughter of entire populations really did demoralize the defenders of other Islamic towns. Clearly the Muslims regarded the Mongols as even more terrible and barbaric than did the Chinese, who had long lived with such Turco–Mongol neighbours. Pehaps Mongol armies had learned much about siegecraft from their Uighur allies and their first Chinese foes, before erupting into Islam. Above all, perhaps, was the fact that even the biggest Transoxanian, Iranian and Afghan cities could not compare with the vast walled cities of China.

Genghis Khan's grand design, whether or not it rested upon a carefully worked out strategy, involved invasions and the alteration of ethnic boundaries. Mongol tradition stipulated that a defeated tribe, unless it was a blood enemy like the Tatars, should be absorbed rather than exterminated. Leaders and even a percentage of the entire tribe might be slaughtered, but the enemy's military manpower was too valuable to be thrown away. Once Genghis Khan's empire reached continental proportions, efforts at absorption involved the attempted transfer of populations. For example, the basically Iranian and largely Christian Alans of the northern Caucasus were shifted to the eastern steppes where, however, they were not accepted by the culturally very different Mongol tribes.

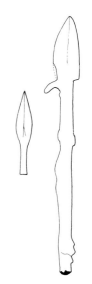

Spears are more common than helmets but are still rarer than the bow fragments and arrowheads which abound in Turkish or Mongol graves. These two examples date from the 13th or 14th century and come from Serai, capital of the Mongol Golden Horde Khanate of southern Russia. The larger is over 80 cms long and has the hook for unhorsing a foe which is mentioned by many of the Mongols' foes (ex-Pletnyeva).

Genghis Khan probably died as a result of internal injuries suffered in a fall while hunting — though he lived for many days after this accident.

Peoples who were judged incapable of a useful military function, which apparently included most of the settled and urban inhabitants of eastern Islam, were simply slaughtered. Yet even here there was a twisted logic in Mongol savagery. The common explanation, that the steppe nomads despised sedentary ways of life and simply destroyed what they failed to understand, does not account for the organized approach the Mongols took to such destruction. Nor did Genghis Khan's men seem particularly sadistic. They generally showed no emotion whatsoever while carefully wiping out a specified proportion of their defeated foes. It seemed as if such atrocities were taken as a normal aspect of war, to be undertaken in as efficient a manner as possible. There was also an apparent contradiction – at least to the modern mind – between, on the one hand, the high moral standard of Genghis Khan's life and the wise, even reflective, attitude he took to government, and on the other hand, a total lack of concern he and his men showed for human life.

A more rational explanation for the Mongol extermination campaign in eastern Islam points to the speedy surrenders that such terrorism often achieved and suggests that Genghis Khan also intended to create 'dead lands' along his south-western border. The Khwarazmshahs had been the only real rivals to Genghis Khan's domination of central Asia and the obliteration of the civilization that had supported their power would

Although Central Asian religious art was highly stylized and hard to interpret, secular art reflected current reality in great detail. On this fragment of wall-painting from Bezeklik, near the Uighur city of Beshbalik, three Uighur princes are shown in all their finery. Belts with such pendant straps became the mark of the military élite wherever Turkish peoples came to power or prominence, though here they are used to hold purses, pen-cases and small knives (West Berlin State Museums).

ensure that no further rivals would emerge for years to come. It also seems likely that, with his eyes firmly set upon China, Genghis Khan had no particular wish to conquer the Muslim Middle East or even to occupy much of the Kwarazmian state. 'Dead lands' posed no threat and, if they reverted to steppe and supported only a rudimentary nomadic population, they would also be easier to administer.

Arms and Equipment

Mongol arms and armour, like their tactics, were in the Eurasian steppe tradition. Most of the evidence comes from written and pictorial sources – the nomadic life did not lend itself to rich archaeological remains. The main cities of the Mongol Empire date from after the death of Genghis Khan, while those tombs and burials that have been excavated mostly date from before the great Khan's rise to power.

Almost all sources agree that the Mongol soldier wore a fur cap with earflaps, a fur-lined or felt coat, thick stockings and soft leather riding boots. Those who possessed armour might have a hardened leather or iron helmet and a lamellar cuirass, usually of hardened leather pieces laced with rawhide thongs. Only the élite would own iron lamellar laced with silk thread. An armoured flap that protected the right arm would, according to some contemporary observers, be unlaced while shooting so as not to encumber the man as he pulled his bowstring. Swords were again reserved for the élite. They were not always curved sabres, as is so

The extravagantly decorated reality behind the stylized military costumes shown in so much Central Asian art is confirmed by this highly detailed Chinese drawing. Here Uighur Turks pay homage to the Chinese leader Guo Zui. Made in the 11th or 12th centuries by Li Gonglin, it shows the curved sabres and straight swords, decorated bowcases, plumed fur-lined hats, lamellar and fabric-covered armours, broad waist-supporting cummerbunds and pendant belts of Turkish warriors. All these features would be seen in later art of the Mongol period, as would the banners, saddles, harness and armour carried by the Uighurs' horses (National Palace Museum, Taiwan).

35

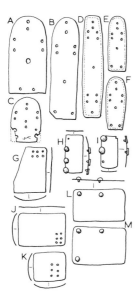

Many different forms of fragmentary lamellar armour have been found across the medieval Eurasian steppes. The variations probably reflect local tradition as well as the use of different shapes to protect particular parts of the body as lamellar armour could be of very sophisticated design. These examples come from: (A) 10th–14th century Turfan area (British Museum); (B) 10th–14th century Gobi Desert (British Museum); (C) 10th–11th century Mongol, Nadezhdin (ex-Gorelik); (D) (F) 11–12th century Mongol, Tangut area (ex-Gorelik); (G–M) 1123–29 AD Abaza area (Regional Museum, Abakan, USSR);

often thought, though even straight swords would normally be single-edged. A decorated cap and sword belt were worn as insignia of rank or command. Small battle-axes and maces were used by some Mongols, while many spears had hooks to unhorse a foe. Lassos of horse-hair rope were widely employed, but the main weapon remained, of course, the bow.

The Central Asian composite bow, like comparable weapons used by Middle Eastern and some eastern European armies, was an extremely sophisticated weapon. It needed much greater strength to pull than the famous English longbow. But, although it was much shorter, and consequently suitable for use on horseback, it had an equally long draw – right back to the archer's cheek. The composite bow also gave a much more regular release of tension when loosed and thus its arrows had about twice the range, with a flatter trajectory and greater accuracy, than English infantry bows. It appears, in fact, that whereas the penetrating power of the longbow relied primarily on the arrow's weight, that of the Asiatic composite bow depended upon the arrow's velocity. Because of this, its effectiveness was comparable to the crossbow which was, however, far slower to operate. Small wonder that it took a long time for gunpowder to have much impact upon the steppes and that 'Tartar' horse-archers from the Crimea, not to mention Ottoman Turks, were still campaigning effectively across eastern Europe well into the seventeenth century.

The Mongol or Turkish version of the Asiatic composite bow was apparently shorter than the 'Scythian' type still used in Byzantium and Russia. But, being even shorter for use on horse-back, it was thicker in section and needed even greater strength to pull – often more than 45 kg of tension. Different peoples used different materials in the construction of their composite bows, though all were built around a wooden core. Many central Asian nomads used four pieces of ram's horn, whereas the Chinese incorporated a single large piece of water-buffalo horn. The belly of the bow consisted of strands of sinew, the Chinese using spinal sinew, the Muslims the Achilles tendon and the nomads whatever they could obtain. Fish glue was preferred for the most important stress points. Many early Mongol bows had angled 'ears' reinforced with bone, as had the larger ancient Hun bows. In the Mongol weapon these were often angled so far forward that the string rested upon them, though the reasons for this development were unclear.

Whereas simple bows such as the English longbow lose their strength if left strung while not in use, the fully composite bow incorporating wood, sinew and horn works better when thus kept under tension. This might explain the existence of two types of bowcase in central Asia. The older form was designed to hold an unstrung bow, the newer for a strung weapon. Both appear to have been in use during Genghis Khan's lifetime, though the unstrung version was dying out. Presumably this indicated that partially composite bows, lacking the horn element, were still in use – perhaps for hunting.

Central Asian arrows and arrowheads were almost as sophisticated as the bows. Some arrows were made wholly or partly of hollow reed. Modern experiments have shown that reed absorbs the shock of release very quickly, the arrow thus soon straightening out and flying more accurately. An extraordinary variety of arrowheads have been found in central Asian graves, most of which are mirrored in the archery manuals of medieval Islam. From a European point of view the most extraordinary were, perhaps, those with wide chisel heads designed to cause broad wounds and generally reserved for hunting. Others had whistles attached, these probably having a signalling function.

Even more important to the Mongol warrior than his bow was his pony. This small animal was incredibly tough – like its owner. With a strong neck, thick legs, dense coat, immense endurance, steadiness and sureness of foot, the Mongol pony was ideally suited not only to its environment but also to the Mongol style of warfare. It flourished in wide grassy plains and could survive even in Russian forests or Alpine regions. Living almost entirely on the pasture it found along the way, it did not need a complicated commissariat to supply it with fodder. On the other hand, it was not suited to the ferocious heat of Middle Eastern deserts or the humid climate of India. Almost as soon as the Mongol armies reached areas that lacked great grasslands, their conquests slowed and were eventually brought to a halt.

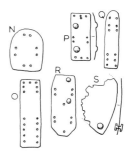

Further examples of lamellar armour: (N) 12th–13th century Mongol, Khara-Knoto (ex-Gorelik); (O) 12th century Mongol, Shaigun (ex-Gorelik); (P) 13th century Mongol from Olelkvo (ex-Gorelik); (Q) 13th century Islamic or Mongol from ruins of Afrasiab mosque, Samarkand (ex-Gorelik); (R) 13th century Mongol from Chernova (Regional Museum, Minusinsk, USSR).

A series of manuscripts known as 'Small Shahnamas' provides some of the earliest representations of Mongol arms, armour and warriors in Islamic art. They were probably made in Iraq around 1300 AD. Like this illustration of Isfandiyar lassoing Gursar, they show doubled pendant ear protections fastened to a helmet's rim as on a surviving helmet from Mongol Central Asia, the probably scale- or mail-lined 'soft armour' of the two leading figures, and the full lamellar cuirass of three other horsemen (British Museum, Dept. of Oriental Antiquities no. 1948–12, f. 11–022).

The Great Battles

An examination of two of Genghis Khan's victories tells much about the skills and organisation of the Mongol fighting forces.

Crushing the Naimans

Genghis Khan's defeat of the powerful and relatively civilized Naiman tribe in 1204 is one of the most fully described of his early battles. The *Secret History of the Mongols* – a unique source in that it is the only surviving account of Genghis Khan's life written in Mongol by a Mongol – devoted no less than seven small chapters to the battle and the events that led up to it.

Genghis Khan had already overcome most of the tribes of Mongolia. Their defeated remnants, as well as others who feared the rapidly growing power of Genghis, gravitated towards the *Tayang* or king of the Naimans. He in turn now became the focus for all anti-Genghis Khan forces and a clash seemed inevitable. The *Tayang's* first move was an attempt to isolate the Mongols diplomatically and to outflank them by winning an alliance with the Öngüt Turks who lived along the Chin frontier in northern China. The Öngüts had frequently found them-selves caught between Mongol raiding and Chin reprisals, so they had little love for the turbulent and fragmented Mongol tribes. However, the Öngüt chieftain decided that his people's interests might be better served if the firm hand of Genghis controlled the warlike Mongols, so he immediately informed the Khan of the Naiman's proposal for an anti-Mongol alliance.

The *Secret History* tells how Genghis organized his army into tens, hundreds and thousands and chose commanders personally known to him for their courage and skill. In this Genghis Khan followed traditional Mongol practice, but he also introduced new elements into his military organization. He created a new rank, of *cherbi*, for an officer in charge of supplies. He also formed a new guard unit or *käshik* – an élite corps at the heart of the army of which only young Mongol aristocrats and free men could be members. He selected, too, a personal bodyguard of one thousand *ba'atur* ('valiant men'), who would always fight in the forefront of battle and who would provide a permanent guard against the kind of sudden attack against a leader or headquarters that had long been a favourite tactic of steppe warfare.

Genghis Khan then summoned a gathering of clan leaders in the spring of 1204. War with the Naiman was agreed, but many of the Khan's chief followers warned him that their horses were weak and thin after a hard winter. They proposed that the campaign be postponed until autumn, by which time their mounts would have been fattened on summer pastures. Others urged an immediate surprise attack, and this was the course that Genghis Khan followed. Sacrifices and offerings were made to Genghis Khan's banner, in which the guardian genius of the army was believed to reside. The army reportedly set out on a 'red circle day' (full-moon) in the Year of the Rat (1204), but the actual month is unknown. It assembled in a well-watered and grassy area on the borders of Naiman territory, where the horses were fattened.

Quite when the fighting started is unclear but Genghis is known to have faced a formidable coalition of Naiman, Jajirat, Merkit and Oirat tribal contingents. The *Tayang* had assembled his large army in the foothills and at first simply awaited the Mongol attack. His plan had apparently been to retreat by stages into the wild Altai mountains, luring Genghis into some defile where he could be caught in a sudden counter-attack. But this cautious plan had to be abandoned when his chief lieutenants taunted him, saying that his father had never shown his horse's rump to an enemy. Some even advised the *Tayang* to stay in the women's tents if he was afraid to fight. Clearly the Naiman army did not have the same iron discipline, nor its leader the same unquestioning obedience, as was seen on the Mongol side. On the other hand the more civilized Naiman warriors appear to have been better equipped and the alliance probably enjoyed numerical superiority.

Meanwhile Genghis sent an advance guard under the faithful Jebe to probe the Naiman position, but also to retreat at the first sign of serious resistance. The Khan himself followed more slowly with the bulk of his troops. Goaded by his lieutenants, the *Tayang* now decided to take the offensive. The clash that followed seems to have taken place in late summer or early autumn, suggesting that the *Tayang* had been able to carry out at least some of his planned manoeuvres before being shamed into a premature and disastrous confrontation.

The battle itself, which was to determine the fate of Mongolia and half the known world, is said to have been fought in the Khangai area, near the site of the future Mongol Imperial capital of Qaraqorum. The *Secret History* states that during their advance the Naimans captured one of Jebe's advance guard. Noting the man's skinny horse and tattered saddle they deduced that the Mongols had advanced before their cavalry was in good fighting trim. Genghis Khan's army, whose horses were indeed both hungry and tired, was now camped on the Sa'ari steppe where they had hoped to give the animals a rest. To keep the Naiman forces at bay Genghis Khan ordered his soldiers to build additional camp fires, up to five per man, so as to make their numbers appear far greater than they were. It worked for a while, for the Naiman alliance paused before the Mongol encampment, whose fires were 'like the stars in the sky'.

The advance guards and outposts of both forces came then into contact, at which point Genghis Khan instructed his army to advance against the enemy in the *qara'ana* march, to face the foe in the 'lake' array and then attack in the 'chisel' fight. This meant that the men would march in dense masses like the thorny *qara'ana*, a desert shrub. On

sighting the enemy they would spread over as wide an area as possible, filling the natural lie of the land. Their attack would be like a chisel striking wood, namely with a major thrust to the enemy centre. Meanwhile the *Tayang* deployed his men along the foot of the hills. The battle itself was extremely ferocious, but few tactical details are recorded in the *Secret History*. Instead this indulges in a series of blood-curdling poems and accounts of personal valour. Describing two Mongol clans, it said;

> *Those are the Uru'd and Mang'ud,*
> *Which, driving before them*
> *The men with lances,*
> *Strip them of their bloody clothing;*
> *Which, pushing before them,*
> *The men with swords, cutting them down and killing them,*
> *Take from them their treasure and clothing.*

The fighting lasted all day and the main laurels seem to have gone to Genghis Khan's fierce younger brother, Qasar, who led the Mongol centre. Genghis himself commanded the wings, whose job was to outflank or counterattack the enemy. These were difficult tasks in the broken terrain where the battle was fought and they demanded excellent control and communication. By evening the *Tayang* had been deserted by some of his allies and had been wounded. Because he was too gravely hurt to reach the tent where his wives and family awaited him, his men carried him to a nearby hilltop. He was too weak to issue orders and his followers were at a loss. All they could do was charge repeatedly down the hillside, keeping the victorious Mongols away from their dying leader. Genghis Khan would have spared them, but they refused to surrender and fought until all were slain. Küchlüg, the *Tayang's* son, managed to escape but most of the Naiman tribe had no alternative but to submit.

Defeat into Victory: Parwan and the Indus

Jalal al Din, son of the tragic Khwarazmshah whose Iranian empire bore the brunt of Genghis Khan's western invasion, had been by his father's side when the latter died in despair on a small Caspian island. Jalal, however, was determined to keep up the struggle. He made his way back east on an amazing journey in which he was often no more than an hour ahead of his Mongol pursuers. Only when he reached the wild hills of Afghanistan did Genghis Khan's men finally give up their chase.

Despite the appalling military losses inflicted by the Mongol invasion, Jalal was soon able to assemble a motley army of some sixty thousand troops. In the spring of 1221, he led these forces north to the head of the Panjshir valley, an area that has reappeared in military history as a major centre of Afghan resistance to the Soviet invasion of Afghanistan. There, at the little town of Parwan, he threw himself into the attack against a Mongol army that was besieging a local castle. So sudden and unex-

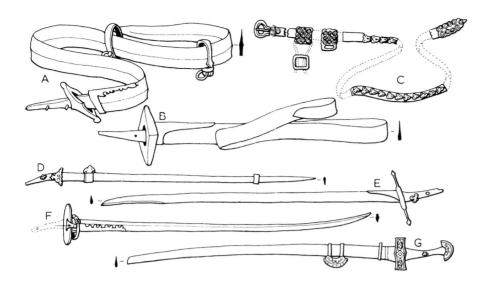

pected was this revival of Muslim resistance that a thousand Mongols are said to have been killed before the rest withdrew across a river, demolishing the bridge behind them. Jalal then established his own base at Parwan while news of the defeat was taken to Genghis Khan in the mountains of Juzjan. The World Conqueror immediately sent 30,000 men under an experienced general, Shigi-Qutuqu, to avenge this setback. With the typical Mongol speed of action, they reached Parwan only one week after Jalal al Din had settled there.

But the Muslims were not content to rest on their recent laurels. They promptly marched out and occupied a position three miles from the town. Jalal al Din took command of the centre; his allies, Amin Malik with his Qanqli Turkish tribal forces and Ighraq with his Turcoman nomads, held the right and left wings respectively. The troops were instructed to dismount, tether their horses and face the Mongols on foot. Clearly the Muslims realized that in terms of horse-archery cavalry tactics they were no match for the fearsome Mongols.

The Mongols in turn hurled themselves first against Amin Malik on the right flank, which was forced back by the ferocity of their attack. Only by sending repeated reinforcements from the rest of his army could Jalal hold the line. The battle then raged until dusk when both sides withdrew to their camps. During the night the Mongols, who appear to have been the smaller army, used one of their favourite ruses by setting up straw men on spare horses. These they then positioned behind their main formation. Dawn's light showed what appeared to be a host of reinforcements on the Mongol side and for a while the Muslim army lost heart. Jalal al Din, however, was an inspiring leader – though in the end a tragic one. The Muslims stood firm and battle was rejoined on this, the second day. The Mongols now concentrated their attacks on the left wing under Ighraq the Turkoman, but this time it was the Mongols who wavered and began to withdraw to their overnight camp. Jalal al Din then signalled his motley army to remount and charge the retreating Mongols who, despite one fierce counterattack, were totally routed.

News of this second defeat reached Genghis Khan, who had already decided that the situation needed his personal attention. It was clearly vital not to allow the Mongols' reputation for invincibility to be seriously dented. On the other side, Jalal al Din was suddenly facing serious problems. Amin Malik and Ighraq had quarrelled over booty from the victory at Parwan. The Turkoman leader, feeling insulted, led his troops away, along with those of another one of Jalal al Din's vital allies, Azam Malik of the Ghurids who ruled Muslim northern India. This was a major military crisis and Jalal, realizing that the wrath of Genghis Khan would soon inevitably fall upon his shrunken army, retreated eastwards. He even abandoned the vital city of Ghazna and marched straight towards the river Indus, hoping to find a refuge beyond its broad waters.

Genghis Khan, though, acted with a speed exceptional even for him. At the head of a vast army, now reinforced by forces commanded by his sons Tolui, Jagatai and Ögotäi, he cut a swathe of appalling destruction across Afghanistan. Pausing at the battlefield of Parwan only long enough to criticize the tactics of both victor and vanquished, the World Conqueror pressed on by day and night so fast that his men often had no time even to cook their food. Reaching Ghazna a fortnight after Jalal al Din had left, he increased the pace of the march and caught up with the retreating Muslim army as it was preparing to cross the Indus. Many boats had, in fact, already been gathered. Effectively hemmed in between the Mongols, the mountains and the river, Jalal had little choice but to fight.

Accounts of the battle of the Indus differ widely. Some described it as one of Genghis Khan's tactical masterpieces. Others saw it as a gallant last stand by the Muslims against overwhelming odds. One thing is, however, certain. The result was a catastrophic defeat for the Muslim army, relieved only by the epic courage of Jalal al Din, upon which all accounts agree. The battle was fought on 24th November 1221, probably near the modern Pakistani town of Kalabagh. Jalal drew his men up in formation, attempting to anchor his left flank on a range of low hills; the right, under Amin Malik, touched the river bank. Meanwhile Genghis Khan took station at the centre of his own army, his position clearly marked by his great standard of nine white yak tails. As he moved about the battlefield, this standard would constantly show his position to his men – and to Jalal al Din.

The Muslims seem to have made the first move, their right wing under Amin Malik forcing back the Mongol left. Judging the situation to be stable on his left flank, which was apparently secure against the hills,

Jalal al Din weakened this wing by sending troops to support Amin Malik's success on the right. He then made a determined charge with his own troops against the Mongol centre. Perhaps he hoped to win a knock-out blow by killing Genghis Khan himself. But such was the high degree of Mongol discipline that the Great Khan felt able apparently to abandon his own centre to fight on as best it could, while he led his black-uniformed personal *kāshik* against Amin Malik's advancing troops down by the river. After a hard-fought struggle, the Muslim attack was driven back, Amin Malik being killed as he attempted to break out in the direction of Peshawar. The victorious Mongols then turned towards Jalal in the centre.

As if this was not bad enough for Jalal al Din, another Mongol regiment of perhaps ten thousand horsemen suddenly erupted from the hills and threw themselves against the Muslims' much-denuded left flank. Unknown to Jalal this formation had been sent around and across the range of low hills by Genghis Khan at the very start of the fighting. Whether Genghis had really anticipated the entire course of the battle, as some of his admiring biographers claimed, or had merely made use of his superior manpower to deliver an unexpected flank attack, is unknown. In the event the arrival of this fresh Mongol regiment virtually encircled the Muslim army, whose only hope of escape now lay across the great Indus river.

Pressed on all sides, Jalal al Din and his surviving troops made a series of desperate charges in hope of breaking out, but this proved impossible. As his army disintegrated around him, Jalal mounted a fresh horse and, with his household troops, made a final charge in order to win a little room. They then turned abruptly. Jalal is said to have thrown off his armour even as he galloped towards the river bank. This would, in fact, have been possible if he wore the laced and buckled lamellar armour used by most eastern Islamic as well as Mongol soldiers. Still carrying his banner in his hand, he urged his horse over what has variously been described as a six- to eighteen-metre high cliff, into the river. Those of his men able to do so also tried to swim for it, but the Mongols were hard on their heels, cutting down men with their arrows and turning the Indus waters red.

'Fortunate the father of such a son!' Genghis Khan reportedly said as he saw Jalal al Din safely reach the other side. Not so fortunate were Jalal's captured children, the eldest of whom was only eight years old. The Mongols hurled all into the river to drown. Only seven hundred of Jalal's army are said to have escaped, yet Jalal al Din's men would still have a part to play in the next few years of Mongol, Muslim and even Crusader history. While Genghis Khan went on to ravage eastern Islam, Jalal made his way west once again, across Iran to Georgia, Armenia and Kurdistan, maintaining a desperate resistance until his murder in 1231. In 1244 the remains of his now leaderless army overran Jerusalem and drove out the

On this detail from the middle of the Freer Gallery's 'Battle Plate', a Turkish horse-archer uses the same kind of composite bow with stiff angled 'ears' as was shown in earlier Central Asian Buddhist art. His mail hauberk, worn beneath an ordinary tunic, can be seen on his chest though no other figures appear to wear armour. Two foot soldiers carry javelins and small round shields (Freer Gallery, Washington).

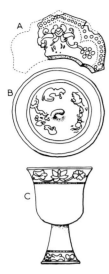

The nomadic peoples of the Eurasian steppes also produced beautiful metalwork for non-military purposes: (A–B) Damaged decorative plaques, probably from a horse harness, Turkish from Sayan-Altai mountains 13th–14th century; (C) Cup from a 13th–14th century Turkish grave, Sayan-Altai mountains. Drinking in so-called Cup Rituals played a vital rôle among the military or political élites of pre-Islamic Turkish peoples and cups of similar form appear in much Turkish art as well as in the art of neighbouring Islamic areas.

Crusaders for the last time, the Holy City then remaining in Muslim hands until 1917.

The Final Years

During the winter of 1222–3 Genghis Khan decided to return to Mongolia. His army had taken huge numbers of prisoners, now of little use and difficult to feed. So tens of thousands of helpless wretches, including skilled craftsmen, artists and scholars, were butchered in a carefully organized one-day operation.

Meanwhile the force of cavalry that had hunted to death the Khwarazmshah, Ala al Din Muhammad, had ridden on, ravaging western Iran and twice raiding Christian Georgia. In late autumn 1221 this army, under Genghis Khan's loyal lieutenants Jebe and Sübötäi, marched up the coast of the Caspian Sea, past the Caucasus mountains and into what is now southern Russia. There they returned to the steppes and clashed with the Kipchak Turks who dominated the area. Faced with this sudden, but not altogether unexpected, invasion the Kipchaks tried to placate the Mongols. They deserted their erstwhile allies, the partly Christian inhabitants of the northern Caucasus, and joined forces with the invaders. But Jebe and Sübötäi, having destroyed the Caucasian peoples one by one, promptly turned upon the Kipchaks. In desperation these nomads appealed to their ancient foes, the Princes of Russia. A huge coalition army from the Kipchak tribes and four Russian Principalities now set out against the Mongols. They were, however, totally outmanoeuvred by the Mongols, who drew them even deeper into the steppes until the allies were exhausted and scattered. Only then did Jebe and Sübötäi strike back, routing the Russians and Kipchaks north of the Sea of Azov.

The Prince of Kiev fought on for three more days until forced to surrender. At first the Mongols treated him with respect, but in the end they put him to death by smothering him beneath piles of carpets. Though this killing was recorded with horror by Russian chroniclers it was, for the Mongols, an honourable means of execution – reserved for royalty whose blood they did not want to shed.

During their inexorable and bloody march homeward, Jebe and Sübötäi defeated all who stood in their path, ransacking Genoese trading settlements in the Crimea, defeating the Volga Bulgars near the Kama river and the Qanqli Turks in the southern Urals. Finally they rejoined Genghis Khan's main army north of the Syr Darya river after what must remain one of the most epic forays in military history.

Genghis Khan was now nearly sixty years old – or maybe even older – yet he was neither allowed nor wished to find peace. Despite quarrels within his family, in 1226 the old conqueror decided once again to invade China. This time the Hsi-Hsia kingdom of western China felt the full fury of an even more powerful and ruthless Mongol Empire. Earlier the

Hsi-Hsia ruler had refused to send troops to help the Mongols in Transoxania and now his country paid the price. Methods of terror perfected against the Muslims were turned against the Chinese inhabitants, who were hunted down in the caves and mountains where they sought refuge. Then, quite suddenly, Genghis Khan died, apparently after an illness of only eight days. In fact he had been thrown from his horse during a hunting expedition at the very start of the campaign, suffering severe internal pains and fever for some time afterwards. But the grim old destroyer had refused to defer the attack on the Hsi-Hsia, saying that 'After such words [a defiant reply from the Chinese], we can no longer draw back. If it means my death . . . I will go to them.'

News of Genghis Khan's death was kept secret for a while as his closest followers took his body to be buried in the Kentei mountains. There young Temüchin had first made his solemn pact with Tängri, supreme deity of the Eternal Blue Sky. Those accompanying the funeral cortège killed all they met along the way, saying 'Go serve our master the Khan in the hereafter.' Three days of ceremonies and great sacrifices were later offered in his honour. Thus Genghis Khan's grave eventually included forty of the most beautiful girls from leading Mongol families, together with many horses and all that a World Conqueror would need in the other world. In accordance with his last wishes, the army had continued its campaign of genocide against the Hsi-Hsia, news of their final extermination being announced during Genghis Khan's funeral rites. The place where he lay then became taboo, so that the forest soon covered Genghis Khan's tomb, the exact location of which remains unknown to this day.

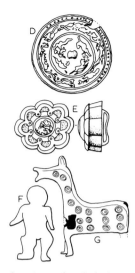

Some items, though also beautiful metalwork, appear little more than toys: (D–E) Decorative plaques or buttons from 11th–14th century graves in Kazakstan. (F–G) Bronze figure and horse, about 3 cms high, from 13th–14th century Golden Horde urban sites along the lower Volga river. (All ex-Pletnyeva).

Impact and Achievements

The creation of the Mongol Empire was the last great nomad expansion in European and Asian history. There were to be steppe empires in the future, but from the decline of the Mongols the nomads were on the defensive against settled civilizations that, for a variety of reasons, gradually and inexorably tipped the balance of power in their own favour.

While nobody can deny the impact that Genghis Khan had on history, assessments of his achievement have tended towards extremes. On one side there is the view that he was simply the greatest gangster of all time and that the Mongols' career of conquest consisted of nothing more than a worldwide rampage of death and destruction. At the other extreme some historians have portrayed Genghis Khan as the noble savage who, illiterate as he was, recognized a single God in the form of the Eternal Blue Sky and whose genius alone took the Mongols from primitive obscurity to the pinnacle of world power. Such extravagant views are largely based on nineteenth-century interpretations of the evidence. Twentieth-century experience of the barbarism to which even the most civilized peoples can sink has tended to put Genghis Khan's behaviour in a new perspective. Genghis Khan, it seems, was just another ruthless empire builder and moral judgements about Genghis Khan tend to obscure the reality of his achievement rather than illuminate it. He was a ruthless empire builder, but he was a man of his time, his culture and his circumstances. He was also, without doubt, a military genius who used available resources to cataclysmic effect.

Those who wrote about Genghis Khan during or immediately after his life often seem to have been more objective than modern scholars. The horror of the massacres was recorded as a matter of fact, while men like Marco Polo could state that his death was, 'a great pity, for he was a just man and a wise one.' The peace that the Khan imposed was bought at a horrible price, but it was peace none the less. On one hand the Arab historian Ibn al Athir wrote:

The Tatars have done things utterly unparalleled in ancient or modern [thirteenth-century] times. . . . May God send a defender to the Muslims for never since the Prophet have they suffered such disasters.

Meanwhile, the Persian al Juwaini declared, with some exaggeration:

In the Muslim countries devastated by Genghis Khan not one in a thousand of the inhabitants survived. . . . If from now until the Day of Resurrection nothing hindered the natural increase of the population it could never reach one-tenth of its density before the Mongol conquest.

In complete contrast, the Muslim chronicler Abu'l Ghazi wrote that:

Under the reign of Genghis Khan, all the country between Iran and the land of the Turks enjoyed such peace that a man might have journeyed from the land of sunrise to the land of sunset with a golden platter upon his head without suffering the least violence from anyone.

Perhaps all the robbers were dead! Whether peace was worth such a price again begs moral questions. One thing is clear. As in so many other cases, the conqueror bears the burden of guilt for the death and destruction he wrought. His successors enjoy the praise for building new and sometimes enlightened civilizations in the 'new world' that he left to them.

Genghis Khan was also one of the most successful empire builders because, unlike the ephemeral states set up by many nomad conquerors, that of the Mongols did not fall apart upon the death of its founder. In this Genghis Khan was more effective than both Alexander the Great and Charlemagne. He left not only an empire and a splendid army but the foundations of an administration and the basis of a legal code, his *yasaq*. He also left a family, the Golden Clan, whose respect for the memory of Genghis Khan was such that, instead of quarrelling over his inheritance,

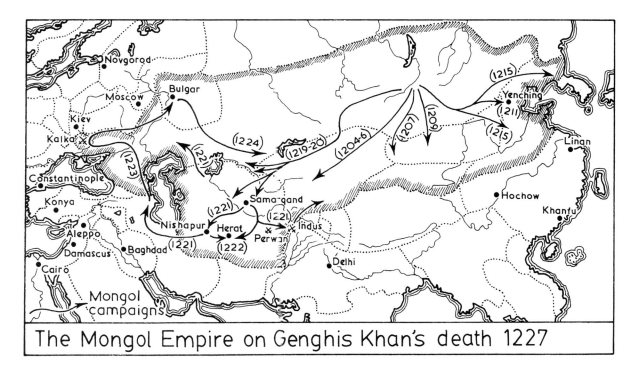

The Mongol Empire on Genghis Khan's death 1227

they generally managed to agree upon the succession. When fragmentation became inevitable they also restructured the Mongol Empire into a galaxy of Khanates, which retained at least the semblance of unity under a recognized senior member of the family. This did not save the Mongols, other than those who remained in their original homeland, from being absorbed by their numerically greater followers. At first this meant the Turcification of the Mongol élite. Later, in densely populated and civilized areas, even these Turco–Mongols were largely absorbed by their teeming subjects.

There was an obvious and dramatic drop in the population of many areas as a direct or indirect result of Genghis Khan's campaigns. Most contemporary accounts were understandably exaggerated and the destruction was also more localized than has often been realized. But the Mongol invasion remained a monumental catastrophe in those areas worst hit. It was not just the size of the slaughter and the destruction of cities that left its mark on areas like Transoxania and eastern Iran. Europe suffered far worse localized destruction during the First and Second World Wars, but has recovered from both disasters with incredible speed. The fact was that, unlike a green and temperate land like Europe or a densely populated country like China, the civilization of eastern Islam was built on a very vulnerable agricultural foundation. Here, perhaps, lies the secret of the destructiveness of the Mongol conquest. Agriculture relied upon irrigation, most obviously on long underground

A 9th–10th century painted fabric clearly designed to be hung vertically. It comes from Toyuq in what was the Uighur khanate, not far from Mongol territory. The figure represents Buddhist lokapala *and wears* cuirassa, *partly of lamellar construction, having buckled shoulder pieces. (West Berlin State Museum).*

canals known as *qanat*. This system was of great antiquity and, despite invasions, political turmoil and earthquake, had been constantly repaired and frequently extended right up until the arrival of the Mongols. These new conquerors destroyed not only crops and grain stores in an obvious attempt to create famine and further reduce the enemy population. They also slaughtered large numbers of peasants in a new form of total war. These victims were just the people who had maintained the *qanat* for centuries and without their constant attention the system rapidly deteriorated. When the *qanat* ceased to function, the irrigation stopped, the land reverted to steppe or desert, the remaining people starved or moved away, thus leaving even fewer survivors to maintain the *qanat*. A vicious circle was set up so that the horror of the Mongol invasions continued to be felt long after Genghis Khan's death. Even today it is clear that, as al Juvayni predicted, provinces like Khurasan have still not regained their previous fertility.

The Mongol impact on China was more patchy. Long-term destruction was limited to the north and west, though pestilence – that eternal companion of war – is believed to have reduced the Chinese population from over one hundred million in pre-Mongol times to seventy million by the late thirteenth century. In Russia the impact of the Mongol conquest was even more unfairly spread, with some areas escaping entirely and even profiting from the 'new world' created by the Mongols. Perhaps the density of the Russian forests not only channelled the passage of Mongol armies but contained the devastation they caused. The Mongol conquest even seems to have tied medieval Russia yet closer into the web of international commerce that, like all nomad conquerors, the Mongols enthusiastically promoted. Paradoxically, perhaps, the centuries of Mongol domination greatly strengthened and enriched the Russian Orthodox Church. Russian culture was, however, further separated from that of Catholic Europe.

The effects of the Mongol conquest on the sprawling Eurasian steppes have not been so carefully studied. The power of Genghis Khan's empire inevitably made it rich and this can be seen in the higher material culture of some nomadic regions. Cities were built where they had not been seen before, and stone architecture emerged in zones where previously the only buildings had been of wood. Above all there was an enormous expansion of Turkish-speaking peoples at the expense of non-Turkish nomadic and semi-nomadic tribes. Perhaps the fact that the Turkish language benefited in this way, rather than the Mongol tongue, remains the ultimate paradox of Genghis Khan's career and of the great Mongol conquests.

The Great Khans

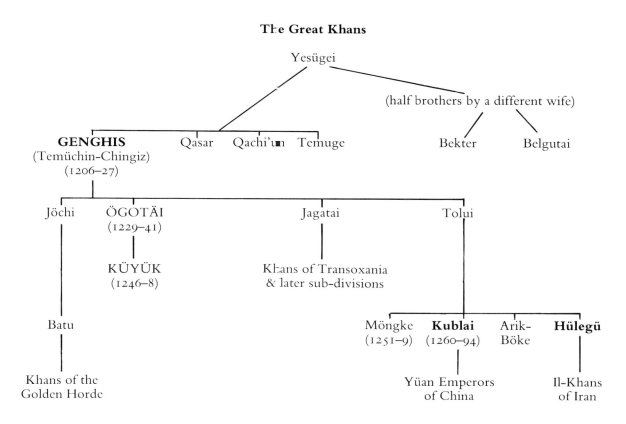

Bibliography

Cleaves, F.W. (ed. & trans.) *The Secret History of the Mongols* Cambridge, Mass. & London, 1982.

Derevyanko, A.P. and Natsazgdorzh, Sh. (eds) *Arkheologiya, Etnografiya i Antropologiya Mongolii (Archaeology, Ethnography and Anthropology of the Mongols)* (in Russian) Novosibirsk, 1987.

Fox, R. *Genghis Khan* London, 1936.

Gaunt, G.D. & A.M. 'Mongol Archers of the Thirteenth Century' *Journal of the Society of Archer Antiquaries* XVI pp. 20–21 1973.

Grousset, R. (trans. Sinor, D. and MacKellar, M.) *Conqueror of the World* Edinburgh & London, 1967.

Grousset, R. (trans. Walford, N.) *The Empire of the Steppes, a History of Central Asia* New Brunswick, 1970.

Lattimore, O. 'The Geography of Chingis Khan' *Geographical Journal* CXXIX, pp. 1–7 1963.

Martin, H.D. *The Rise of Chingis Khan and his Conquest of North China* Baltimore, 1950.

Martin, H.D. 'The Mongol Army' *Journal of the Royal Asiatic Society*, pp. 46–85 1943.

Morgan, D. *The Mongols* Oxford & New York, 1986.

Nowgorodowa, E. *Alte Kunst der Mongolei* Leipzig, 1980.

Pletnyeva, S.A. *Stepi Eurasi v Ehpoxu Spednevekovya (The Eurasian Steppes in the Middle Ages)* (in Russian) Moscow, 1981.

Prawdin, M. (trans. Paul, E. & C.) *The Mongol Empire, its Rise and Legacy* London, 1940.

Ratchnevsky, P. *Cinggis-Khan, Sein Leben und Wirken* Wiesbaden, 1983.

Saunders, J.J. *The History of the Mongol Conquests* London, 1971.

Sinor, D. 'The Inner Asian Warriors' *Journal of the American Oriental Society* CI–CII pp. 133–144 1981.

Spuler, B. *The Mongols in History* London, 1971.

Vladimirtsov, B. Ya. (trans. Carsow, M.) *Le Régime Social des Mongols* Paris, 1948.

Vladimirtsov, B. Ya. (trans. Prince D.S. Mirsky) *The Life of Chingis-Khan* (second edition) New York & London, 1969.

KUBLAI KHAN
LORD OF THE CELESTIAL EMPIRE

Kublai Khan, grandson of Genghis who became Great Khan in 1260. His main interests lay, however, in China itself where he reigned until 1294 and founded the Yüan dynasty. One of a series of anonymous portraits from the Chinese Imperial Portrait Gallery (Coll. of the National Palace Museum, Taiwan).

Tun-huang oasis, site of a series of Buddhist cave-temples known as the Caves of a Thousand Buddhas. There was also a Nestorian Christian parish and a Manichaen centre at Tun-huang. Here, near the northern foothills of the Tibetan plateau and the eastern edge of the Takla Makan desert, Chinese, Tibetan and Turco-Mongol Central cultures came into contact and frequent conflict. Before its conquest by Genghis Khan in 1227 the area fell within the Hsi-Hsia kingdom of western China.

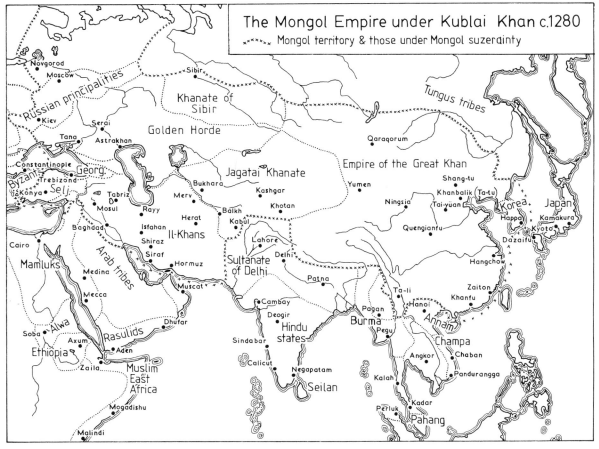

The Mongol Empire under Kublai Khan c.1280
×-×-×-× Mongol territory & those under Mongol suzerainty

In Xanadu did Kubla Khan
A stately pleasure dome decree;
Where Alph, the sacred river, ran
Through caverns measureless to man
Down to a sunless sea

Ancestral voices prophesying war

Kubla Khan
(S. T. Coleridge)

The Supreme Ruler

Kublai Khan is best remembered, outside China, as a fabulously wealthy and almost legendary figure rather than as a great military commander. Coleridge was, in fact, historically correct when he wrote that 'in Xanadu did Kublai Khan a stately pleasure dome decree', though this dome was more of an oversized and highly decorated Mongol tent than a palace. Westerners also know Kublai Khan through the writings of Marco Polo, the thirteenth-century Venetian traveller who revealed the Far East to barely believing European eyes.

Yet the real Kublai, grandson of that bloody conqueror Genghis Khan, by military campaign and conquest added huge areas and vast populations to the already immense Mongol domains. He also made Peking the capital of a world empire that stretched from the Pacific to the Danube, from Siberia to the Indian Ocean.

Kublai Khan and the new Yüan dynasty that he founded in China remained acknowledged suzereins of all those Mongol khanates that had grown from Genghis Khan's massive conquests. Coleridge's Xanadu was in reality Shang-tu, Kublai's summer palace. There, in 1260, Kublai had himself proclaimed Great Khan or supreme ruler of the Mongol world and there, as described in awe-struck detail by Marco Polo, he indeed built a magnificent palace alongside an enormous and well-stocked hunting park. Unlike his conquering grandfather, Kublai dedicated his life to reunifying China under Mongol rule and extending Chinese influence over the surrounding countries. China's unity had, in fact, been lost centuries earlier with the fall of the T'ang dynasty.

While Kublai's predecessors sought solely to enrich the Mongols, Kublai seems to have had two aims. He wished, of course, to maintain and extend Mongol rule, but at the same time he tried to serve China in his rôle as the new Son of Heaven and heir to nineteen previous Chinese dynasties. His new Yüan dynasty, set up in 1272, was the twentieth in China's long and illustrious history. Yet, however much Kublai Khan admired Chinese civilization, he remained a Mongol and a warrior. He

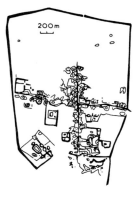

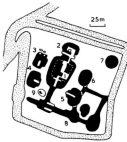

was, in fact, a typical educated barbarian ruling an ancient and cultured society. Under Kublai Khan's rule, the Mongol military élite in China adopted many Chinese habits and even began to grow soft in some respects. This trend only became apparent under his successors but even Marco Polo noted that the Mongols of China, like those of the Middle East, were, by the late thirteenth century, already adopting the ways of those they had conquered.

Kublai Khan was, again according to an admiring Marco Polo, of middle height with a figure of 'just proportion'. His face was somewhat red, which may have resulted from the addiction to food and drink that became a feature of his later life. Marco Polo also regarded him as:

the most powerful of men, in subjects, lands and treasures, that there is on earth or ever was, from the time of our first father Adam to this day.

An Islamic historian, Wassaf, was similarly full of praise, saying that Kublai's power eclipsed that of all previous rulers anywhere in the world, and:

One thing which demonstrates his wit and intelligence is the fact that he was on intimate terms with men of merit and masters of science; that he liked their company and welcomed them more than any other set of people.

On the other hand Kublai Khan's life saw setbacks as well as victories and he seems to have died a sad and lonely figure. His two humiliating defeats at the hands of the Japanese are perhaps remembered more widely than his victories over many other foes. Perhaps Kublai's tragedy is that no human being could live up to the awe-inspiring reputation given him by his contemporaries, particularly as his memory is also overshadowed by that of his daunting grandfather, Genghis Khan.

Mongols Over China

Kublai did not inherit an easy situation. Chinese resistance to the Mongol invasion had stiffened during the early years of Ögotäi, Genghis Khan's easy-going but drunken successor as Great Khan of the Mongol Empire. The Chin rulers of northern China had been battered but certainly not defeated by Genghis Khan and only a full-scale campaign using almost all available Mongol resources finally succeeded in capturing the last Chin province of Ho-nan in 1234. This grim struggle was a war of cities in which Ögotäi's Mongols used their new-found skills in mining, siege engineering and perhaps even gunpowder.

The age-old rivalry between northern and southern China had obviously weakened Chinese resistance to the Mongols. But now the north had fallen and the Mongols faced a very different kind of foe in the densely populated, rich and fertile regions south of the broad Hwai river.

The Chin of northern China had been of relatively recent nomadic origin – rather like the Mongols themselves. The Sung dynasty of southern China was, however, purely Chinese and had a very long, highly civilized history. The Mongol assault on the Sung began in 1236. It would last forty-three years and only be completed by Kublai Khan himself. Meanwhile the Mongols continued raiding Korea in the north, winning suzereinty over the Koreans, defeating a rebellion and eventually installing a Korean defector as their governor in P'yongyang. Even so the Koreans would continue to give the Mongols a great deal of further trouble in the future.

Realizing that their sprawling World Empire needed an administrative centre, if not a great urban capital, the Mongols had built a new city at Qaraqorum in Mongolia. This was not a very large or splendid affair. Qaraqorum seems, in fact, to have been more of a walled camp site with a few buildings attached, its most notable feature being a huge hunting park. Yet the little city served a vital function as the nerve-centre of an increasingly elaborate government postal system. This in turn grew out a simpler organization created by Genghis himself. Ögotäi's postal service was now based upon way-stations one day's ride apart and stretching throughout his vast realm.

In 1241 alcohol finally caught up with Ögotäi, despite his promise to his brother to drink no more than a limited number of cups of wine per day – a promise that he evaded by using unusually large cups! On Ögotäi's death the Mongol Empire was thrown into confusion and virtual civil war until the descendants of Genghis Khan's son Tolui seized the throne in a bloody coup d'état in 1251. Möngke, eldest brother and leader of the family, became Great Khan. His brother Hülegü took responsibility in the Middle East while Kublai took command of Mongol forces in northern China. Möngkë's accession to the throne was also to have a profound impact on the course of Mongol, and world, history for it turned the Mongols' attention firmly eastward. The brief

A Chinese painted silk showing Mongol nomads on the march. Here a Bactrian camel carries a heavy load on its wood-framed pack saddle. Though Central Asian nomads occasionally fought on camelback, their two-humped camels were essentially beasts of burden, unlike the much faster single-humped Arabian dromedary which was both a riding animal and a beast of burden.

55

Mongol invasion of Europe was not repeated and even Hülegü's epic struggle against the Muslims was to remain something of a side-show as far as the Great Khans were concerned.

The Young Kublai

Fragments of a bronze belt with small pendant bells from a medieval grave in northern Manchuria, undated (ex-Derevyanko).

While Genghis Khan's childhood is shrouded in legend, Kublai's early life is well recorded. He was born in 1215 and was much influenced by his mother, a woman of exceptionally strong character named Sorkhakhtani. Women played a prominent rôle throughout Mongol history. Many fought at their husbands' sides. Others ruled as regents, served as counsellors and even saved entire tribes through their inspiration. But Sorkhakhtani was more than this. As a young woman she had been almost the only person to stand up to Genghis Khan's overpowering personality. Yet she never seems to have been criticized by him. As a niece of Togrul, last independent ruler of the Kerait tribe, she had been given to Genghis Khan's son Tolui as a wife when Togrul had been defeated by the great conqueror. Her elder sister became one of Genghis Khan's own wives. When Tolui died, Sorkhakhtani refused to marry the Great Khan Ögotäi's son. Instead she declared that she would dedicate her life to her four sons – Möngke, Hülegü, Kublai and Arik-böke. Sorkhakhtani was herself a Nestorian Christian but although Hülegü was educated by a Nestorian priest Kublai was taught by a Chinese sage.

Genghis Khan had a very high regard for Kublai; he recognized the child's intelligence and once said to his followers; 'If you are ever in doubt what to do, ask this boy Kublai'. On another occasion Genghis Khan met Tolui's sons when they were on one of those great Mongol hunts. Kublai, aged eleven, had just shot his first hare, while the nine-year old Hülegü had brought down his first wild goat. Thereupon, the Great Khan personally smeared the boys' right, shooting, thumbs with the blood and fat of their victims in a ceremony foreshadowing the blooding with a fox's tail that is still practised in European style hunts.

After he became Great Khan, Möngke offered his younger brother territory in China. Kublai checked with his Chinese advisers and chose an area that was fertile but relatively under-populated. Möngke, knowing little of agriculture, was surprised that Kublai had selected an area that seemed to offer little in the way of military manpower, so he added some extra territory in the Ho-nan area. Möngke was himself a stern and warlike man. Although a Mongol through and through, he further strengthened the civil administration as well as the army, making the

Mongol Empire into a remarkably centralized state. Möngke employed a Nestorian Christian as his chancellor but also favoured Taoists. Buddhism he regarded as 'the palm of the hand' to which other religions were 'like the five fingers'.

Mongol expansion also started anew under this grim ruler. A great tribal gathering or *quriltai* sent Hülegü to Iran, while Möngke and Kublai jointly set about the conquest of Sung China. Mongol forces were already campaigning in Korea. In 1257 the Koreans abandoned all hope of buying off their oppressors and began to fight back hard, particularly from the sea. Meanwhile huge Mongol forces were arrayed against the Sung, Kublai being placed in command of one of the four armies entrusted with this campaign. For his part Kublai dedicated himself totally to the task, but it was still to be the Mongols' toughest war. The Sung Chinese showed themselves to be the most resilient of foes. Southern China was not only densely populated and full of strongly walled cities. It was also a land of mountain ranges and wide fast-flowing rivers. This was terrain in which the nomad horse-archers of the Central Asian steppes found themselves somewhat at a loss. Instead the Mongols had to learn new techniques of Chinese warfare, which they succeeded in doing remarkably quickly. They also had to employ great numbers of Chinese soldiers, mostly infantry, as well as specialist troops from all over the Mongol empire. Southern China also threatened her invaders and their horses with new diseases and an unfamiliar climate. Sung cities were sometimes vast. The capital in what is now Hangchow had an estimated population of one and half million. Venice, one of the greatest of European cities at that time, only numbered some hundred thousand inhabitants.

Before attacking the Sung heartland, Möngke decided to crush the mountainous and largely non-Chinese kingdom of Nanchow in the far south-west of what is now China. If successful, this operation would outflank the Sung and also cut off some of their lucrative overland trade with Burma and India. Kublai was given responsibility for this vital campaign and in September 1253, at the age of thirty-six, he set out on what was his first major military operation as an independent commander. This was quite old for a Mongol prince, many others having proved themselves in war at a far earlier age. Perhaps for this reason Kublai took no chances and showed all the careful preparation and planning that were to become a hallmark of his military career. He ensured that his army was fully supplied and equipped to face the daunting natural obstacles that faced it. Kublai himself, with his old Chinese teacher Yao Shu at his side, led one half of the army, while the other was commanded by Uriyangkhadai, son of Genghis Khan's brilliant general Sübötäi.

To reach their objective, in a classic example of the indirect approach, these two armies had to cross three great rivers and numerous mountain

Ögotäi Khan, son of Genghis, who ruled the Mongol World Empire from 1229 to 1241. This picture by an unknown artist once formed part of the Chinese Imperial Portrait Gallery (Coll. of the National Palace Museum, Taiwan).

Anonymous portrait of the Yüan Empress Ch'e-po-erh. Female court costume of basically this type appears in art of the Mongol period from China to Iran (Coll. of the National Palace Museum, Taiwan).

ranges. The two forces would then unite before the walls of Ta-li, capital of the kingdom of Nanchow, which would thus be caught in a pincer. There was plenty of hard fighting on the march, yet the real brilliance of Kublai's invasion was logistical. Nanchow had previously maintained its independence behind mountain walls, but Kublai got his armies to their objective across country that had previously been considered impassable. Every valley had to be fought for as each aboriginal tribe defended its ancestral territory. Each was, however, defeated and each then in turn supplied guides, provisions and sometimes troops for the advancing Mongol forces. The Mongols were not completely unfamiliar with such warfare, however. The inflated sheepskin rafts that they used to cross rushing mountain torrents reflected a technique long used by Central Asian nomads when campaigning or migrating through the steppes, mountains and forests of their original homeland. The making of these rafts was supervised by a senior officer named Bayan, who in later years would become one of Kublai's most trusted and successful generals.

When at last the Mongol armies converged on the Nanchow capital of Ta-li, the inhabitants might well have dreaded a massacre such as those that had characterized previous Mongol victories. Yet it was not to be. Chinese historians claim that, just before the Mongols entered Ta-li, Kublai's old teacher and adviser, Yao Shu, told his pupil a Chinese moral tale about an ancient Chinese general who had tricked his troops into taking a conquered town without killing any of the inhabitants. Kublai, they claim, then leapt to his feet crying, 'What you have been describing is merely a fable, but tomorrow I shall make it real!' The Mongol soldiers then hung huge silken banners beneath the city wall proclaiming, 'On pain of death do not kill'. The commandants of Ta-li slew the three Mongol officers whom Kublai sent to demand their surrender but even so the Mongol army, which had by now broken into the city, rode behind other banners proclaiming the same message, 'On pain of death do not kill'. In the end no Mongol and no defender was hurt, except for the three unfortunate Mongol envoys, the two Ta-li commandants who were executed for defying Kublai's order, and the chief minister who ruled Nanchow. How much credit should really go to Kublai's teacher, Yao Shu, is unknown, for Kublai was already proving himself civilized enough to realize that mercy could be as effective a weapon as massacre had been.

The conquest of Nanchow took fifteen months, but the Mongols were now in a position to attack the mighty Sung from both north and west. Meanwhile Kublai's general, Uriyangkhadai, remained in Nanchow from which he pacified almost all the tribes of what is now south-west China and even raided into Tibet. In 1257 Uriyangkhadai tried to take Annam in northern Vietnam and defeated a huge Vietnamese army that included war elephants. In this remarkable battle the Mongols' horses had refused to face these huge and unknown beasts, so Uriyangkhadai's man dismounted and attacked the elephants with fire-arrows. The elephants panicked and stampeded back through the ranks of their own men, crashing into the jungle and tearing the wooden castles from their backs. Although the local ruler agreed to pay tribute to the Mongols, the climate, disease and continued guerrilla attacks forced Kublai's general to return to China. Only 20,000 of the original Mongol army of 100,000 are said to have survived this appalling campaign. But, despite such losses, Kublai's first big military operation had been a resounding success. He had proved himself to be a first-rate commander as well as a fine strategist.

Kublai's handling of the Nanchow campaign showed just how much he had been influenced by Chinese civilization and Chinese military thinking. This was even more apparent in the way he ruled northern China as the Great Khan's viceroy. Here he was greatly influenced by a Buddhist monk, Liu Ping-chung, and the two men appear in Chinese histories as the ideal Wise Ruler and his Virtuous Minister so popular in Chinese legend. The reality is, however, more difficult to pin down. We know that Liu was a fine artist, a reasonable poet and an excellent mathematician. Kublai greatly valued the monk's advice on many subjects and they probably shared responsibility for the idea of building a new capital ten days' journey from Peking. This would be strategically sited on the cultural and ethnic frontier between the Mongolian steppe and the Chinese agricultural zone. In 1263 this palace-city, the Xanadu of Coleridge's poem, was renamed Shang-tu or 'Upper Capital'. Kublai's old tutor, the Chinese sage Yao Shu, also continued to wield influence. It is he who is credited with convincing Kublai to concentrate on military affairs while leaving the business of government to experienced officials. This he did, both as viceroy and later as Great Khan himself, though developments like the establishment of military farms run by Chinese soldiers showed that military and civil affairs could not always be kept separate.

Unfortunately Kublai's obvious admiration for the Chinese way of doing things made him enemies among more traditional Mongols at his

A Central Asian chieftain's ger tent within an enclosure, exactly as described by Marco Polo. This picture, from a long scroll-painting of The Story of Lady Wen-chi, *was made in the early Ming period just after the Mongol Yüan dynasty had been overthrown. Other details include a canopy erected in front of the tent, the wickerwork internal structure of the ger itself and the typical saddles of the Mongol ponies waiting outside (Met. Museum of Art, no. 1973.120.3, New York).*

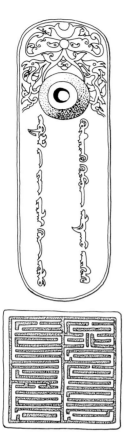

(upper) *bronze* paiza *or tablet of authority with an Uighur inscription from the western regions of the Mongol empire.* (lower) *bronze seal for stamping documents. It belonged to a Mongol officer in command of one hundred to one thousand cavalry and was fished up in Hakata Bay, Japan, from the wreck of Kublai Khan's invasion fleet, sunk in 1281. The maze-like pattern is in the Mongol script.*

brother's court. Möngke could also have been jealous of Kublai's growing prestige within China and may even have seen Shang-tu as a possible rival to the Mongol imperial capital at Qaraqorum. Whatever the reasons, Möngke had his brother's vice-regal government investigated in 1257 and many of Kublai's Chinese officials were executed. The strains steadily grew worse and Kublai even considered rebelling against his elder brother. Again the old scholar Yao Shu is credited with dissuading Kublai from such a suicidal action, saying:

You are your brother's first subject and you must set an example of subordination and obedience. Send your wives and children to him and go yourself in person to offer him all you own and your life.

Kublai did go to Möngke, made his peace and returned to continue ruling as viceroy over the Mongol possessions in China. Perhaps both men, being hard-headed realists, knew that civil war would benefit neither. Instead they seem to have agreed on an all-out invasion of southern China, to crush the Sung once and for all.

This time Möngke took charge of the campaign while leaving the youngest of his brothers, Arik-böke, to govern Qaraqorum. Sacrifices were first laid at the grave of Genghis Khan to beseech his blessing on the forthcoming invasion. A four-pronged offensive was then launched. Möngke advanced from the north-west, Kublai from the north and general Uriyangkhadai from the south-west, while a smaller, fourth force struck from the west. They hoped thereby to overrun central China, seize Sung territory in the south-west and, by isolating the Sung heartland in eastern China, force the Sung to surrender. Such elaborate and sophisticated strategy also aimed to reduce the losses that would be inevitable in a prolonged war and again showed how far the warlike Mongols had come since the days of Genghis Khan. At first things went well, though Möngke's army made slow progress against determined resistance. Kublai was besieging Wuchang when the unexpected news arrived that Möngke was dead – either from an arrow wound suffered in the taking of Ho-chou or from dysentery contracted during that same siege. The entire Mongol empire was once again thrown into turmoil and the Sung were saved – for a while.

Son of Heaven

Kublai's commitment to the war against the Sung is shown by his insistence on pressing ahead across the broad Yangtze river, even after hearing of his brother's death and despite being invited to return to Mongolia. There a new Great Khan was to be elected at a *quriltai* gathering of Mongol leaders and members of Genghis Khan's Golden Family. 'We have come here with an army like ants or locusts,' he replied, according to Rashid al Din, 'How can we turn back, our task unfinished, because of mere rumours.' Of course Kublai knew that the *quriltai* could hardly go ahead without him, and a triumphant attack across the Yangtze would impress those attending the gathering. So, against the advice of his generals, who preferred to await better weather conditions, the flags were raised, drums beaten and Kublai's army sailed across the mighty river. Once they reached the other side the weather suddenly improved. A fierce but victorious battle was fought against Sung defending forces and the Mongols established their bridgehead. In so doing they also succeeded in cutting the Yangtse, a vital artery for the Sung kingdom. Only now did Kublai make a temporary peace and hurry north before getting bogged down in a war that would inevitably consist of endless bitter sieges.

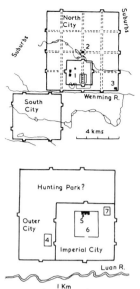

Plans of Kublai Khan's capitals at Ta-tu (Khanbalik), now Beijing (upper) *and Shang-tu* (lower). 1 – Yüan Palace; 2 – bell-tower; 3 – observatory; 4 – palace; 5 – inner palace; 6 – Forbidden City; 7 – possible site of temple.

The election of a new Great Khan was not as simple as it might have seemed. Kublai was the eldest surviving son of Tolui but other branches of Genghis Khan's family also had a clear claim to the throne. Many more traditional Mongols were also suspicious of Kublai's flirtation with Chinese civilization and his increasing reliance on Chinese advisers, not to mention Chinese troops. In the event, however, only Kublai and his younger brother Arik-böke had enough military might close to where it mattered – Mongolia, site of the vital *quriltai*. So only they could make an effective claim to the title of Great Khan. That Kublai three times refused the title was merely a matter of good manners. In reality he, like his brother Arik-böke, was a hard-headed politician who had every intention of becoming Great Khan if he possibly could.

Kublai promptly arranged his own somewhat irregular *quriltai* at Shang-tu. There, on 4th June 1260, his own army proclaimed him leader of the entire Mongol world. He was then forty-four years old. Back in Mongolia, Arik-böke replied by having himself similarly proclaimed as Great Khan by the more traditional Mongol leaders. A brief civil war followed, which Kublai quickly seemed to have won – he had, of course, far greater military resources than his brother. Nevertheless the fraternal blood-letting flared up a year later. Kublai constantly refused to pursue his defeated young brother and not until 1264 did Arik-böke finally surrender. Thereafter, he was kept as a privileged prisoner until his death in 1266.

Knowing that his position was shaky among many of the Mongols, Kublai Khan also had himself crowned as 'Son of Heaven', Emperor of China in the Chinese manner. He similarly issued a proclamation declaring that, although the Mongols were superior warriors, they needed Chinese skills in government. Both these actions were a transparent attempt to win Chinese support. The fate of the Mongol world empire was now clearly linked to that of China. Mongol affairs in the Middle East and eastern Europe became ever more marginal as far as the Great Khans were concerned. Nevertheless the traditionalists, soon to be led by Khaidu and the descendants of Genghis Khan's other son Jagatai, were to remain a thorn in Kublai's side for the rest of his life.

Despite his undeniable admiration for things Chinese, Kublai Khan clung firmly to his Mongol heritage. In this he was helped by another remarkable woman, his ambitious and very practical wife, Chabi. She took a close interest in practically everything from military organization to agricultural development and the design of clothes. Despite the staggering wealth of her husband's court, Chabi tried to instil a sense of economy by getting her women to weave rugs from the threads of worn out bow-strings. She also designed a new type of Mongol hat with a brim against the fierce southern sun and a sleeveless tunic suitable for archers to wear in battle. On a number of occasions Chabi also saved the families of defeated foes from humiliation or execution. Meanwhile Kublai Khan had huge hunting parks marked out beside his palaces so that he could still keep hunting in traditional Mongol style. The 'stately pleasure dome' of Coleridge's poem, a gigantic and highly decorated Mongol tent, was set up in the middle of this park while a smaller piece of steppe grassland was also laid out in front of Kublai's palace in Peking, to remind the Great Khan of his nomad origins.

Kublai Khan's other brother, Hülegü, had supported Kublai during his struggle with Arik-böke but Hülegü had been unable to do much because of his own problems in the Middle East. There the Mongols had suffered their first significant defeat at the hands of Egypt's Mamluks at the battle of Ayn Jalut in 1260. Although he was eventually recognized as Great Khan by virtually all Mongols, Kublai was never able to control central Asia effectively. Even the Uighur lands were eventually lost to his western cousins, though Mongolia, being closer to China, was held as a rather privileged province of what had now become a Chinese empire.

Conquest of Southern China

In 1264 Kublai Khan turned once again to the conquest of the Sung in what was to prove the greatest military achievement of his career. By his side were two skilled generals who already had considerable experience of fighting against the southern Chinese. These were the Mongol Bayan, son of Kublai's old comrade Uriyangkhadai, and the Uighur Arigh Khaya. Once more Kublai ensured a carefully planned and meticulous campaign. It would be his own private war and he wanted to take southern China intact, not as a wasteland. Chinese aristocrats who offered loyalty to the new régime were left in possession of their lands. Cities were not sacked and destruction of agriculture was kept to a minimum. Nevertheless the Sung were once again to be the Mongols' most formidable foes.

Mongol troops still faced particular problems in southern China. There remained the perennial problems of parasites, disease and unsuitable terrain for large-scale cavalry warfare. Even the Mongols' hardy steppe ponies suffered from the hot, humid climate and there was virtually no open grazing to feed them. Mongol losses rose alarmingly and gaps in the ranks had to be filled with native Chinese levies, most of whom were infantry. At first these troops were despised by their Mongol overlords but they rapidly proved themselves to be not only hardy fighters but better able to cope with the debilitating climate. Progress was, however, painfully slow. The Sung capital of Hangchow fell only in 1276 and it took a further three years for Sung resistance finally to end. Attitudes were also different from what they had been in Genghis Khan's day. Prisoners were usually treated moderately well and Kublai did all that he could to encourage defections from the Sung side. This was particularly successful where the powerful Sung navy was concerned, a vital factor in a war where ships provided communication and transport not only around the coast but up the broad rivers of southern China.

Meanwhile Bayan proved himself a master of siege warfare, a branch of the military art in which the nomad Mongols had now become world leaders. The most epic siege was that of Hsiang-yang, which lasted no less than five years and was to be the turning point in Kublai's conquest of southern China. Hsiang-yang was held by one of the most tenacious

63

This portrait of an unnamed Yüan Emperor illustrates the basically Central Asian style of costume worn by the rulers of China throughout the period of Mongol domination (Coll. of the National Palace Museum, Taiwan).

of Sung commanders, Lü Wen-huan. Because the city stood on the banks of the wide Han river, the Mongols had to use their new-found nautical skills in an attempt to stop Sung supplies and reinforcements from reaching the garrison. Even if this could be achieved, and even if all overland relief efforts could be defeated, Hsiang-yang would eventually have to be stormed. To keep casualties to a minimum the Mongols therefore needed the very best available siege artillery. Experts were recruited throughout the Mongol Empire, from northern China, Korea and even from far distant Muslim Iraq. Meanwhile many battles were fought in the surrounding countryside and on the Han river, but still the city did not fall, for the Sung realized that the fate of their kingdom hung upon that of Hsiang-yang. The Mongol noose steadily tightened but a full-scale assault remained a very hazardous option. Newer, bigger siege machines were erected and an almost constant bombardment was maintained until, late in March 1273, Lü Wen-huan at last surrendered.

The loss of Hsiang-yang was a devastating blow to Sung morale. City after city now fell, until at last Kublai Khan's armies closed around the Sung capital of Hangchow itself. This, the so-called Venice of the East, had a huge population, an enormous garrison, mighty walls, stone towers in nearly every street and a network of urban canals said to be spanned by 12000 bridges. It was a besiegers' nightmare! By this time, January 1276, the old Sung Emperor had died, a child was on the throne and the land was ruled by the widowed Empress Dowager. General Bayan had a long list of victories to his credit, yet even he must have felt relieved when the Empress Dowager agreed to hand over the Sung Imperial Seal in an unmistakable symbol of surrender – Hangchow would not have to be besieged after all. Instead of a Mongol sack and massacre, Kublai's officers made a peaceful yet triumphant entry into the ancient Sung capital. There they proceeded to collect all official seals, the finest works of art, books and maps to be sent to the Great Khan's court.

Despite the Empress Dowager's surrender, the Chinese of the deep south kept up the struggle. The last flicker of resistance was by a Sung fleet, aboard which was a nine-year old boy, Ti-ping, the last Sung Emperor. Even after the Mongols had captured every port along the coast this heroic fleet fought on from bases in coastal islands. But now the Mongols also had a navy of their own and on 19th March 1279 the enemy was trapped near Yai-shan. Only nine Sung ships broke out. That of the little Emperor was not among them. They say that the Sung admiral took the child in his arms and, shouting out 'An Emperor of the Sung chooses death rather than imprisonment!' leapt into the sea, drowning both himself and the boy ruler.

With this, the final defeat of the Sung, Kublai Khan reunited China for the first time since the fall of the T'ang dynasty in the tenth century. Despite a turbulent history, mainland China has never since lost this unity. To the Mongols, Kublai had achieved a long cherished dream, for

Genghis Khan himself smeared the thumbs of his grand-children, Kublai and Hülegü, with the blood of animal's they killed in a Mongol archery initiation rite.

those nomads who regarded themselves as 'Sons of the Grey Wolf and the Hind' had finally become masters of all China.

Defeat in Japan

Much of Kublai's army was dispersed after the defeat of the Sung, but the Great Khan's military ambitions were far from ended. He went on to demand homage from all neighbouring states that had once acknowledged Chinese suzereinty – plus some that were only thought to have accepted such a status. Kublai was thus set on a collision course with practically every independent kingdom in eastern Asia. No other power was in a position to threaten Kublai's empire, but many petty rulers and chieftains were prepared to raid areas where Mongol rule was as yet still weak. Further conquests would also reinforce his shaky position among the warlike but traditional Mongols of central Asia, while at the same time stabilizing newly won but unsettled frontier provinces.

Kublai had already brought Korea finally into the Mongol orbit in 1273, though the Korean royal family was still permitted to rule in the Great Khan's name. For decades Japanese pirates had been carrying out freebooting raids on the Korean coast but these had ceased with the Mongol occupation of the peninsula – the Japanese had no wish to quarrel with the mighty Kublai Khan. Unfortunately the Great Khan had other ideas and he sent a series of embassies demanding that Japan recognize him as overlord – a move that would eventually lead the Mongols to their most humiliating defeat. Kublai's first such demand was sent in 1266 but it never reached Japan, being stalled in Korea. A second embassy finally arrived in 1268 and it caused near panic as well as considerable shock in a court that regarded its own Emperor as virtually divine.

Japan might have been, as Kublai wrote, 'a small country', but it was a very warlike one. A period of relative stability had followed the Minamoto clan's victory in their epic power struggle with the rival Taira family. Japan was now ruled by a military dictator or *shogun*, with the Emperor as titular ruler. By the mid-thirteenth century even the *shogun* had become little more than a figurehead, controlled by a family of regents. Yet the situation was stable under a military council known as the *bakufu* and the country was prosperous.

Receiving no satisfactory reply, Kublai prepared for invasion. Korea was ordered to build a fleet and raise an army, but that war-ravaged country was in no condition to obey. Even an advance guard of a few thousand Mongol troops had to be sent home because there was not enough food for them. When at last an invasion fleet did set sail in 1274 it consisted of hundreds of ships and perhaps forty thousand assorted

In addition to weapons and fine bronze objects, a number of very crudely made storage jars have been brought up from Hakata Bay. Many are distorted, reflecting the urgent need for supplies when Kublai Khan's invasion fleet was hurriedly assembled.

After hearing a story about the cunning and compassion of an ancient Chinese general, the young Kublai Khan declared that he too could capture a city without shedding blood

Mongol, Korean and northern Chinese troops and sailors. The Koreans were not at all happy about fighting for Kublai Khan and, despite initial successes on the small islands of Tsushima and Iki, the expedition turned into a disaster. The Mongols made a bridgehead at Hakata Bay in November and drove off all Japanese attempts to dislodge them. Then the weather turned against the invaders. A massive storm was clearly brewing. The Korean sea captains persuaded the Mongol officers to re-embark their men and ride out the storm at sea. It was a disastrous decision. A terrible typhoon struck the fleet and up to two hundred ships foundered, with the loss of some thirteen thousand lives. The survivors made their way straight back home.

Although it had been the weather that finally defeated Kublai Khan's invasion, his army had also been unable to expand its bridgehead. This perhaps accounted for the Mongols' willingness to accept Korean advice and re-embark aboard the fleet. On the other hand the Japanese had also faced problems. Their forces had not fought a full-scale battle for many decades. The Japanese warrior code of *bushido* had much in common with that of medieval European chivalry. It emphasized individual combat between champions and professional *samurai* who would fight only opponents of similar rank after declaring their names, titles, ancestry and exploits. The grimly professional Mongols fought in disciplined formations and also enjoyed superior weaponry. Not only was the Mongol composite bow greatly superior to the simple Japanese longbow but Kublai Khan's army also used assorted crossbows and pyrotechnic weapons, probably including primitive forms of gun-powder. Nevertheless the Great Khan had obviously under-estimated Japanese powers of resistance and was determined not to make the same mistake next time.

Kublai's second invasion of Japan had to await the final defeat of the Sung and for a while it looked as if the Japanese would seize the offensive and attack Korea. As it turned out the *bakufu* limited itself to building a fleet of small coastal warships, plus a twenty-kilometre-long defensive wall around Hakata Bay. For his second invasion Kublai Khan hoped to build a thousand ships and raise an army of 170000 men – an unre-alistically ambitious figure. Yet an invasion force was assembled, though the poor workmanship of many objects retrieved from the sunken wreck of this second fleet show that corners were cut and preparations hurried.

This time it was to be a two-pronged attack from northern and southern China, converging on the island of Iki. But the commanders quarrelled, the southern fleet was delayed and the northern invasion force pressed on without them. It landed north of the new Japanese defensive wall while the southern fleet eventually beached near the southern end. Even so the Japanese were able to prevent both invading armies from breaching their defences. The Chinese and Korean troops fought without enthusiasm and the Mongols were still not used to

Bronze statuette of the Buddha, also recovered from the site of Kublai Khan's wrecked fleet in Hakata Bay and now in a shrine on Takashima island.

maritime warfare. The Japanese took the naval offensive and their small warships often forced Kublai's less-manœuvrable vessels to chain themselves together for security. Fighting continued from 23rd June to 14th August 1281. Then, on 15th and 16th August, another typhoon struck. Both invasion fleets were smashed against the coast. A third of the northern army drowned while over half of the southerners perished. Those who were trapped ashore were either slaughtered or enslaved by the Japanese. Not surprisingly the Japanese have, from that day to this, regarded the *Kamikaze* or Divine Wind as a mark of heavenly favour. For Kublai Khan this second disaster was a crushing blow to his prestige and he wanted to make a third, overwhelming effort. Only the unanimous opposition of his advisers and his own eventual death stopped this third attempted invasion of Japan. Huge losses had also been suffered in terms of casualties and sheer expense, while the myth of Mongol invincibility had been shattered throughout eastern Asia.

Although the invading Mongols, their Chinese and Korean allies, are shown with monotonous uniformity throughout most of the Japanese Mongol Invasion Scroll, this magnificent painting does show the kind of humble soldiers that formed the bulk of many of Kublai Khan's armies. Here infantry, who, judging by their large rectangular cane shields, are more likely to be southern Chinese rather than Koreans, retreat under a hail of Japanese arrows. In reality Mongol archery, though not necessarily that of their allies, was more effective than Japanese bowmanship. Troops in this picture mostly wear 'soft armour' of felt or buff leather.

The South-east Asian Campaigns

Kublai's attacks on Indochina and Burma had more success on the battlefield but also suffered setbacks. When compared to the wide-sweeping victories enjoyed by the Mongols under Genghis Khan these campaigns look like second-rate affairs. But in reality Kublai Khan's armies triumphed over enormous climatic, geographical and logistical problems never faced by their predecessors. Earlier Mongol armies had fought largely in terrain comparable to that of their native central Asian homeland, without having to face the tropical heat and rain, dense jungle and unknown diseases that Kublai's men met. Mongol horse-archery tactics were often completely unsuited to such conditions and many historians have judged Kublai Khan's efforts to conquer south-east Asia as foolish. Yet the Great Khan persisted with a skill and determination worthy of his mighty ancestor.

Indochina was, at that time, divided into four large kingdoms; Chinese-influenced Annam around what is now northern Vietnam; largely Buddhist Champa in what is now southern Vietnam; similarly Buddhist Khmer centred upon modern Cambodia; and the much larger but again Buddhist Burmese Empire. Annam had already been raided by Uriyangkhadai but Champa was Kublai's first major target. This state had accepted Mongol suzereinty, but its king refused to humble himself personally at Kublai's Court. In 1281 a small army of only five thousand men in one hundred ships set sail for south Vietnam. Like later invaders, they easily seized a bridgehead but the Champa king merely retreated inland. When the Mongol-Chinese army followed him it found itself entangled in jungle-covered hills, pursuing an elusive foe and constantly harassed by guerrillas. Kublai sent a further one and a half thousand men the following year but they also got bogged down. Even his ablest commander, the famous Uighur general Arigh Khaya who had won resounding victories against the Sung, was unable to make progress in this green hell.

Perhaps sending an army overland would help. Such a force would, of course, have to pass through Annam in northern Vietnam, but Annam had accepted Mongol suzereinty. Nevertheless the Annamese king was still not prepared to let the Mongols pass unmolested – so Kublai now found himself at war with both his southern neighbours. In purely military terms the Mongols had much greater success in the north than the south, sweeping aside the Annamese army with relative ease. But the Annamese then adopted the guerrilla tactics of the Champa. The morale of Kublai's tiny expeditionary army was steadily sapped as it suffered mounting losses in both men and supplies. Isolated and dispirited, the Mongols decided to withdraw – but very few made it. Near the Annam-China border they were surrounded and crushed in 1285, in one of the very few full-scale battles of this campaign. Kublai could not let such a humiliation go unavenged. The following year a massive raid into northern Vietnam reached the capital of Hanoi, yet again the climate forced his army to withdraw. On the credit side, both Annam and Champa were also weary of war and their rulers agreed to send tribute to Kublai Khan, if only to keep the Mongols off their backs.

68

This Chinese or Korean ship is in Japanese illustration of the hero Suenaga slaying a Mongol commander. The winch at the stern is probably based on verbal reports of the system which raised and lowered the stern rudders of larger Chinese vessels. The costume, arms and armour of the Mongols or Koreans are also more stylized and less varied than those of their Japanese foes. The picture comes from the Mongol Invasion Scroll, commissioned from a Japanese artist by Takezaki Suenaga, who is shown performing various heroic feats.

Kublai's quarrel with Burma was in some ways more serious. It also ended in a clear though expensive victory for the Mongols. The kingdom of Pagan in Burma had previously paid tribute but when, in 1271, Kublai demanded that this be continued his ambassadors were insulted by the Burmese king, Narathihapate This extraordinary monarch described himself, somewhat extravagantly as 'supreme commander of thirty-six million soldiers, swallower of three hundred curries daily, and mate of three thousand concubines.' Two years later the Burmese king felt that another Mongol embassy had been disrespectful and had them summarily executed. Apparently they had refused to remove their shoes in his presence. It is interesting to note that this question of shoes came up again at the outbreak of the Anglo-Burmese war of 1824–6, when a British representative failed to remove his footwear in the sacred Shwehsandaw pagoda.

With his hands full elsewhere, Kublai was prepared to let even this incident pass for a while. Then, in 1277, the Burmese themselves suddenly attacked a border principality. This was the so-called 'Golden Tooth' state of Kaungai, whose ruler had submitted to the Mongols. The war that followed was, for the Burmese, an epic struggle between their relatively small state and the world empire of the Great Khan. For Kublai it was, however, little more than a troublesome frontier incident to be dealt with by the provincial troops of south-western China.

Yet Burma was no mean military force. Its very large army included cavalry, infantry and war elephants, though the bulk of Burmese soldiers appear to have been barely trained local levies. Before battle, priest-magicians sometimes painted magical signs of sun and moon on the elephants' heads, horses' withers and warriors' spears and shields. To face the forthcoming Mongol invasion the Burmese king is said to have raised an army of 400000 men (an impossible figure) led by the generals Anantapaccaya and Randhapaccaya. With their perhaps ramshackle

69

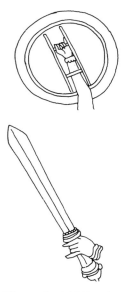

The sword and shield are from a frieze, Angkor Wat, 12th century.

army the generals erected a large fortified encampment, surrounded by ditch and palisade, in the Bhamo valley, there to await their foe. For his part Kublai Khan ordered his Muslim military governor of Yunnan, Nasir al Din, to lead an expedition to Pagan and there avenge the death of his envoys. Nasir al Din was the son of a Turkish cavalry leader from Bukhara in Transoxania who had been captured by Genghis Khan. He proved to be a loyal and capable commander, well able to adapt to the different military conditions his men faced in Burma.

With only ten thousand men, Nasir, however, was seriously outnumbered. Worse than that, he found that his cavalry could not advance against Narathihapate's elephants, just as Uriyangkhadai had found when he raided Annam some years ealier. Two thousand of these great beasts formed the front rank of the vast Burmese army, which now advanced from its fortified encampment. The Mongol and Chinese horses simply panicked at the sight of them and tried to gallop into the surrounding forest. Perhaps Nasir al Din showed admirable quick thinking or perhaps he had anticipated this problem. Whatever the case, Nasir's men were ordered to dismount and tether their horses, then line up as infantry archers and await the Burmese advance. The mixed Mongol and Chinese army thus found itself fighting in a way that was unfamiliar, at least to the Mongols, yet their discipline was such that they stood impassively watching the ponderous Burmese advance. As soon as the unarmoured war elephants came within range, Nasir al Din's men showered them with arrows. The Burmese also had archers, but their weapons were much inferior to the powerful central Asian composite bow. Now the great beasts panicked in their turn, crashing back through their own ranks of cavalry and infantry. Yet the battle was still hard fought and long. The outnumbered Mongols had placed their flanks against the surrounding jungle and when at last the Burmese began to fall back they remounted their horses, charged the enemy and turned Narathihapate's defeat into a rout.

Marco Polo gave a graphic description of the battle, clearly based on the accounts of men who had been present. He went on to say that:

The elephant is an animal with more wit than any other. . . . They [the Mongols] caught more than two hundred of them. And it was from this time forth that the Great Khan began to keep numbers of elephants.'

Other chroniclers say that only twelve elephants actually reached Kublai's Court.

It was a notable victory, but the kingdom of Pagan had certainly not been conquered. The Burmese continued to raid Kublai's frontiers, the Great Khan replying with invasions deep into Burma in 1283 and 1287. On the latter occasion the Mongols marched down the Irrawaddy valley to capture and plunder the Burmese capital itself, but not until ten years later did a new king of Pagan, Kyozwa, finally acknowledge Kublai's suzereinty.

70

Kublai's invasion of the distant island of Java was even more dramatic, if somewhat pointless. Ostensibly it was in retaliation for the mutilation of another of the Great Khan's envoys, but in reality it probably had more to do with control of the rich spice trade of the Molucca island, which both states coveted. In 1293, using the experience painfully gained against Japan and in Indochina, Kublai Khan sent a force of 20000 men under Mongol, Chinese and Uighur generals to the eastern end of Java. Armed with a year's supply of grain and huge amounts of silver to purchase local supplies, they joined a Javanese rebel force to defeat the local king. But the Mongols' Javanese ally then turned against them and forced them to abandon the island. All that they gained from this spectacular expedition were a few shiploads of spices, perfumes, incense, ivory, rhinoceros horns, maps and a register of the local population – hardly enough even to cover campaign expenses.

Cambodian relief carvings show the kinds of troops, including war-elephants, faced by Kublai Khan's armies during their invasions of Indo-China. This is the battle between Khmer and Champa warriors, from Angkor Thom, 13th century.

Rebellion and Revolt

Kublai's overseas wars had little effect on his position as Great Khan, but the problems he faced in central Asia were much more serious. Here he endured the constant enmity of Khaidu, grandson of Ögotäi and leader of those Mongol traditionalists who feared and resented Kublai Khan's increasing identification with Chinese civilization. Khaidu has been described as the living opposite of Kublai, both in his attitudes and in his way of life. He also posed a far greater threat than Kublai's young brother Arik-böke had ever done. From a power base in the mountains east of Lake Balkash, Khaidu first humbled the Mongol Khans of Transoxania and thus made himself effective master of central Asia. A clash with Kublai became inevitable and from around 1271 until 1288 there was almost constant friction and frequent open warfare between the forces of Kublai and those of Khaidu. Yet there were very few major battles, the fighting largely consisting of raids and minor engagements.

Kublai's troops concentrated on keeping their long and vulnerable supply routes open across the steppes and deserts, but they were hampered by frequent quarrels among their leaders. While Khaidu's men fought in a traditional nomad style, raiding then retreating into the mountains, forests and steppes, Kublai concentrated on garrisoning the main towns, extending agriculture and winning the support of members of the settled population. These in turn became the inevitable target of Khaidu's raids. Kublai Khan set up new military colonies supplied with seeds, tools and weapons. Self-sufficiency remained an elusive goal for Kublai's garrisons, but lack of food caused even greater problems for his enemy.

The Great Khan's tactics were, in fact, those that had been used against central Asian nomads by Chinese emperors for thousands of years. Instead of pursuing Khaidu into the mountains and steppes, Kublai set up a military cordon around the enemy heartland in an attempt to contain their raids. His troops seem to have reacted only if Khaidu's men broke through this line. Gradually, almost inexorably, Kublai's westernmost garrisons found themselves isolated and vulnerable as the agricultural infrastructure declined and canals and dams were destroyed. Eventually Kublai had to recognize the inevitable. He abandoned most of what is now the Chinese autonomous province of Sinkiang-Uighur and concentrated on holding Mongolia, where he was much more successful. In Mongolia Kublai Khan won over the people of a war-ravaged region by sending convoys of food from China and setting up more military-agricultural colonies. The government postal service was made yet more efficient and a supply of craftsmen was even sent to teach Mongol artisans new skills.

Khaidu maintained his resistance until seven years after Kublai Khan's death – he was finally defeated and killed in 1301. In 1287 Kublai faced yet another rebellion by traditional forces, this time in Manchuria. It was led by Nayan, a Nestorian Christian descended from one of Genghis Khan's half-brothers. Much of Nayan's army was also Christian and, according to Marco Polo, had the Cross upon its banner. This revolt proved to be so serious that Kublai himself led the expedition to crush it. The Great Khan had, as usual, been very careful. A relatively small mixed force was gathered, consisting of cavalry and infantry, while

Kublai himself rode in a palanquin carried by four elephants. Marco Polo stated that these elephants were protected by leather armour covered in cloth of gold. Crossbowmen and archers he said, also accompanied Kublai Khan within the wooden palanquin, which was surmounted by a banner bearing the signs of sun and moon. By now the Great Khan was seventy-two years old and suffered from gout, rheumatism and various other ailments. Meanwhile the Mongol fleet had shipped supplies to the Liao river, close to where the rebel army was encamped. The subsequent battle was long and hard, but in the end the Great Khan's combined force

On this Chinese silk-painting of the Yüan period, entitled 'The Spring Rider', a mounted archer wears Chinese rather than nomad Central Asian costume (National Palace Museum, Taiwan).

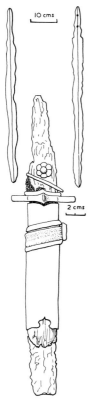

of cavalry and infantry won the day, Nayan being captured and executed.

Further south, in Tibet, Kublai was offered nominal suzereinty, though most of that bleak and mountainous land remained outside his real control. In the warmer but equally mountainous regions south-east of Tibet, Kublai's authority was more real and he succeeded in considerably extending China's frontiers. Despite setbacks and rebellions in central Asia, Kublai also remained the recognized Great Khan of the Mongol world. In this capacity he often intervened – at least diplomatically – in the affairs of the western Mongol khanates. Early in his reign he had negotiated an end to a war between his brother Hülegü in Iran and Berke, his cousin who ruled the Mongol Golden Horde in southern Russia. Kublai later intervened in a succession crisis in Mongol Iran, ironically in favour of traditionalist forces against those who were accused of having 'abandoned the ways of their forefathers and having accepted the Law of the Arabs'. On another occasion his disapproval was in itself enough to have a proposed peace agreement with the Muslim Mamluks of Egypt abandoned.

The Great Khan's Army

The army of Kublai Khan differed considerably from that of Genghis Khan in its recruitment, organization and tactics. Not only had the Mongol world empire changed over the previous half century, but so had the foes that it faced. Kublai ruled a well-organized and highly civilized state based upon China, whose culture was one of the oldest, and certainly the most continuous, in history. During the first phase of the Mongol conquest of northern China huge areas were given to various Mongol princes and generals as virtually autonomous fiefs. Kublai Khan is, however, generally believed to have centralized the military administration. How far this went in practice is not at all clear. Centralization may, in fact, have remained an ideal rather than a reality in almost all aspects of the Great Khan's government. Nevertheless, direct government control was certainly seen around the capital of Peking and in the thinly populated, non-Chinese or nomadic regions on the fringes of China.

In 1263 Kublai Khan set up a Privy Council or *Shu-mi Yüan* to deal with all military matters. Like other government agencies it had, in all provinces of his Empire, branches charged with carrying out central government orders. Beneath the major departments of state were six ministries organized along remarkably modern lines. One was the Ministry of War, which dealt with military commands, military colonies and the vital government postal system. In theory it was also responsible

Blades of straight swords (upper), perhaps of Chinese manufacture and found in the Amur river area on the northern borders of the Mongol empire. Troops in Kublai Khan's armies used both Chinese-style straight swords and Central Asian curved sabres (ex-Derevyanko). Remains of a probably curved sabre (lower), perhaps of Chinese origin, found in a grave at Troitskogo in the Amur river basin and dating from a few centuries before the Mongol conquest of Manchuria (ex-Derevyanko).

74

for military training, though in practice the Privy Council seems to have had a direct hand in such matters. Theoretically the Privy Council controlled the army but again, in reality, the opposition of Mongol commanders, who had traditionally enjoyed considerable independence, meant that Kublai had to set up a separate military system for them. Troops under the Great Khan's personal control were known as the *Meng-ku chün* or Mongol Army. Other provincial units, over which he had less direct authority, were given the Mongol name of *tammachi*. Both *Meng-ku chün* and *tammachi* consisted primarily of cavalry. A third, less prestigious but in some ways more vital, division of Kublai Khan's army consisted of ethnic Chinese infantry.

Within the highly sophisticated government apparatus of Mongol China there were various agencies that had a major or minor military rôle. Some were among those directly attached to the Emperor's Court and had their offices in one of the twin capital cities, Peking and Shang-tu. These included the 'Court of the Imperial Stud', which not only supplied Kublai Khan with mare's milk for his highly alcoholic *qumis* but was also in charge of the state horse herds. It naturally worked closely with the 'Court for the Imperial Tack', which dealt with harness, saddles and so on. Both of these in turn collaborated with such departments as the 'Directorate of Animal Feeds', the 'Directorate of Leathers

In the hot summer months Mongol and other steppe nomads wore less heavy clothes than the double-breasted coats shown in most pictures. Here a Mongol archer, painted in the Ming rulers after the fall of the Yüan period, has his right arm completely exposed for ease of shooting. He also wears a loose turban of almost Islamic appearance (Victoria and Albert Museum, no. E33–1964, London).

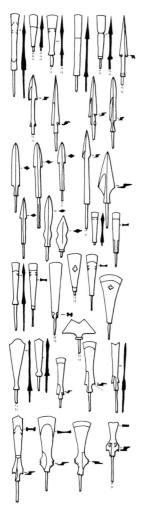

The arrowheads found in warrior graves in Manchuria and the Amur region along the north-eastern frontier of the Mongol World Empire are even more varied than those from Central Asia. Troops from these regions also served in Kublai Khan's armies and their weaponry traditionally showed a high degree of Chinese influence (ex-Derevyanko).

and Furs' and the 'Directorate of Felt Manufacturers'. The 'Ta-tu (Peking) Construction and Protection Office' and the 'Shang-tu Construction and Protection Office' presumably had some responsibility for the fortifications of the capital cities. Peking also had a police force directed by an office with the appalling bureaucratic title of 'The General Commandery of the Ta-tu Circuit Constabulary'. Agencies that offered the Great Khan advice or expertise included, in addition to those dealing with history, religion, medicine and astronomy, a 'Bureau of Imperial Insignia', which was responsible for flags and banners.

The Privy Council also went beneath the title of 'Bureau of Military Affairs' and, together with the Central Secretariat and Censorate, was the most powerful instrument whereby the will of Kublai Khan's government was imposed on his sprawling Empire. It worked hand in hand with the 'Chief Military Commission' or *Ta tu-tu fu*, which supervised the Great Khan's four personal guard units and controlled the 'Armaments Court' or *Wu-pei ssu*, which both manufactured and stored weapons in its arsenals. Meanwhile the grimly named Censorate, *Yü-shih t'ai*, served as a form of secret police or surveillance service.

The heir-apparent had his own virtually separate military administration, including guard units. Lesser princes were aided in the administration and defence of their huge fiefs by various Imperial advisers – who probably also kept a close eye on their activities. In reality the Great Khan's authority over the more distant fiefs and provinces varied considerably. Beyond the metropolitan region around Peking, Mongol government was probably much more pragmatic or even ramshackle than the idealized central administration of Kublai Khan's Court would suggest. Even the vital 'Bureau of Military Affairs' had direct control only over the thirty-five imperial units and other military organizations based in or around Peking, though it did also control élite units stationed in the key centres of Ho-nan, Shensi and Liao-yang. Elsewhere the Great Khan's army was controlled by smaller local replicas of the main 'Bureau of Military Affairs'. Generally speaking, these local military administrations were among the first agencies to be set up in newly conquered territory. Theoretically they should have been temporary, to be replaced by branches of the central Bureau as soon as possible. In reality some lasted well into the fourteenth century.

The bulk of the troops were, as always, under regional rather than central command. Apart from those around Peking, most were stationed in vulnerable frontier provinces. Elsewhere there were often almost no imperial troops to be seen, local order being maintained by local forces or by the military-agricultural colonies. The three main divisions of the army, consisting of the Great Khan's own Mongol Army, the regional *tammachi* and the Chinese infantry, were very large – even when compared to the tribal armies of Genghis Khan. Chinese armies had always been big, but they had also been slow and cumbersome compared to their Central Asian nomadic foes. Now the stolid endurance of the spear- and shield-carrying Chinese foot soldier had been reinforced by the power and mobility of the Mongol horse-archer. He in turn was now much more disciplined and almost certainly better equipped than in the old days. These armies could also move at remarkable speed, with infantrymen frequently riding pillion behind each horseman, though of course dismounting to fight.

Military organization continued to follow the decimal system established by Genghis Khan, with troops being subdivided into groups of ten, one hundred, one thousand and ten thousand. This, as Marco Polo explained, made command relatively simple: 'By this arrangement each officer has to attend only to the management of ten men or ten bodies of men.' The almost blind obedience of the Khan's subjects to their superiors naturally strengthened the command structure. The absolute power of the Mongol aristocracy over their inferiors and the fact that everything – people, animals and possessions – was considered ultimately as the Great Khan's property, were noted by other observers, including the Franciscan friar Carpini. Unauthorized retreat in battle was said to be punishable by death. Even a soldier's comrades would be punished if they failed to prevent him fleeing. The same would apply if a unit failed at least to try and rescue captured comrades. How far such severe penalties applied in practice is, however, unknown.

The effectiveness of Kublai Khan's military organization is shown, not in his over-ambitious forays across the sea or into the steaming jungles of south-east Asia, but in triumphant campaigns like that against the Sung of southern China. This had demanded far greater planning and logistical skill than any earlier Mongol conquest. Many of these massive and far-reaching campaigns required not only Mongol cavalry but the close coordination of such horsemen with Chinese infantry, not to mention the more-than-supporting rôle played by Kublai Khan's newly formed Mongol navy. Contemporaries certainly recognized the Great Khan's military capabilities. Marco Polo said he was 'brave and daring in action, but in point of judgement and military skill he was considered to be the most able and successful commander that ever led the Tartars [Mongols] to battle.'

One of the biggest problems that Kublai Khan's army faced was that of recruitment. All adult male Mongols were still liable for military service, but Kublai had also encouraged many nomads to settle down and take up agriculture in strategically sited colonies. Such men could not be called to the colours as easily or quickly as their purely nomadic predecessors had been. The same applied to men who had been given land in return for good service. Yet those Mongols who did fight for Kublai were clearly quite as effective as their fathers and grandfathers had been. Although they were exempted from most taxation, they had to provide their own military equipment and perhaps other supplies as

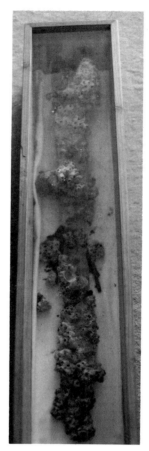

The blade of a straight sword found, stuck vertically into the sandy bed of Hakata bay, by Japanese underwater archaeologists. Though very corroded and encrusted with marine deposits, it is one of the most important military finds yet recovered from the wrecks of Kublai Khan's invasion fleet (photo Prof. Taroa Mozai).

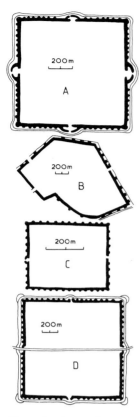

Plans of 10th to 13th century fortifications in northern Manchuria and the Amur basin, showing the strong Chinese influence felt in this area: (A) Bali castle; (B) Sandoatin castle; (C) castle in the estuary of the river Khulani; (D) fortress of Takhuchehn (after M.V. Vorobevy).

well. Such warriors now formed a kind of military caste, but these settled Mongols were by no means an aristocracy. Their burdens, both military and financial, remained extremely heavy. The same applied to those Chinese families whom the government had declared to be 'hereditary military households'. They too had to supply soldiers and supplies to the Great Khan's army. On the other hand nomads of the steppes remained a vital source of readily available troops and there were still references to warrior women fighting for and against Kublai, as they had done in the tribal past.

Yet the Mongols remained a small people, numbering only a few hundred thousands when compared to the teeming millions of their Chinese subjects. Not surprisingly, the Chinese were mistrusted by their Mongol conquerors, despite the fact that Chinese military manpower had become vital. The bulk of the population also continued to regard the Great Khan as a foreigner, though no longer perhaps as a barbarian. Kublai rotated his élite regiments and garrisons every two years to ensure that they were not corrupted by local loyalties, while senior posts were filled by Mongols, Uighurs, Tibetans, Turks or Iranians but never by native Chinese.

Garrisons in sensitive or vulnerable areas generally consisted of Mongol troops, or of native troops under reliable Mongol officers. Such garrisons could often be very large. Each of the twelve gates of a big city like Yen-king is said to have been guarded by one thousand troops and many such gate-guardians were certainly native Chinese. Kublai Khan is known to have recruited from among immense numbers of prisoners-of-war taken during his conquest of southern China. At times of crisis he had even opened the prisons and pressed common criminals into his army. Whatever their origins and quality, the majority of such Chinese soldiers fought as infantry. Of course some Chinese troops served on horseback. Those of southern China appear to have ridden with long stirrup leathers and almost straight legs in the same manner as European cavalry. Mongols and most other Asian peoples rode, of course, with short stirrups and bent legs. According to Marco Polo such southern Chinese cavalry wore buffalo-hide armour and fought with spears, shields and crossbows, though the latter are unlikely to have been used on horseback. Perhaps what Marco Polo recorded were mounted infantry rather than true cavalry, though crossbows are known to have been used by horsemen in the medieval Islamic world.

Aboriginal non-Chinese troops were similarly recruited from the warlike tribal peoples of the deep south. Many had joined the Mongols during Kublai Khan's first triumphant invasion of the Sung empire. Towards the end of Mongol rule in China a force of such troops, known as the Miao army, was still largely responsible for garrisoning the rich but troublesome provinces of Hangchow, Wu-hsing and Soochow. Non-Chinese would also have been needed, at least in the early days, to

78

control and look after the war elephants used by Kublai Khan's army after his invasions of Indo-China and Burma. The Mongol and Uighur peoples of central Asia naturally continued to provide Kublai's most reliable troops. Many were Nestorian Christians, while other Christians in the Great Khan's service included men from as far afield as Syria and the Caucasus.

Muslims were equally prominent, particularly in technical rôles. These were recruited from both central Asian and Middle Eastern peoples. Some were descended from prisoners, others entered Kublai Khan's service voluntarily. There is even a suggestion that the Great Khan planned to settle large numbers of Muslims in the economically and militarily strategic southern province of Yunnan. This region was, in the thirteenth century, still sparsely inhabited by a largely non-Chinese population. Though the scheme apparently came to nothing, Yunnan was nevertheless governed by a Muslim, Sayid Ajall Shams al Din, one of the very few Muslim rulers in Mongol China and a very trusted servant.

Two stone grinding mortars brought up from the bed of Hakata Bay. Though they might have been for the making of medicines or other ointments, these mortars could also have been for the grinding of saltpetre and other ingredients to make gunpowder. The Mongols are known to have used highly sophisticated explosive devices during various campaigns, including their two failed invasions of Japan (photo Prof. Taroa Mozai).

Among the most prominent foreign experts to serve in Kublai Khan's armies were Muslim scientists and engineers from the Middle East. This might seem surprising given the fact that China is normally regarded as the source of so many of the Middle Ages' developments. China was certainly seen in this light by Muslims themselves, who had been instructed by the Prophet Muhammad to 'Seek knowledge even unto China'. In military matters, however, even the Chinese clearly had something to learn from the Middle East.

Among the best-known such experts were two siege engineers from Iraq, Ala al Din from Mosul and Isma'il from Hilla, who in 1272 were brought to the siege of Sung-held Hsiang-yang by Kublai's brilliant Uighur general, Arigh Khaya. Their huge stone-throwing engines had an immediate effect on that particular battle and thus on the whole course of the Mongols' campaign against the Sung. Muslim doctors similarly served in two hospitals at the Imperial Court, while Muslim scientists and astronomers arrived with an extraordinary array of instruments, including a celestial globe showing the position of the stars and a terrestrial globe – which proves that they at least knew the world to be round! A Muslim also designed Kublai's new capital at Ta-tu, the foundation of that archetypal Chinese 'Forbidden City' in Peking.

Many Muslims would have been numbered among Kublai's four personal guard regiments, most of whom were recruited from the Turkish Kipchaks of the western steppes. One such guard unit consisted, however, of up to thirty thousand Alans. The fathers of these Christians of the Greek Orthodox rite had been transferred from the northern slopes of the Caucasus to the east by Genghis Khan and his immediate successors. An entire corps of such Alans was massacred by the Sung at Chenchow in 1275, but many more survived. Their descendants even sent a letter to Pope Benedict XII in 1338, submitting to his religious authority and asking for priests to guide them. All these guard units formed Kublai Khan's *keshig* or *käshik*, which was a private cavalry army rather than a mere bodyguard such as that with which Genghis Khan had surrounded himself. According to Marco Polo the four guard units served in rotation, three days and nights on duty, nine days off.

One would have expected military supplies to pose few problems in a rich and fertile land like China, yet there were difficulties. The establishment of military colonies, where garrison troops also lived as farmers, solved the problem of feeding some soldiers. This was a very suitable solution where Chinese troops were concerned, particularly if they were stationed in bleak and otherwise uncultivated border regions. The government also kept strict control over vital military supplies. These included some perhaps unexpected products like bamboo, where the government maintained a strict monopoly, since bamboo was used for spear shafts, bows, arrows and other weapons. The central 'Armaments Court' supplied arms and armour to units around Peking, while its provincial branches, each with its own corps of armourers and artisans, supplied some provincial troops. Most provincial forces were, however, probably equipped by independent local arms manufacturers.

One very serious problem was the shortage of horses. The Imperial Stud could generally supply only forces stationed around Peking, plus providing the mounts needed by the Postal Service. Elsewhere China had never been renowned, or even suitable, for the raising of large numbers of horses. Instead the government turned to the people, insisting that one out of every hundred horses throughout Kublai Khan's Empire be sold to the government at an officially set price. Sometimes animals were simply requisitioned without any payment whatsoever. 'What need have the monks . . . , sitting in their temples, of horses', Kublai once remarked. There were also severe penalties for concealing horses or for smuggling them out of China.

Supplying an army in the field remained difficult, even for such a sophisticated administration as that of Mongol China. In 1260, for example, 10,000 additional horses had to be sent to a force preparing to march from Peking against a nomad threat from the steppe. In addition, no less than 13,300,000 pounds of rice had to be supplied for the men. A few weeks later 10,000 outfits, each consisting of a fur hat, boots and trousers, were sent from various parts of China for this army. Despite such apparently huge quantities of food and equipment, the Mongol soldiers – and probably the Chinese infantrymen as well – travelled light, at least to European eyes. Anything that could not be carried by the troopers' own horses normally went in carts, whose light, sturdy construction and weatherproof character clearly impressed Marco Polo. On campaign the men lived in tiny felt tents.

Kublai inherited a concern for communications from his predecessors.

When Kublai Khan's army invaded Vietnam, it faced war-elephants and dense jungle such as his Mongol warriors had never met before.

The frequency with which Mongol military officers sought out local maps whenever they captured a town suggests that they were following standing orders. Two 'Bureaus for Transmission Services', in Peking and Shang-tu, dealt not only with official messages but also with official supplies. A third such Bureau was set up in the south immediately after its conquest from the Sung. The most important 'Imperial roads' were kept in good repair and were even lined with shady trees wherever possible. More than 20000 post-horses were distributed among way-stations built at twenty-five to thirty mile intervals along these routes. Bridges were also built, passes widened and major obstacles removed. The most important Imperial messengers would wear bells around their belts so that the way-stations could hear their approach and thus get fresh horses ready before they arrived. Some main roads were also under the direct control of the army, presumably to keep down banditry and inhibit enemy raids. Even the Grand Canal, which Kublai built for 1100 miles from Hangchow to his new capital at Peking, served a military purpose. Apart from enabling vast quantities of food, primarily rice, to be shipped from the fertile south, it could transport heavy military equipment and other supplies.

Nor was the spiritual and moral side of military affairs neglected. Kublai Khan habitually consulted seers and astrologers before a major battle. Ritual sacrifices were also made, such as the scattering of milk from his special white mares on the ground around the Imperial Palace. Military insignia were carried with pride by officers and those entrusted by the Great Khan with special duties. Marco Polo mentions tablets or warrants-of-command of silver for those commanding one hundred men, silver-gilt for those commanding a thousand, and solid gold bearing a lion's head for those commanding ten thousand troops. Just such a military seal has been recovered, demonstrating the reliability of Marco Polo's account of his long stay at Kublai Khan's court. It belonged to a Mongol officer in command of one hundred to one thousand men.

The vessels that plied China's great rivers were, of course, very different from those that sailed the oceans as far as India and Africa. Here the artist Wu T-ing-Hui shows a dragon-boat race during the Mongol Yüan perid. The highly decorated boat remains, however, basically a typical river craft of the kind which ferried huge volumes of food northwards up the Grand Canal or Mongol armies into southern China (National Palace Museum, Taiwan).

Marco Polo served Kublai loyally for several years, and later wrote detailed descriptions of the armies he had seen pass by in review.

Similar gold or gilded metal seals were used as passports, indicating that a particular individual was on the Great Khan's business. One of these was given to Marco Polo's brothers so that they could demand hospitality and protection from Mongol authorities during their long journey back to Europe.

Naval Power

Kublai Khan's naval expeditions

Kublai Khan inherited a powerful fleet from the defeated Sung of southern China. This he used to conquer the coastal islands, reduce piracy and attempt to force his suzereinty on distant lands which had once paid tribute to China. Chinese naval power and overseas trade had, in fact, grown enormously under the Sung, while there had been dramatic advances in naval technology. Some resulted from the influence of Arab ships arriving from Iraq, southern Arabia and Egypt, while others were purely Chinese developments that in turn influenced the naval technology of the Islamic world. Flourishing shipyards could now be found in Hangchow, Canton, Ming-Chou and Wen-chou. The Sung even had special government departments dealing with river patrols and coastal defence. All this was now available to Kublai Khan who had already established a rudimentary navy in northern China, as well as being able to draw upon Korean maritime resources.

Mongol nomads took to the sea with remarkable alacrity, just as the desert-dwelling Arabs had done during their period of empire building six centuries earlier. In fact a number of Arabs played a leading role in the development of Kublai Khan's navy. One came from a long-established merchant family resident in Kuang-Chou. He is known only by the Chinese version of his name, P'u Shou-keng. This merchant first rose to become the Sung's Superintendent of Maritime Trade and was later promoted as Kublai's military commander of the vital coastal provinces of Fukien and Kwantung. Despite their humiliating defeats at the hands of the Japanese – which were largely a result of the weather being on Japan's side – the Great Khan's navy achieved some remarkable results.

Chinese ships of this period also deserve mention, if only because archaeology has again confirmed Marco Polo's description of both the design and huge size of the Khan's ships. This Venetian traveller was, of course, an expert on shipping, and he stated that the largest vessels needed a crew of up to three hundred men. They were much larger than anything seen in Europe and also had a sophisticated internal structure of watertight compartments, making them much harder to sink. A ship of this kind, dating from around 1277, was found near Quanzhou, the medieval Zaitun, in 1973. She was an ocean-going vessel with a deep keel and had originally been around one hundred and twelve feet long. Judging from the remains of her cargo the ship was returning

from the East Indies when she was wrecked. Though only four weapons were found aboard this peaceful trading craft, comparable vessels sailed the pirate-infested eastern oceans as far as Sri Lanka, Arabia and perhaps east Africa. Others carried Kublai Khan's troops to the shores of Japan, Indo-China, Java and, according to a probably legendary source, even the Philippines.

Reconstruction of a 13th century Chinese ocean-going ship of the kind described by Marco Polo, remains of which have been found at Quanzou. Such vessels had thirteen watertight compartments, a crew of over one hundred and fifty men and a stern rudder which, though also known in the Muslim world, was as yet rare in Europe. These were the ships that took Kublai Khan's invading armies to Japan, Vietnam and Indonesia.

Arms, Armour and Equipment

Even in the days of Ögotäi the Mongols were already using sophisticated siege tactics during their Chinese wars, including mobile towers, stone-throwing mangonels and mining. Their foes, particularly the Chin dynasty of northern China, replied with various incendiary devices such as rockets. The Mongols remained, of course, among the finest archers

Mongol helmets: (upper) peaked segmented form from Plosko, 1290–1313 AD (ex-Gorelik); (lower) segmented helmet with ring on side probably to support circular ear defences, from Altai mountains early 14th century (local museum, Biyskiy Kraevedcheski, USSR).

in the world, but by Kublai's time the Mongol army had more abundant weaponry. Excellent swords, maces, war-axes and spears of various kinds were used by most troops. The armour worn by common soldiers, and that used to protect horses, was generally of hardened leather. Mongol armour had, of course, been influenced by Chinese styles for hundreds of years, though it should also be pointed out that central Asian forms of weapons and armour had, in turn, influenced China. There has been a perhaps natural tendency to assume that advanced civilizations like China or Iran were the sources of most military-technological developments. Yet the archaeological and even pictorial or written evidence indicates that the nomadic cultures of Turkish and Mongol central Asia also had considerable military influence on their more settled neighbours.

Where China and Mongolia are concerned it seems probable that such nomads were the source of most advances in cavalry equipment, from saddles and harness to bows for horse-archery. China was, meanwhile, the source of most new ideas in infantry warfare, siege engineering and pyrotechnics. An extraordinary variety of infantry weapons had long been used by the Chinese. Some eventually seem to have spread to the Islamic Middle East as a result of the Mongol conquests. The metallurgical industry of southern China had developed to a very high degree under Sung rule, with iron mining and smelting being a state monopoly using slave labour. China, of course, already had its own rich tradition of arms and armour. A form of coat-of-plates, in which small iron scales were fastened inside a linen or silk jerkin, had supposedly been invented by a T'ang Minister of War in the late eighth century. Lamellar armour of iron or hardened leather was more widespread and had been known at least since the seventh century, perhaps having been adopted as a result of nomad influence. Lamellar itself was invented in the ancient Middle East but in China it largely faded from use during the fourteenth century. In its place various forms of the essentially Chinese coat-of-plates became the standard type of armour. The Franciscan friar Carpini gave a most detailed description of the manufacture of Mongol lamellar, in both leather and iron, which shows it to have been identical to the fragments found in earlier central Asian graves as well as similar to lamellar used in the Muslim world. Only a wider use of rawhide rather than hardened leather might have set the Mongols slightly apart.

Mongol and other troops in Kublai's army also wore a form of armour made from several layers of ox-hide pressed together, though whether this type of protection stemmed from Mongol, Chinese or even Korean tradition is as yet unclear. Some scholars have interpreted the banded armour illustrated in so much Chinese and Central Asian art as consisting of metal lames laced together on the inside of a flexible leather or fabric garment. They are, however, much more likely to be stylized representations of ordinary lamellar or to show lamellar covered in rows

84

of decorative fabric, as appears in a more realist manner on fourteenth century Persian illustrations.

More surprising, given the obvious technological sophistication of the Chinese armour tradition, was an almost total lack of mail armour. In other regions, such as the Eurasian steppes, a lack of mail has been put down to supposed backwardness. But such an explanation cannot apply in Mongol China. Here one can only assume that mail was lacking because it was either not needed or was regarded as unsuitable in an area where archery dominated warfare. The vulnerability of mail to powerful bows, such as the composite Asiatic weapon or the European crossbow, is apparent throughout medieval European and Middle Eastern history. Those few illustrations or records of mail in China indicate that it was regarded as a Western (i.e., Turkestani or Iranian) form of defence. The import of armour from Mongol Iran to Mongol China was probably on a small scale, perhaps only for the use of Kublai's Kipchak and Alan guard units, many of whom originally came from the west.

Among items found amid the wrecks of Kublai's invasion fleet off Japan was a straight, single-edged sword. It was probably for use by a cavalryman. This weapon had much in common with swords found in central Asian graves and the fact that it was straight need not point to a Chinese rather than Mongol style. Marine archaeologists predict that, once a full exploration of these wrecks is conducted, a huge amount of well-preserved weaponry will be found. In the meantime virtually no helmets seem to have survived from Mongol China. Mongol helmets are, however, believed to have been taller and more pointed than the traditional Chinese type. Helmets of so-called Mongol style continued to be used in Korea and even Japan well into the sixteenth century. These helmets were characterized by a small subsidiary dome on top of the skull. Such a feature is also found on helmets, and representations of helmets, from both the western and eastern ends of the Eurasian steppes dating back at least to the sixth century AD.

Initially the Mongols learned the art of siege warfare and siege engineering from the Chinese, or at least from Chinese-influenced people like the Uighurs. Various sizes and forms of crossbow, listed in the Mongol armoury and almost certainly used by soldiers of Chinese origin, clearly stemmed from the Chinese military tradition. Such devices were common in Europe and, although they were used in the Muslim Middle East, they never found much favour in the Islamic world. Crossbows had, however, been common in China for a thousand years.

By the time of Kublai Khan the Mongols were also learning from the Muslims. The most important 'western' engine to be used in Kublai's China was the *hui-hui p'ao*, mangonels designed by Ala al Din and Isma'il, the two specialists from Iraq. Isma'il also invented a long-range rock-throwing weapon known in China as a *chü shih p'ao*. Considerable

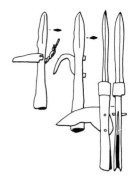

Three spearheads from the Amur area. Probably dating from the 11th or 12th centuries, they include the hook for un-horsing a foe that was also associated with the Mongols. Unlike a similar spear from the western end of the Mongol World Empire, however, these hooks are riveted to their sockets rather than being cast in one piece (ex-Derevyanko).

85

argument revolves around the precise nature of these weapons. Some say that they were simply advanced mangonels, probably of the counter-weight type known in Europe as the trebuchet, which had been invented in the Middle East during the twelfth century. Others suggest that at least the *chü shih p'ao* employed gunpowder or was a form of Greek-fire flame-thrower using relatively advanced pyrotechnics. *Hui-hui p'ao* were also used at sea with devastating effect against the Sung fleet, and stone balls of various sizes have been found in the wrecked Mongol fleet off Japan. These could, however, equally have been shot from man-gonels or primitive fire-arms. The only contemporary description of the *hui-hui p'ao* states that it was more powerful than ordinary *p'ao*, but not that it was a fundamentally different kind of weapon. The *hui-hui p'ao* had a framework of huge timbers. It hurled rocks several feet across and it incorporated some element that could be moved back and forth to alter the weapon's range. This sounds like the most advanced Middle Eastern trebuchet, which had just such an adjustable weight on its beam-sling to increase or reduce range.

The whole question of whether real gunpowder was known in thirteenth-century China and in the Muslim world remains very con-fused. By the year 1000 the Chinese certainly had flame-throwing devices like those used by the Byzantines. By 1132 they used bamboo tubes filled with incendiary powder, but these may again have been one-man flame-throwers as known in Byzantium around the same time. Just over a century later it seems that, in China, small bullets could be shot from such tubes. In other words, they were primitive hand-guns. Both pictorial and written sources suggest that the *hui-hui p'ao* threw hollow iron balls that exploded, almost certainly being filled with gunpowder. This did not, of course, mean that the *hui-hui p'ao* were themselves firearms. Paper-covered fire-crackers, which spread lime like a fog, had been known in the early twelfth century and soon appear to have developed into true grenades (*huo-p'ao*). Yet it is still unclear whether these exploded or merely set a target on fire. By the time of Kublai's abortive invasion of Japan they clearly did explode, with a resounding bang and abundant smoke; they were used against fortifications and against troops in open battle. There is even reference to a *huo-ch'iang*, probably a bamboo tube filled with incendiary material, being used on horseback by two Chinese soldiers against a senior Mongol officer in the year 1276.

Kublai Khan's leading expert on fire weapons was a certain Chang Chun-tso. Though he was himself a Chinese, he learned his trade from his father, who had accompanied Genghis Khan on his invasion of Muslim Transoxania and Iran. Perhaps the use of gunpowder as a propellant, in other words the invention of true guns, appeared first in the Muslim Middle East, whereas the invention of gunpowder itself was a Chinese achievement.

As protection against these devastating new siege engines the Chinese suspended multiple layers of four-inch-thick rope made from rice stalks down the outside of their city walls. In other places the fortifications were overlaid with clay to absorb the shock of projectiles. One may be sure that the Mongols learned these defensive tactics, yet under such circumstances it is surprising to find that Mongol-Chinese fortifications were not particularly highly developed. Those of the Outer City of Shang-tu consisted of a rectangular earthen embankment eighteen feet high, with six towers on each side and a total of six gates. The Inner City containing the Imperial Palace was roughly square in plan, being surrounded by a brick wall ten to sixteen feet high plus four turrets on each side. The defences of Peking again relied on an earthen rampart and two inner walls. The eleven gates were perhaps more imposing and consisted of three-storey towers. On the other hand, Kublai's army remained primarily an offensive force and the heart of the Empire surely did not expect to face serious invasion. These Imperial cities were also erected at considerable speed, Kublai Khan holding his first audience in the Palace less than seven years after his workers broke the first ground.

A stone ball, either to be shot from a mangonel or primitive cannon. A number of these stones have also been recovered from Hakata bay but until the machines that shot them are discovered the question of whether Kublai Khan's armies actually had cannon must remain unanswered (photo Prof. Taroa Mozai).

The Great Khan's Battles

The Siege of Hsiang-yang

The Mongol capture of the Sung city of Hsiang-yang is an excellent example of the sophisticated siege techniques used in Kublai Khan's time. It was also described in some detail by the Great Khan's main biographers, as well as by Marco Polo.

The twin cities of Hsiang-yang and Fan-ch'eng stood on opposite banks of the Han river in what is now the Chinese province of Hupei. The site was strategically important as these were the last Sung strongholds blocking a Mongol advance down the Han to the huge Yangtze, some distance to the south. If they fell, the cities could also serve the Mongols as strong bases from which to invade the Yangtze plain. For this reason the Sung had already fortified both, Hsiang-yang having a strong castle, stout wall and deep moat. Lü Wen-huan, an experienced commander, held them for the Sung Empire.

At first the Mongols hoped to starve the garrison into surrender, but to make any blockade effective they would need a river fleet to control the Han down to its junction with the Yangtze. The strength of the fortifications also meant that the very best siege artillery would be needed if Mongol casualties were not to become unacceptable. Kublai therefore selected his field commanders with care. They came from a variety of ethnic backgrounds, as did the troops they led, and they also had a variety of particular skills. Liu Cheng, a recent defector from the Sung, and Shih T'ien-tse were both Chinese. Arigh Khaya was a Turkish Uighur from central Asia, while A-chu was a Mongol. Ismai'l and Ala al Din were specialist siege engineers from Iraq. Koreans and ex-Chin craftsmen from northern China built the five hundred small boats that would patrol the lower Han river.

The siege itself took almost five years (1268–73). To start with, the blockade was gradually tightened around the two cities, but the inhabitants had already taken in huge stocks of food. Sung ships were sometimes also able to slip through with additional supplies. Fighting was clearly not continuous and even the blockade seems to have been lifted occasionally, though the reasons remain unknown. Within a few months Liu Cheng, Kublai Khan's renegade Chinese general, ordered field fortifications to be built south of the cities overlooking the Han river. These were designed to stop supplies reaching Hisiang-yang from this direction. When A-chu and his Mongol forces arrived in October 1268, the Sung defenders seem to have panicked and, on 6th December, they tried to break out. In this they totally failed, being driven back with heavy losses. Thereafter the Sung garrison sat tight and awaited supplies or reinforcements. In August next year a Sung general named Hsia Kuei attacked one of the Mongol fortifications overlooking the Han river, supposedly with up to three thousand boats. This attempt was again routed, fifty Sung boats being captured by Kublai Khan's men.

But Kublai Khan was also growing impatient and so sent 20000 reinforcements to help A-chu and Liu Cheng. The second Chinese general in Kublai's service, Shih T'ien-tse, suggested that the field fortifications south of Hsiang-yang be linked by a long earthen rampart. This was done while thousands of small boats and even greater numbers of troops arrived to strengthen the Mongols' blockade. Yet the increasingly isolated Sung garrison would still not submit and a stalemate persisted.

Meanwhile the Sung Court offered big rewards and promotion for

men who could smuggle messages in or out of Hsiang-yang. They also did what they could to get supplies into the suffering city. The garrison appears, in fact, to have had enough food and water but lacked clothing, salt and various other less important items. Occasional attempts to break through the Mongol lines were mostly unsuccessful. One attempt on 18th March 1270 was undertaken by ten thousand infantry and cavalry accompanying more than a hundred boats. The Mongols were, however, ready and the Sung attempt to burst through their field fortifications was driven back with heavy loss. Some attempts to break in did succeed, though one such effort in October 1270 was crushed with the loss of thirty boats. A further attempt in August 1271 cost the Sung two thousand dead, but in September 1272 about three thousand Sung troops did battle their way into Hsiang-yang. In so doing they lost one of their senior officers and most of the supplies they had brought with them. Furthermore these men were now trapped in the city.

By now the Mongol blockade was virtually perfect, although the besiegers were still not strong enough to assault the massive defences of Hsiang-yang. It was at this point, late in 1272, that the two Iraqi engineers appeared on the scene. They first erected their massive modern mangonels against the second city of Fan-ch'eng. After a few days of battering it fell to an overwhelming assault by Arigh Khaya's men. The fall of Fan-ch'eng seems to have convinced Lü Wen-huan, Sung commander in Hsiang-yang, that his position had become hopeless. The Iraqi engineers had, by this time, re-erected their mangonels opposite the south-eastern corner of Hsiang-yang, which they bombarded with massive rocks. Possessing no answer to such fire-power, the defending commander finally surrendered and the road to the Sung heartland lay open to the Mongols.

The Defeat of Nayan

Kublai Khan's defeat of the Mongol rebel Nayan in 1287 was a rare triumph for him in an otherwise sad old age. During this campaign the Great Khan once again displayed the care and the vigour of the military campaigns of his youth.

Reconstruction and arrangement of internal scales of a Mongol fabric-covered body armour, 13th–14th century from Abakan region of upper Yenesi river (ex-Gorelik). Reconstruction of typical Turco-Mongol lamellar horse-armour (ex-Gorelik).

The rebellion of Nayan, a Nestorian Christian, erupted in Manchuria and appears to have been coordinated with the activities of Kublai's long-standing rival in central Asia, the Mongol khan Khaidu of Sinkiang. Kublai clearly felt that Nayan's threat was serious, for he rapidly raised a considerable army. One detachment was sent to prevent the forces of Khaidu linking up with those of Nayan. Another marched into southern Manchuria, where more dissidents were threatening trouble. But the bulk of Kublai's forces he himself led against Nayan, who had established a base near the mouth of the river Liao.

Marco Polo's estimates of the size of the Great Khan's army – 360000 cavalry and 100000 infantry – is wildly exaggerated, as the terrain in which the campaign was fought could not have supported so many horses, let alone the men. But the proportions of more than three horsemen to each foot soldier may be correct. Meanwhile supplies were sent to the mouth of the Liao river by Kublai Khan's navy.

Having completed his arrangements with great speed and some secrecy, Kublai immediately marched north-eastward and was apparently able to catch Nayan off guard. The Great Khan, who was now seventy-two years of age and wracked by numerous ailments, insisted on taking part in the battle in a wooden tower carried by four elephants. According to Marco Polo he reached Nayan's position after a forced march of twenty-five days. Nayan's men appear to have been encamped within a double line of wagons, a time-honoured form of nomad field fortification. Yet for the next two days Kublai's army is said to have rested near a range of hills that separated them from Nayan's force. This would surely have lost them any advantage of surprise. On the other hand unrecorded negotiations might have taken place or Kublai may now have been confident of the outcome as his rapid mobilization and even speedier march meant that he could now overpower Nayan with greatly superior forces. During these two days Kublai Khan also consulted various astrologers who, not surprisingly, informed him that he would win the forthcoming battle.

Early on the third day Kublai's men marched over the hills and, according to Marco Polo, found Nayan's troops unprepared and with few sentinels posted. Nayan himself was even said to be asleep in his tent. Kublai's troops attacked in three divisions with their flanks extended so as to envelop the enemy camp. In front of each battalion of cavalry marched a relatively small number of infantry armed with swords and short spears. Their task was to attack the enemies' horses but, if the fight turned against them, they could be carried out of danger behind the saddles of their own horsemen. The sound of wind instruments signalled the start of battle, the men then joining in with warlike songs. But not until the drums rolled and cymbals crashed did the soldiers advance, the right and left wings being the first to do so.

As soon as the two armies came within range they poured volleys of

arrows into each others' ranks, after which they met with spears, swords and maces. Marco Polo appears to have been a witness of this battle, for he noted that many more horses than men were slain. The struggle continued until noon, for Nayan's men fought with great devotion although they were seriously outnumbered. Eventually, however, Nayan realized that he was virtually surrounded and so attempted to escape, but was cut off and captured.

After being taken before Kublai Khan the unfortunate rebel was executed bloodlessly, which means that he was either smothered by, or violently tossed in, heavy carpets. The surviving members of his army then came to make their submission to the Great Khan.

Court ladies, grooms and standard-bearers on a painted Chinese scroll of the Yüan period, second half of the 13th century (Freer Gallery of Art, no. 57.14.2A, Washington).

Legacy and Legend

Kublai's later life was dogged by personal tragedy as well as mixed military fortunes. His beloved chief wife Chabi died in 1281 and this loss apparently devastated the Great Khan – without her steadying influence his political decisions became increasingly erratic. Four years later his favourite son and chosen heir, Chen-chin also died, throwing Kublai's plans into disarray and leading to further depression. From then on Kublai Khan steadily withdrew from active government, leaving everyday affairs to officials who were not always as honest or capable as they might have been. His own appearance also changed. He became grossly fat, though he still indulged in regular hunting on the broad expanse of steppe grassland that had been laid out near his palace. No longer able to draw a bow, Kublai hunted with a trained cheetah which rode on the crupper of his horse in a manner seen among Asian nobility for a thousand years. At other times he hunted from a howdah carried on the back of one or two elephants, from where he watched his hawks swoop upon cranes or his trained tigers tear down a bear, boar or wild ox.

Kublai Khan had long worn Chinese rather than Central Asian costume, but he was still a true Mongol in his enormous consumption of food and alcohol. Delicate fruits were brought to his table across vast distances, while his own special *qumis* was fermented from the milk of a herd of ten thousand spotless white mares. This exotic brew could be shared only by descendants of Genghis Khan himself. Small wonder that Kublai developed gout and needed special boots made from a particularly soft kind of fish-skin sent as tribute by the rulers of Korea.

When the fabled Kublai Khan finally died, dispirited and depressed on 18th February 1294, he was laid to rest near the tombs of his grandfather, Genghis Khan, and his brother, Möngke. Already a wood was growing around the single great tree that had marked the World Conqueror's grave. Soon the whole hill would be covered by a dense forest so that these tombs were lost forever. Today even the identity of the hill once known as Burdan-kaldun is forgotten and the resting place of two of the greatest figures in Asian history remains hidden.

The Great Achievement

Kublai Khan may not have been the most successful of Mongol rulers in merely military terms. His greatness lay in a mixture of wide conquests, the establishment of a new dynasty in China, the promotion of arts and trade, and perhaps above all in the fact that he earned the admiration of almost all his contemporaries. Few rulers have had their deeds so lavishly praised by such a variety of chroniclers from such an assortment of different cultural and religious backgrounds. Marco Polo spread his fame in Europe, Rashid al Din in the Muslim world. Chinese and Korean courtiers did the same in the Far East, while even a Syrian doctor of Jewish origin recalled his wise policies with unrestrained enthusiasm. Kublai achieved, in fact, something that even Genghis Khan himself failed to earn. He successfully portrayed himself as a truly Universal Ruler and was recognized as such by his subjects and by those who lived continents away.

At a time when religious identity was more important than land of birth or language spoken, Kublai remained something of a religious chameleon. His personal preference was for Buddhism, or rather for the slightly unorthodox Tibetan lamaist version of that religion. But his own faith normally remained a private matter – itself an unusual state of affairs in an age when religion led to more wars than any other cause. Such toleration was also a boon when it came to ruling the Great Khan's

Kublai Khan as an aged man, on a hunting expedition to the steppes north of his capital. Note that the hunters shoot at birds while their ponies are standing still. The horseman at the bottom of the picture has a trained hunting cheetah behind his saddle (Nat. Palace Museum, Taiwan).

diverse domains. The Confucian élite of China regarded him as the righteous upholder of their ancient cultural system. To Buddhists he appeared as *Manjusri*, the Boddhisattva of Wisdom, while to Christians like Marco Polo, Kublai Khan always seemed to be on the point of converting to their faith. For their part, Muslims saw the Great Khan as a wise and normally respectful protector – even, sometimes, as a patron.

In purely military terms Kublai Khan added the rich and powerful Sung state of southern China to the Mongol Empire, along with its estimated population of fifty million souls. This alone ranked him among the greatest of Mongol commanders. His other campaigns ranged from the brilliantly successful to the undeniably catastrophic. Kublai's ambition and determination seemed, at least in his early years, to be boundless and in this he was a true descendant of Genghis Khan. On the other hand, under him the Mongols in China began to lose their separate identity, just as their cousins in the Middle East were beginning to lose theirs. This was hardly Kublai's fault, for it was inevitable that a few hundred thousand nomad conquerors would soon be absorbed by a huge civilization such as that of China.

The new Yüan dynasty that he founded was relatively short-lived and left little mark on the government or legal system of China. Yet the Yüan period was to be very rich in terms of the visual arts, literature and, above all, theatre. Despite being recognized as Great Khan, Kublai lost any real control over the other Mongol khanates to the west of China. Yet this was again probably an unavoidable process of imperial fragmentation. Even his dream of a Mongol Empire in China started crumbling soon after his death, signs of weakness having become apparent in Kublai Khan's own lifetime.

Untarnished Glory

Yet everything about Kublai Khan seemed destined for legend. On one hand, he remained a warlike Mongol with an enormous appetite for food, drink, hunting, women and colourful display – not to mention war. On the other, he displayed typically Chinese ultra-refinement in art, clothes and domestic tastes. Kublai Khan ruled wisely and tried hard to repair the damage caused to China by half a century of war. He showed concern for the welfare of the poor, as well as for his soldiers. He promoted education, transport, trade and famine relief. A later Chinese historian typically praised Kublai Khan for recognizing Chinese superiority in the art of government, for, he wrote, 'He thankfully accepted the advice given him by learned men, and he truly loved his people.' Nobody ever said that about Genghis Khan!

Perhaps the best epitaph for Kublai Khan was written by his most recent biographer, the American scholar Morris Rossabi, who wrote: 'Kublai's dream for a world empire was not fulfilled, but his glory remains untarnished.'

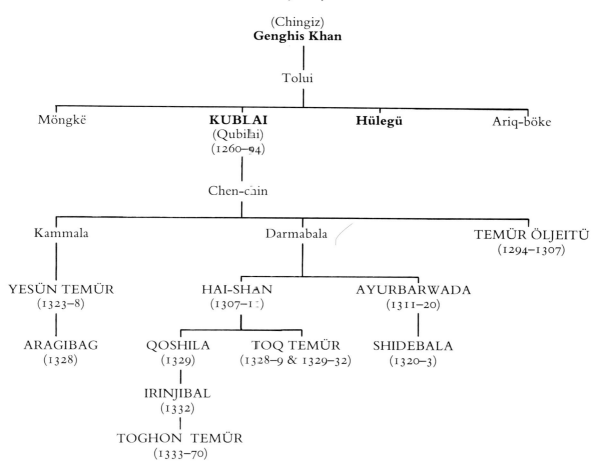

The Yüan Dynasty of China

(Chingiz)
Genghis Khan

Tolui

Möngkë   **KUBLAI**   **Hülegü**   Ariq-böke
(Qubilai)
(1260–94)

Chen-chin

Kammala   Darmabala   TEMÜR ÖLJEITÜ
(1294–1307)

YESÜN TEMÜR   HAI-SHAN   AYURBARWADA
(1323–8)   (1307–11)   (1311–20)

ARAGIBAG   QOSHILA   TOQ TEMÜR   SHIDEBALA
(1328)   (1329)   (1328–9 & 1329–32)   (1320–3)

IRINJIBAL
(1332)

TOGHON TEMÜR
(1333–70)

Bibliography

de Hartog, L. *Genghis Khan: Conqueror of the World* London, 1989.

Goodrich, L.C. and Fang Chia-sheng, 'The Early Development of Firearms in China *Isis* XXVI/2 (1946, pp. 114–23.

Goodrich, L.C., 'Firearms among the Chinese: A Supplementary Note,' *Isis* XXXIX/1–2, pp. 63–4 1948.

Green, J. 'Kublai's invasion of Japan' in *History from the Sea* (ed. Throckmorton, P.) pp. 166–7, London, 1987.

Green, J. 'Looking for Khubilai Khan' (article on the sunken fleet in Imari Bay, Japan) *Geo Magazine* Dec. pp. 59–69 1983– Jan. 1984.

Groeneveldt, W.P. 'The Expedition of the Mongols against Java in 1293 A.D.' *China Review* IV (1875–76), pp. 246–54.

Grousset, R. (trans. Walford, N.) *The Empire of the Steppes: A History of Central Asia* New Brunswick, 1970.

Hsiao Ch'i-ch'ing *The Military Establishment of the Yüan Dynasty* Cambridge, Mass., 1978.

Lo Jung-pang 'The Emergence of China as a Sea Power during the Late Sung and Early Yüan Periods.' *Far Eastern Quarterly* XIV, pp. 489–503, 1954–1955.

Marco Polo (ed. & trans. Masefield, J.) *The Travels of Marco Polo the Venetian* London & Toronto, 1908.

Marco Polo (ed. & trans. Moule, A.C. and Pelliot, P.) *Marco Polo: The Description of the World* London, 1938.

Morgan, D. *The Mongols* Oxford & New York, 1986.

Prawdin, M. (trans. Paul, E. & C.) *The Mongol Empire: Its Rise and Legacy* London, 1940.

Rossabi, M. *Khubilai Khan: His Life and Times* Berkeley & London, 1988.

Spuler B. (trans. Drummond, H. & S.) *History of the Mongols Based on Eastern and Western Accounts of the Thirteenth and Fourteenth Centuries* Berkeley, 1972.

Werner, E.T.C. *Chinese Weapons* Shanghai, 1932.

به یک نگاه تو رستم زننگ می‌سی خوش

خوش اکر سوی من افتد نگاه دمبدت

HÜLEGÜ
DESTROYER OF BAGHDAD

The steppes of Azerbayjan near Malakan in north-western Iran. This area is still home to Turkish tribes who raise enormous flocks of sheep on its relatively fertile grasslands. In the Middle Ages and earlier, the Azerbayjani steppes served as a base area for the Il-khans and many nomadic invaders of the Middle East.

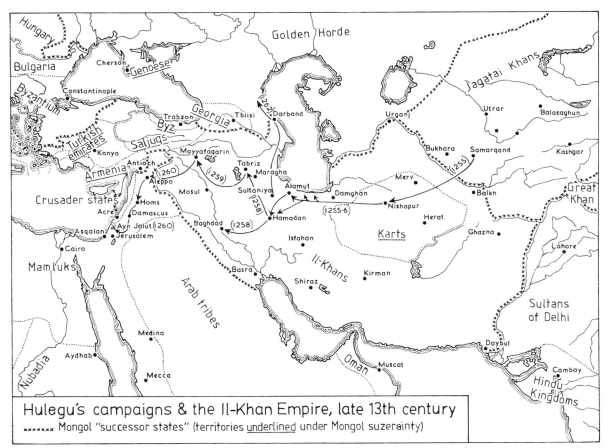

Hulegu's campaigns & the Il-Khan Empire, late 13th century
✕✕✕✕✕ Mongol "successor states" (territories <u>underlined</u> under Mongol suzerainty)

He has sacked all the cities of the Muslims and, without consulting his kinsmen, has brought about the death of the Caliph. With the help of God I will call him to account for so much innocent blood!

(Berke of the Golden Horde)

Destroyer and Builder – Winner and Loser

Like his grandfather, Genghis Khan, Hülegü was a warrior and conqueror, and his story may be simply told if he is considered only as an empire builder in the old Mongol tradition, as the destroyer of one Muslim power after another. At the head of an enormous army he first almost eliminated the Muslim sect of the Assassins, captured Baghdad and massacred its citizens and destroyed the Abbasid Caliphate. Moving into Syria, he took Aleppo and Damascus. His triumphant progress was brought to a halt only by Egypt.

But as well as a destroyer he was also something of a builder. The Il-Khan dynasty that he established in Iran and Iraq played a significant part in shaping the later medieval history of the Middle East. He extended Mongol dominion to the shores of the Mediterranean while his successors, unconsciously perhaps, did a great deal to re-establish a sense of Iranian national identity. The rulers of Persia, as it was then known, were no longer mere governors of one or more Islamic provinces. They ruled a state which, for the first time since the fall of the Sassanian Emperors in the seventh century, entered into direct and separate diplomatic relations with Europe and China. The centralizing policies of the Il-Khans also paved the way for the Iranian nationalistic attitudes of the sixteenth century Safavids.

Nevertheless the Mongol conquest remained a cultural and economic disaster. It also failed as far as the Mongols themselves were concerned, for Il-Khan rule was short-lived. The Mongols, unlike the less barbarous but still culturally primitive Arabs who had previously conquered Iran, failed to create a Mongol-Chinese civilization comparable to that of the Arab-Islamic Caliphate. While the Arab Empire endured for centuries and left an indelible cultural mark upon the entire Middle East, the Mongol Empire fell apart in less than a hundred years and left little more than destruction in its wake. Mongols and Arabs had both been tribal and unsophisticated societies compared to the peoples they conquered, but whereas the Arabs had a 'higher' religion in the shape of Islam and an immensely rich language, the Mongols had virtually nothing except a borrowed veneer of Chinese civilization. The glories of the Il-Khan period remained Islamic with the addition of those few aspects of Chinese or Central Asian culture that the Iranians, Arabs and Turks themselves chose to adopt.

Grandson of Genghis

Relatively little is known about the early life of Hülegü. He was born around 1217 and was, like the Great Khan Kublai, a son of Tolui and a grandson of the world conqueror Genghis Khan. His name of Hülegü meant 'the one in excess' or 'the overflowing' and while his brother Kublai soon earned a reputation for intelligence, Hülegü's talents seem to have been more bellicose. The two boys were personally blooded by Genghis Khan in an ancient Mongol hunting ritual after making their first kills with a bow. But while the eleven-year-old Kublai only brought down a wild hare, the nine-year-old Hülegü bagged a wild mountain goat. Nevertheless Hülegü was given a better education than most Mongol princes, as his mother had huge ambitions for her sons. He developed an interest in philosophy, alchemy and astrology and liked to surround himself with learned men. Yet he always remained unpredictable and at times displayed appalling savagery. This cannot be put down solely to his Mongol heritage, for his brother Kublai grew into a remarkably tolerant and humane ruler. Perhaps it is true, as some chroniclers claimed, that Hülegü was epileptic and that this affected his temper.

Hülegü's Inheritance
Many years passed between Genghis Khan's descent upon the Muslim Middle East and Hülegü's arrival in the region where he would carve out his own claim to fame. Jalal al Din, last of the Khwarazmshahs, had kept up a desperate fight against the Mongols until his death in 1231 – murdered in the mountains of Kurdistan after his army melted away in despair. Yet Muslim resistance did not end, for two of Jalal al Din's former generals fought a guerrilla campaign around Nishapur for some time. Meanwhile the Abbasid Caliphs of Baghdad still ruled Iraq and were even extending their influence now that the Khwarazmshahs had gone. The most dangerous foes still to defy the Mongols in Iran were, however, the Assassins in their mountain fastness south of the Caspian sea.

These Assassins were, in fact, an extreme Shi'a Islamic sect more properly called Isma'ilis. They had broken away from the Shi'a Muslims who ruled Egypt before the days of Saladin and they now controlled a

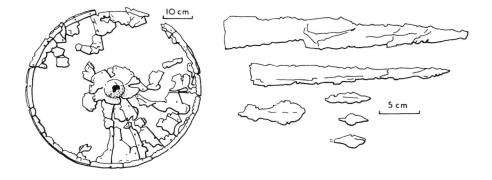

series of castles in two of the most inaccessible regions of the Middle East. The Assassin headquarters was at Alamut, high in the Alburz range north-west of modern Tehran. Another branch of the Assassins, under the 'Old Man of the Mountain', held castles in the Syrian coastal range between Crusader and Saracen territory. The nickname of Assassin came from their supposed indulgence in hashish and entered various European languages through the Isma'ilis' terrifying use of murder to achieve their political or religious ends.

There is no doubt that the surviving population of conquered Iran was cruelly treated by its Mongol masters and the country was in a state of virtual chaos. A rudimentary administration had been set up by the governors Körgüz and Arghun Aqa, the latter even restoring some devastated towns. Another man, who would later become Hülegü's most famous general, had meanwhile consolidated Mongol military control and had even captured some outlying Assassin castles. This was Kit-Buqa, a Nestorian Christian who was said to be descended from one of the Three Wise Men.

From the start the Mongols had allowed some local rulers to remain as vassals. Among these were the Afghan Karts, who now held Herat. This Kart dynasty would, in fact, outlast the Mongols themselves. In southern Iran other vassals struggled to maintain their autonomy in Kirman, Fars and Shiraz. Near Isfahan the Caliph of Baghdad's army had even defeated the invaders in battle, while numerous Mongol attempts to capture Isfahan failed until that city finally fell in 1237. The following year a Mongol army invaded Iraq but was again defeated by the Caliph's forces near Samarra. Although the Mongols immediately returned and conquered northern Iraq, the Caliph's record of resistance would have an influence on events just over twenty years later when Hülegü himself descended upon Baghdad.

During the intervening years, however, a new Caliph came to the throne. This weak and vacillating man, named al Musta'sim, was doomed to be the last of a line that stretched back five centuries and included such famous names as al Mansur and Harun al Rashid. The Mongol hold on northern Iraq now cut Baghdad off from the independent Muslim areas of Syria and Egypt, except by the virtually impassable Syrian desert. Al Musta'sim had also allowed the Caliph's small but efficient army to deteriorate while he ruled over a court riddled by factionalism and treachery. The once great city of Baghdad had shrunk to a series of separate and squabbling suburbs, frequently beyond the Caliph's control. Drainage systems had fallen into disrepair so that even these suburbs were frequently flooded. Nevertheless Baghdad remained an enormous city by medieval standards.

To the west, in Syria, the Ayyubid descendants of Saladin still held power, though the country was divided among petty princes with al Nasir Yusuf of Damascus and Aleppo as the most powerful. The coast was dominated by now drastically reduced Crusader States while in Egypt the Mamluks, one-time slave soldiers of the Ayyubids, had seized control in 1250. Mongol armies had already penetrated Syria, being bought off beneath the walls of Aleppo in 1244 and demanding a tribute of three thousand virgins from Bohemond V, the Crusader Prince of Antioch (Antakya). Bohemond proudly refused and as yet there was no question of the Crusaders seeing Mongols as potential allies against the surrounding Muslims. The Mongols were, in fact, regarded as barbarous infidels and a serious military threat. Native Syrian Christians perhaps took a more positive view of the invaders than did the Catholic Crusader States. They knew that many Mongols were themselves Christians and followed rites similar to those of some Middle Eastern sects. For their part the Mongols viewed the Crusaders with caution and kept themselves informed of plans for any new Crusades.

Mongol raids continued, however. In 1252 one captured a valuable caravan taking six hundred loads of Egyptian sugar to Baghdad. Four years later a second Mongol defeat of the Saljuqs of Rum (Anatolia) confirmed the Saljuqs' status as vassals of the Mongol world empire and caused further alarm in Syria and the Crusader States. When Küyük was proclaimed Great Khan in 1246 Saljuq princes, as well as Ayyubid, Abbasid, Isma'ili, Byzantine, Russian and Armenian delegations, hurried to bow at his feet. Christian Georgia was now a vassal of those Mongols who ruled southern Russia and who would later become known as the Golden Horde, while the Christian Armenians of Cilicia had also voluntarily placed themselves under Mongol suzereinty. By so doing, the Armenian King Hethoum hoped to win back lands lost to the Saljuqs and perhaps harness Mongol might to a great revival of Christian fortunes throughout the Middle East. The Great Khan Möngke is even said to have promised Hethoum that he would destroy Baghdad and the Caliphate, described as the 'mortal enemy' of Christians. This, like the story that Möngke would restore the Holy Land to Christendom or that Hülegü himself made a pilgrimage to Jerusalem, is a fable. Yet Hethoum

and various other Eastern Christian leaders did try to sow the Mongol wind for their own advantage and in return reaped a whirlwind of Muslim vengeance.

Destroying the Assassins

In 1251 Möngke, the new Great Khan, held a *quriltay* or gathering of Mongol leaders. This would decide the fate of almost half the known world and among its decisions was that of sending Möngke's younger brother Hülegü to be viceroy of the chaotic provinces of Iran. Möngke instructed him to:

Establish the usages, customs and laws of Genghiz Khan from the banks of the Amu Darya river to the ends of the land of Egypt. Treat with kindness and good will every man who submits and is obedient to your orders. Whoever resists you, plunge him into humiliation.

First among Hülegü's tasks was the destruction of the Isma'ili Assassins. Secondly he must reduce the Caliphate of Baghdad to obedience, for the Mongol vision of world domination could not accept the existence of a leader who claimed allegiances higher than that to the Great Khan

A series of Turkish and Mongol tomb-towers, known as gunbads, can still be seen at Maraghah in north-western Iran. Some like this, the early 14th century Gunbad-i-Jafariyah, are decorated with blue tiles. Maraghah and Tabriz together served as the capitals of the Il-Khan Mongol state set up by Hülegü.

103

himself. The Assassins would be shown no mercy; the Caliph, however, would be attacked only if he refused Mongol suzereinty.

Hülegü's army was given a splendid send-off. Möngke, Hülegü and the other senior Mongol princes each laid on great feasts with drinking, gambling and gifts of robes. The Great Khan then sent jewels, money, more robes and fine horses to Hülegü, his wives, sons and military commanders before the vast army set out on 19th October 1253. Hülegü's second son, Jumghar, was placed in immediate military command as his father's deputy while Hülegü's other sons, Abaqa and Yeshmut, stayed by his side. Kit-Buqa, now with the rank of *bavurchi* or steward, had already set out with 12000 men to harass the Assassins, while Hülegü's main army supposedly consisted of two out of every ten available Mongol soldiers. Khan Jagatai and Batu of the Golden Horde also sent contingents, while a thousand engineers and infantry skilled in siege warfare came from northern China.

This huge force split into four divisions, which travelled at a leisurely pace by different routes so that their animals had enough pasture as they marched. Hülegü himself reached Samarqand in the autumn of 1255 and was entertained for forty days in an enormous white felt tent presented by the regional governor. Not until the first day of 1256 did his army finally cross the Amu Darya (Oxus river) over a series of enormous boat-bridges into Khurasan. There Hülegü went hunting on Bactrian camels and bagged ten tigers. He also received the homage of most of the governors and rulers of Iran in yet another splendidly embroidered linen tent. It was at this time that the famous historian Ata-Malik al Juvayni entered Hülegü's service. The rest of that winter was spent in military preparation and seemingly endless drinking sessions before, as Juvayni put it:

orders were given for the fastening of banners and standards [to the spears] and the massing of troops for Holy War and uprooting the castles of heresy.

The heretics in question were, of course, the Isma'ilis and during the spring and summer Hülegü continued his unhurried march, obliterating the rebellious town of Tun (modern Firdaus) on the way. But the Isma'ilis did not simply cower in terror. They sent their *fida'i*, or in modern terms 'fedayeen', to harass Hülegü's army, although nothing could now stop the Mongol juggernaut. After being feasted in yet another tent (this supposedly making the sun dim and the moon wear a sulky expression in envy of its magnificence) Hülegü entered Isma'ili territory. His main force consisted of a centre and two wings, each of which again took different routes. Meanwhile a Mongol army stationed in Iraq headed for Alamut, the chief Assassin castle.

The troops ranged against the Isma'ilis were not all of Mongol origin. In fact, local Iranian vassal forces played a major part, those of Kirman and Yazd being sent against outlying fortresses. Some of these lesser

castles resisted for a very long time. According to legend Girdkuh, over three hundred kilometres to the east, surrendered only when the garrison's clothes wore out and the castle is still surrounded by the siege wall erected by the Mongols. The previous Isma'ili Grand Master had already been murdered by his own courtiers in a vain hope of averting Mongol wrath. Now the new Grand Master, Rukn al Din, evacuated five outlying castles and attempted to buy time by negotiating. He also tried to spin things out until winter snows made a full-scale assault impossible, even sending one of his younger illegitimate sons as a hostage. But Hülegü was in no mood to be patient and sent the child back as too young and of doubtful parentage. Instead he threw his full strength against the extraordinary cave fortress of Maymun-Diz where Rukn al Din had taken refuge.

Most of Hülegü's generals wanted to postpone the attack because winter was close at hand and it would become extremely difficult to supply a besieging army so high in the Alburz mountains. A minority urged an immediate all-out attack and this was the course that Hülegü followed. The siege was hard fought, although it lasted only a fortnight. The size of the besieging army was enough to terrify the defenders and Rukn al Din surrendered. He was at first well treated by Hülegü – he still, of course, had his uses. In return the Grand Master sent his own emissaries to the other fortresses, ordering them to open their gates to the Mongol invaders. Most obeyed the order and had their defences razed. Lammasar, the Isma'ili capital of Alamut and Girdkuh to the east, Assassin bases in Afghanistan, and the Syrian branch of the Isma'ili sect,

Few relics of Central Asian Christianity survive, despite the major role Nestorian and Jacobite Christians played during the Mongol period. In the Middle East, however, Christian minorities still thrive, particularly in what was once known as the Jazira region of Syria, south-eastern Turkey and Iraq. Not far from Mardin in Turkey stand the two Jacobite-Syriac monasteries of Mar Gabriel and Derzafaran. Derzafaran (above) is the larger and stands in the Tur Abdin hills. Part of the structure dates back to late Roman and pre-Islamic times.

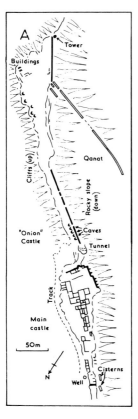

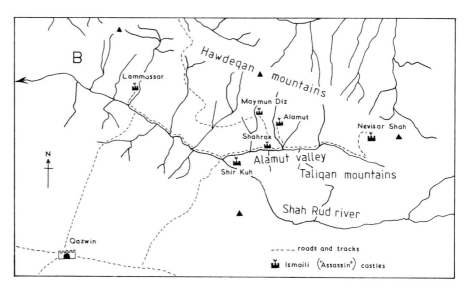

The Isma'ili, the so-called Assassins, of northern Iran were among the Mongols' fiercest foes. They held castles in many of the most inaccessible mountainous regions of the Muslim Middle East, the Isma'ili headquarters being in the Alamut valley north of Qazwin (above right). A plan of the castle of Alamut, capital of the Grand Master of the Assassins (above left), shows how it consisted of a main fortress, the lower 'Onion' castle and a small town, all straddling a rocky ridge. Cut into the mountainside was a qanat or channel designed to collect rainwater as it poured down the slope. B the Isma'ili castles in the mountains of northern Iran surrounded the main fortress of Alamut and threatened the rich trade route through Qazwin.

far away in the mountains overlooking the Mediterranean, ignored Rukn al Din's messengers.

The defenders of Alamut were promised safe conduct and, according to the historian Juvayni, 'all the inmates of that university of wickedness and nest of Satan came down with all their goods and belongings.' Alamut had been a centre of considerable learning and Juvayni saved both the library and the scholars who worked there. Many, including the famous astronomer Nasir al Din Tusi, had been held in Alamut against their will for years, though they had been able to continue their scholarly work. While Hülegü's soldiers demolished the defences of Alamut, Juvayni got permission to salvage what he could from the famous library, keeping Korans, non-heretical religious books and those dealing with science or history. The rest he burned. Juvayni also collected an interesting array of scientific and astronomical instruments, including astrolabes and globes showing the positions of the stars. Some of this equipment probably ended up in the famous observatory near Maragha, where Nasir al Din Tusi would one day continue his scientific work for Hülegü.

For Rukn al Din himself the end was now near. While Hülegü directed the siege of stubborn Lammassar, the captive Grand Master was given a Mongol wife for company and teams of Bactrian fighting camels to watch. Eventually, however, it became obvious that even Rukn al Din's personal orders to surrender would have no effect on the garrisons of Lammassar and Girdkuh, so his usefulness was at an end. Instead the Grand Master was given permission to visit the Great Khan Möngke but once he reached the Imperial Capital of Qaraqorum he was humiliated and maltreated as his attendants deserted him one by one. On the return

journey Rukn al Din was murdered in circumstances that remain unclear. Some say that this, the last of the Assassin Grand Masters, was
kicked to a pulp before being finished off with a sword.

Now the Mongols turned upon those Isma'ilis who had already
surrendered. First of all Rukn al Din's family was wiped out, then all the
garrisons who had surrendered, including their families. Over one
hundred thousand people were probably slaughtered. The Isma'ili sect
survived, though, both in Iran and elsewhere – in 1275, a decade after
Hülegü's death, they even managed to retake Alamut for a short while.
Many fled to Sind in what is now southern Pakistan. There they survived
almost as an underground sect before emerging once again as a much
more peaceful community, today headed by the fabulously wealthy
Agha Khan. The Syrian Isma'ilis similarly survived their apparent
destruction by the Mamluks later in the thirteenth century and they still
inhabit picturesque villages, dominated by crumbling castles, in the
coastal mountains of Syria.

The famous Round City of Baghdad, site of so many Arabian Nights tales, has disappeared entirely and was already ruined when Hülegü's Mongols captured Baghdad in 1258. Little can be seen of the city sacked by the Mongols, the only surviving gate being the Bab al Wastani built in 1123 and now serving as the Iraqi Military Museum. Like most Mesopotamian architecture it is built of brick. A wide moat also ran around the entire city from the Tigris.

Conquest of the Caliphate

Hülegü's next target was the Abbasid Caliphate in Baghdad. The Mongol world empire already included many Muslim subjects and the Sunnis among them still looked to the Caliph for spiritual leadership. This spiritual leader must, therefore, either be brought under Mongol control or be destroyed. Compared to the immense size of the Mongol Empire, the Caliphate looked a puny foe, yet it could – theoretically – call upon the support of millions of Muslims across the world. Even if such support was now no more than a myth, Baghdad itself remained a large and rich city guarded by what had, until recently, shown itself to be a formidable army of up to sixty thousand troops with a record of admittedly minor victories over the Mongols. At its peak the population of Baghdad was probably over a million, though this had certainly declined by the mid-thirteenth century. Even Kufa and the port of Basra had once held around four hundred thousand souls and they remained great cities. The settled and irrigated parts of Iraq had an enormous and frequently warlike population, as the density of settlement in Islamic areas like lower Iraq, the Nile valley and parts of Syria was much higher than anywhere else in the world except northern India and parts of China.

Yet the Caliph's army had been neglected in recent years. It was now ill-equipped, barely trained and of doubtful loyalty. While its commander demanded emergency defence measures and additional troops, the Caliph al Musta'sim seemed more concerned with frivolous pleasure. Even al Musta'sim's *wazir* or chief minister was in touch with the Mongols and, as a Shi'a Muslim, is unlikely to have had much loyalty to a Sunni Muslim Caliph. Nevertheless Hülegü proceeded with extreme caution. He feared treason among his own Muslim vassals and viewed the actions of the Muslim rulers of Syria and Egypt with caution. Hülegü was also a very superstitious man and his astrologers were deeply divided in their opinions. Some foretold Hülegü's own death if he raised his hand against the Caliph, but Nasir al Din Tusi, the astronomer who had now entered Mongol service, compared the military strengths of the two sides and made a blunt prediction. 'What will happen?' Hülegü asked. 'Hülegü will reign in place of Musta'sim,' came the scientist's simple reply.

First Hülegü marched towards Iraq, then returned to Hamadan. Next he retired to Tabriz before going back to Hamadan, which now became the Mongol forward base for their invasion of Iraq. Meanwhile the Mongol and the Caliph exchanged letters and threats. But al Musta'sim's warnings of Divine retribution had no effect on the largely shamanist, Buddhist or Christian Mongol leaders and the Caliph's final offer of tribute but not homage was refused by Hülegü. The governor of the Caliph's frontier castles was also persuaded to turn traitor. The die was

Soldiers at the Holy Sepulchre and the Crucifixion in a Syriac Gospel of the mid-13th century. Though basically in Byzantine style these pictures, like those of other oriental Christian manuscripts, show the influence of Islamic art. They also illustrate warriors in full lamellar armour, perhaps reflecting the arrival of the Mongols or of those defeated eastern Islamic armies who fled before them (Office of the Syriac Metropolitan, Mardin).

now cast and, in November 1257, Hülegü set out once again from Hamadan. This time he did not turn back. Reinforced by contingents that came from the Golden Horde, from a Mongol force already stationed on the borders of Anatolia and by Georgian vassal cavalry eager to strike a blow against the greatest of all Muslim cities, Hülegü's armies converged on Baghdad.

Many of the Shi'a Muslims of southern Iraq went over to the invaders, who now put Baghdad under close siege. Conditions inside the city were terrible, with hordes of refugees having flooded in from the surrounding villages. Al Musta'sim was at his wits' end. A negotiated peace was now out of the question and the Muslims had no realistic hope of driving off the Mongols. Yet they put up a determined resistance for almost a month before surrendering. The garrison was then murdered in cold blood, as were huge numbers of ordinary men, women and children. Exaggerated estimates of the casualties vary from eight hundred thousand to two million. The real figure was probably well over one hundred thousand, a large proportion probably being refugees who had fled to Baghdad.

The Caliph al Musta'sim, like the Isma'ili Grand Master before him, was for a while treated well. Various stories are told of the manner of his death. Nasir al Din Tusi, who may actually have been present, tells how a tray of gold was set before the Caliph. 'Eat!' demanded Hülegü. 'It is not edible,' answered al Musta'sim. 'Then why did you keep it and not use it to pay your soldiers,' asked Hülegü, 'And why did you not make these iron doors into arrowheads and why did you not come to the river and try to stop me crossing?' 'That was God's will,' the Caliph replied.

Another of Baghdad's gates survived until 1917 when it was blown up in an accidental explosion. This was the Bab Tillism which was decorated with a fine Saljuq carving of a 'hero' subduing two dragons, a popular motif in Turco-Islamic art (Staatliche Museen Berlin.

109

'What will now happen to you is also God's will,' was the Mongol's chilling response. Some say that the Caliph was then locked in a tower with his own treasure and starved to death, but this is almost certainly a myth. Others speak of him being cut down by Hülegü himself, or by his commander Ilge Noyan or by Prince Hasan Brosh, who led the Georgian cavalry. The most convincing account tells how al Musta'sim was wrapped in a carpet and kicked to death; a much more likely Mongol method of execution for someone of noble blood.

The Mongols certainly seized enormous treasure and other booty in Baghdad, some of which Hülegü sent to his brother Möngke. Nor was the great city totally destroyed. Hülegü even ordered some buildings to be restored before he and his army returned to Hamadan. Al Musta'sim's treacherous *wazir* and some other officials were confirmed in office by the conqueror, who told them to clear away the dead and reopen the bazaars. The Christian community and its churches had also been spared and the Nestorian Patriarch, Makikha, was given one of the Caliph's old palaces as his residence. In fact the Christians of Baghdad prospered, further fuelling the resentment of their surviving Muslim neighbours. Many Middle Eastern Christians now came to see the Mongols as saviours and to predict the total destruction of Islam, while even the Shi'a Muslims rejoiced at the fall of the Sunni Caliphate.

Sunni Muslims were, on the other hand, appalled. The cultural cost of the Mongol invasion was already enormous in terms of cities, libraries and schools destroyed and teachers and scholars killed or dispersed. The damage wrought to Iraq's irrigation system is only now being reversed with twentieth century technology and oil wealth. Some scholars have even suggested that the rise of Western European civilization, from a position of cultural and technological inferiority to world domination, was in part due to devastation inflicted on the Muslim world by the Mongols, coming so close after the Crusaders' sack of Byzantine Constantinople in 1204.

More immediately, the fall of Baghdad sent ripples of panic throughout northern Iraq, Syria and Anatolia. This was more from fear of Mongol power than concern for the fall of the Caliphate, which seems to have had little impact. Muslim leaders now flocked to Hülegü's Court to pay their respects or throw themselves upon his doubtful mercy. Among the first was the Atabeg or governor of Mosul, Badr al Din Lu'lu, who was over ninety years old. When his followers expressed fears for his safety, Lu'lu is said to have replied that he might even take the fearsome Mongol by the ears. Sure enough, among the gifts that the Atabeg of Mosul brought to Hülagü were a pair of ear-rings set with enormous pearls. The Destroyer of Baghdad graciously permitted Lu'lu to fasten them to the royal ears, which the Atabeg did – with a sideways glance to his trembling attendants. Next came the two Saljuq Sultans of Rum (Anatolia). Kai Kaus II, the ruler of western Rum, presented

Hülegü with a pair of stockings on whose soles his own face had been painted. 'Your slave,' muttered the grovelling Kai Kaus, 'dares to hope that his king will condescend to honour his servant's head by placing his august foot upon it.' Even the Mongols are said to have been shocked by such fulsome flattery!

Mosul, the second city of Iraq, was ruled by a Turkish atabeg or governor of Armenian origin at the time of the Mongol invasion. This was Badr al Din Lu'lu and the ruins of his palace still stand on the banks of the Tigris, above the remains of massive defensive walls of an even earlier date.

Into Syria

Hülegü next prepared for the third part of his task in the Middle East, the conquest of the Jazira (Upper Mesopotamia), Syria and Egypt. Many local rulers had already offered token submission to the Mongols but Hülegü wanted total control. First a rebellion had to be crushed in Georgia, but once this was done Mongol and vassal forces were assembled on the broad grasslands of Azerbayjan. Among this mixed army were a corps of Chinese soldiers commanded by a certain Kuo K'an, probably siege engineers like those who had helped subdue the Isma'ili castles. The leading Ayyubid prince in Syria, al Nasir Yusuf, had already made contact with the Mongols, perhaps hoping for an alliance against rival Syrian princes or against the Mamluks of Egypt. Hülegü, however, had no intention of becoming a pawn in other rulers' rivalries and the various Ayyubids soon realized that they must either become humble vassals or meet the Mongols head on.

Hülegü's invasion force was massive, numbering perhaps 120000 men. It included Turkish, Armenian and Georgian contingents and once again marched in four separate divisons. The first target was a tiny Ayyubid principality at Mayyafaqarin in the mountains west of Lake Van. Its ruler al Kamil had proudly refused to accept Mongol domination. Hülegü's son Yoshmut besieged the town, which fell early in 1260, Armenians and Georgians playing a leading rôle in the attack. Mayyafaqarin's Muslim population was then massacred and al Kamil was forced to eat chunks of his own flesh until he died. The local Christians were, however, spared. Other Mongol units seized Nisibin, Harran and Urfa. Not all the cities of the Jazira suffered as badly as Mayyafaqarin. The Turkish Artuqid dynasty of Mardin was, for example, allowed to remain as Mongol vassals, despite defying the Mongols throughout a lengthy siege, and even managed to extend its territory. Meanwhile Bohemond, the Crusader Prince of Antioch, also hurried to submit to Hülegü.

The people of Syria knew that they would be next and in January 1260 the Mongols suddenly appeared before Aleppo. The city fell in less than a week, although the huge citadel held out until 25th February. The subsequent massacre was, as usual, thorough and methodical. The Mongols' Armenian allies also burned down the Great Mosque, though this appears to have been against Hülegü's orders. Al Nasir Yusuf had meanwhile assembled an army in Damascus and had summoned the aid of his cousins, the Ayyubid princes of Hama and Karak. Yet the fall of Aleppo appears to have shaken his nerve. Through his vacillation al Nasir gradually lost the confidence of those military commanders who wanted to face the Mongols in battle. Many began shifting their allegiance to the Mamluks of Egypt, taking their troops with them. Among them was Baybars, the man who would soon have an important part in

defeating the Mongols at Ayn Jalut and who would eventually rule both Egypt and Syria as one of the greatest Mamluk Sultans.

As panic spread throughout Syria, Homs and Hama surrendered without a fight. Al Nasir Yusuf abandoned Damascus and fled towards Egypt. Hülegü's general Kit-Buqa entered Damascus on 1st March 1260, but the city's citadel held out for another month. Its governor was then personally beheaded by Kit-Buqa, who went on to take almost all of Palestine as far as Gaza on the Mediterranean. Only the Crusader-ruled coastal strip to the north remained outside Mongol control, though the invaders do not appear to have reached Jerusalem. Al Nasir, deserted by almost all his disillusioned followers, sought sanctuary among the Mamluks but they feared that an Ayyubid prince could stir up trouble in Egypt and so turned him away, eventually to be captured in Jordan and sent to Hülegü.

The Muslim collapse in Syria appeared to be irreversible but then came news which would change the situation entirely. Hülegü heard that his brother, the Great Khan Möngke, had died the previous August and so he hurried back to Azerbayjan from where he could watch events in Mongolia, decide his next move and, at the same time, keep an eye on his rival, Berke of the Golden Horde. Kit-Buqa was left in charge of Syria with a much reduced army of around twenty thousand troops. His task was to mop up remaining resistance and establish an administration. Kit-Buqa, as a Nestorian Christian, is reputed to have shown considerable favour to his co-religionists and to have treated the Muslims with contempt. Yet the available evidence seems to show that Kit-Buqa followed the old Mongol practice of treating all subject peoples equally, showing no particular favour to any one religion. For his part Hülegü issued an order from far-away Azerbayjan recognizing the rights of Christians, Muslims, Jews, Magians, Zoroastrians and even Buddhists in Damascus. Nevertheless many of the previously dominant Muslim élite of Syria now fled as refugees to Egypt and, paradoxically, to the Crusader States.

Defeat by the Mamluks

The fall of Muslim Syria was by no means an unqualified blessing for the Crusader States. Western or Latin Catholic Christians did not see the Mongols as potential liberators but as barbarians who had already devastated parts of eastern Europe. Nor did the Mongols yet regard the Crusaders as natural allies. In fact a force sent to Gaza by Kit-Buqa was intended to hinder cooperation between Egyptian Mamluks and the Crusader States. Despite his apparently small army, Kit-Buqa also began preparations for the invasion of Egypt that Hülegü had been contemplat-

After the fall of Baghdad, Hülegü supposedly taunted the captured Caliph with the gold found in the enemy's palace, asking why the Caliph had not used it to hire more soldiers.

ing before he heard of the death of Möngke. The Mongols' information service seems, on this occasion, to have let them down, and they did not realize that, in military terms, Mamluk Egypt was quite unlike fragmented Syria. The Mamluk Sultans of Egypt had, of course, yet to show their mettle. Even the Crusader States, who would eventually be destroyed by these same Mamluks, so far felt little concern about Egypt.

The Crusader lord of Jbayl (Byblos) had, however, already offered to conquer Egypt for Hülegü if only the Mongols would add ten thousand to his own one thousand horsemen. There was also a division of opinion between the northern and southern Crusader States. Bohemond VI of Tripoli and Antioch, along with his neighbour and father-in-law, the Armenian King Hethoum of Cilicia, had become vassals of Hülegü. Both had received extra territory in return for their submission. Antioch's action was, however, denounced in the Crusader Kingdom of Jerusalem and Bohemond was not particularly well treated by his new Mongol overlord. His lands were still ravaged by Mongol raiders and, in the words of his contemporaries, he 'tasted the baseness of Tartar slavery'. Later stories of the honour in which Bohemond was held by Hülegü appear to be fables, like the story that Bohemond accompanied Kit-Buqa during the capture of Damascus, where he converted a mosque into a Latin church. Meanwhile the Crusader Kingdom of Jerusalem watched the Mongols with some alarm, while both Hülegü and his deputy Kit-Buqa were cautious in their dealings with this, the strongest Crusader State. The Mongols were well aware of the Europeans' fearsome military reputation and of European power. They knew all about the Crusading movement and may even have known of King Louis of France's plans for a new Crusade.

In later years Christian chroniclers would bemoan a lost opportunity in which Crusaders and Mongols might have joined forces to defeat the Muslims. But they were writing with the benefit of hindsight, after the Crusader States had been destroyed by the Muslim Mamluks. Few at the time – certainly not those in the Crusader Kingdom of Jerusalem – thought in such terms while Hülegü still aimed to extend Mongol rule over the entire known world. The Great Khan's claim to universal domination was blasphemous to the Crusaders and they had no intention of dismantling their vital fortifications, as Kit-Buqa demanded. Kit-Buqa did try to avoid a direct clash with the Crusaders, but on 17th August 1260, his troops seized and sacked the port of Sidon. The reasons for this attack remain unclear but the city's walls were razed, as was the frontier cave-fortress of Cavea de Tyron. The operation may have been in reprisal for a Crusader raid, or a clash in which Kit-Buqa's nephew was killed, or it could just have been a demonstration of strength. Other minor clashes ended with the best available Crusader troops, including Templars, being mauled by Mongol auxiliaries. Basically, however, Kit-Buqa knew that he could not conquer the Crusader states until

Hülegü returned with adequate troops. Before that happened the Mamluks made their move.

The death of the Great Khan Möngke diverted Hülegü's attention away from Syria. It also led to the establishment of a new Mongol state, that of the Il-Khans, which, though technically still part of the Mongol world empire, was effectively independent. Möngke's death was followed by a war of succession between Hülegü's other brothes, Kublai and Arik-Böke. Hülegü made no claim of his own to the Great Khan's throne but instead helped Kublai by keeping an eye on Berke, Khan of the Golden Horde, whose sympathies lay first with Arik-Böke and later with another of Kublai's rivals, Khaidu. The Mongol world empire was, in fact, beginning to fall apart.

Meanwhile the Mamluks of Egypt decided to act and, for the first time in many years, a major Muslim power took the offensive against the Mongol invaders. The Mamluk Sultan, Sayf al Din Qutuz, was a hardened old soldier and he had also been reinforced by the arrival of Baybars, the senior ex-Ayyubid *mamluk* slave-soldier who had brought his own troops from Syria. When Hülegü's ambassadors arrogantly demanded Mamluk capitulation Qutuz put them to death, thus making war inevitable. Now the Mamluks gathered their forces and, on 26th July 1260, set out across Sinai and overwhelmed the Mongol advance base at Gaza. Although they knew that the bulk of Hülegü's army had returned to Iran, the Mamluks were unsure how the Crusader States would react to this new situation.

Baidar, commander of the Mongols at Gaza, fled to Kit-Buqa, who was encamped with his main force near Ba'lbak in Lebanon. The Crusaders of the Latin Kingdom of Jerusalem now had to decide what to

Also dating from the Mongol Il-Khan period is the so-called 'Ark' of Tabriz in north-western Iran. Built between 1310 and 1320, it is the remains of the Mosque of 'Ali Shah. These massive brick walls also formed part of the defences of the Citadel in which the mosque stood. The architecture of Mongol Iran was, in fact, characterized by its massive size and monumental style.

do. Many wanted to join the Mamluks and fight these terrifying, barbarous Mongol invaders. Others urged a more cautious policy. Some sources suggest that the Crusader barons rejected an alliance with Qutuz but gave the Mamluks provisions and free passage up the Palestinian coast. Others indicate that the idea of an alliance came from the Crusaders, but that Qutuz only wanted their oath of neutrality. Clearly neither side wanted to be seen as proposing a pact between old adversaries – Qutuz because he presented himself as the Champion of Islam against an infidel menace, and the Crusaders because they feared Mongol vengeance.

Meanwhile Kit-Buqa gathered his forces, crushed a rising by the Muslims of Damascus and marched down into the Jordan valley. It has generally been assumed that Kit-Buqa's Mongol army was now much smaller than the Mamluk force encamped outside Acre, but recent research shows that this was probably not the case. The Mamluk army was large, from fifteen to twenty thousand men, but the majority were Turcoman or Arab tribal auxiliaries and poorly equipped cavalry of very mixed origins. The Mamluks themselves formed a small élite of well-armed and highly trained professional warriors. Kit-Buqa's army similarly numbered from ten to twenty thousand, including Georgian and Armenian auxiliaries. The Mongols enjoyed a record of almost unbroken victory and had plenty of experience against other *mamluk* slave-recruited soldiers, but they had not yet met an Egyptian Mamluk force. This was the army of a military state that existed solely for the purpose of maintaining just such an army! The two forces met at Ayn Jalut (the Spring of Goliath) on 3rd September 1260 in a battle that ended in total Mamluk victory, the death of Hülegü's trusted general Kit-Buqa and the complete collapse of Mongol control over Syria.

With hindsight the battle of Ayn Jalut looks like a turning point in world history; certainly in the history of the Mongols and of the Middle East. It was not, of course, the first time that Mongols had suffered defeat at the hands of a Muslim foe but the fact that Hülegü was unable to avenge the death of his lieutenant, or to regain control of Syria, marked this battle as a turning point. It also marked the highwater mark of Mongol conquest in the west. The cities of Syria rapidly reverted to Ayyubid or Mamluk control and Qutuz returned in triumph to Egypt, only to be assassinated by his rival Baybars while hunting hare on 23rd October. Despite his preoccupation with the Mongol succession crisis, Hülegü did try to avenge Kit-Buqa but this resulted in a second Mongol defeat at Hims three months later.

In some respects, this almost forgotten battle was more important than Ayn Jalut, at least in military terms. Hülegü could now only afford to send some six thousand men, but this force retook Aleppo and again massacred many Muslims in reprisal for the death of Kit-Buqa. The Mongols again marched south, but outside Hims they met a small defending army, not of élite Egyptian Mamluks, but of local Ayyubid and ex-Ayyubid forces. There, on 10th December, Hülegü's men were defeated despite apparently outnumbering the Muslim defenders by almost four to one. Syria remained low on Hülegü's list of priorities and no further serious attempts were made to avenge these twin defeats.

The native Christians of Syria now suffered for their recent pro-Mongol sympathies while the Crusader States began to realize that their Mamluk neighbours were a force to be reckoned with. Muslim morale revived and as a result Egypt and Syria were soon reunited for the first time since the days of Saladin. Hülegü, perhaps in frustration, killed his Ayyubid prisoner al Nasir Yusuf, though by removing such a potentially disruptive factor he made Mamluk control of Syria that much easier. Even the Abbasid Caliphate reappeared, though only as a pale shadow of its former self and in a different city. A refugee from Baghdad had turned up in Damascus, claiming to be an uncle of the last Caliph al Musta'sim. Solemnly proclaimed by the Mamluk Sultan Baybars as the the 'Prince of the Faithful,' he was paraded through the streets of Cairo before being sent off to reconquer Baghdad. For a variety of reasons, however, the Mamluks allowed him to take only three hundred cavalry on his daring march across the Syrian Desert. Three hundred bedouin warriors also joined the new Caliph on his journey, but there was no rising in his favour once he reached Iraq. Instead the Caliph's little army met a large Mongol detachment near Anbar, west of Baghdad, and was slaughtered. An Abbasid Caliphate continued to exist in Mamluk Egypt until the early sixteenth century, but its members were mere puppets held under virtual house arrest.

The Mongol threat to Syria remained, though future invasions would be transitory. A major assault was launched in 1281 by an enormous army that again included Georgian, Armenian, Anatolian Saljuq and perhaps even Crusader vassals from Antioch. Again it was utterly defeated at a second battle of Hims. In 1299 a further Mongol invasion succeeded in reoccupying much of Syria before being driven out. The balance of power in the Middle East had, in fact, shifted significantly but, as a result of both Mongol invasions and Mamluk scorched-earth tactics, northern Syria became a virtual desert. The Mamluks also made political use of a deep and bitter quarrel that had developed between the Mongol Il-Khans of Iran and the Mongol Golden Horde of southern Russia. In 1262–3 the Mamluks secured with the now Muslim Golden Horde an alliance that effectively paralyzed Hülegü and his successors.

Against the Golden Horde

Hülegü continued to dominate Saljuq Anatolia but, following the Byzantine recapture of Constantinople (Istanbul) in 1261, a revived

Ceramics from the Mongol Golden Horde of the 13th–14th centuries: (A–E) undecorated locally made pottery; (F–H) glazed pottery, some perhaps imported from Iran or Anatolia.

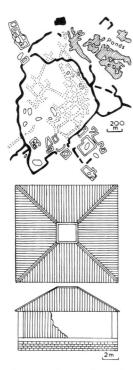

The Mongol way of life after Genghis Khan had built the Mongol World Empire is easier to see in the Golden Horde of the western steppes than in Iran, where it was overshadowed by an existing highly sophisticated Islamic civilization. A series of Mongol towns sprang up along the lower reaches of the mighty Volga river and some have been excavated by Soviet archaeologists. One example is Tsarevskoe Gorodishche (Novi Sarai) about 100 km east of Volgagrad (Stalingrad), shown in the plan (upper) and which consisted of irregular streets within equally irregular defences; (lower) reconstruction of a wooden house on brick foundations of a type found at Tsarevskoe Gorodishche.

Byzantine Empire was also drawn into the Mamluk-Golden Horde alliance. A final element entered this complicated web when the Genoese joined to provide a vital naval link between the Golden Horde and Mamluk Egypt. Hülegü could do little to counter such an extraordinary alliance. The Crusader States still feared the Mongols and were far slower than the Mamluks in grasping the opportunities offered by an increasingly fragmented Mongol world empire. Hülegü certainly tried to make allies among the Crusaders and in Catholic western Europe, while fear of cooperation between Mongols and Crusaders played a major part in the Mamluk decision to obliterate Crusader territory once and for all. Many churchmen in Europe still hoped that the Mongols would become Christian and there were a series of extraordinary contacts between Hülegü, his immediate successors, the Popes in Rome and various European rulers. A letter from Hülegü to Louis IX of France, dated 1262, has been discovered and a year or two later an embassy from Hülegü actually reached Italy. Hülegü's son and successor Abaqa wrote to the Pope and to King Edward I of England in 1273. He also sent various ambassadors but neither the Papacy, France nor England responded to his offers of an alliance. The Catholic monarchs simply could not forget earlier Mongol invasions of Europe and noted that, despite the high status of many Christians at Hülegü's Court, the Il-Khans never became Christian.

There were various reasons for Hülegü's quarrel with Berke. After capturing Baghdad, Hülegü took his army back to Azerbayjan in the far north-west of present-day Iran. Here the broad steppe-like grasslands provided excellent pasture for Mongol ponies while the cities of Maragha and Tabriz served as administrative capitals. Hülegü's Court remained essentially nomadic and the entire area acted as an enormous base camp for his predatory nomad army – a function that Azerbayjan and Hamadan have served throughout history. The vast loot that Hülegü won in Baghdad and elsewhere was deposited on a small island in Lake Urmiah, just west of Tabriz and Maragha. There a special hill-top castle was built at Shahu Tala as a kind of strongly fortified state treasury. An archaeologist who flew over the site shortly before the Second World War described the ruins as still visible 'on the almost inaccessible summit of a great rock rising a thousand feet above the shore of the island'.

Though Hülegü had supported Kublai's successful struggle for the Great Khan's throne, his own position in Iran was not entirely secure. He saw himself as Kublai's loyal deputy, as his successors did after him, and the title of Il-Khan that Hülegü adopted actually meant 'subordinate Khan'. Nevertheless doubt remained about the legitimacy of Hülegü's claim to set up such a separate state. Berke of the Golden Horde clearly saw it as a kind of usurpation in an area that should have fallen under his control, at least where the fertile pastures of Azerbayjan were concerned.

Berke, who had converted to Islam, is said to have been furious at Hülegü's massacre of Muslims in Baghdad and his killing of the Abbasid Caliph, which probably contributed to the growing antagonism between these two Mongol leaders. According to the historian Rashid al Din, Berke had declared:

He has sacked all the cities of the Muslims and, without consulting his kinsmen, has brought about the death of the Caliph. With the help of God I will call him to account for so much innocent blood!

Whether Berke's commitment to the Muslim cause was this genuine has been doubted. The conversion of the Golden Horde and its largely Kipchak Turkish population to Islam remained skin-deep for generations. It did, however, tend to isolate Berke's Golden Horde from the other Mongol powers until the Il-Khans also converted to Islam at the end of the thirteenth century.

Tension worsened after the Mongols' defeat at Ayn Jalut, but open warfare broke out only in 1262. The immediate cause seems to have been the death, under suspicious circumstances, of three Golden Horde princes who had accompanied Hülegü's army during its invasion of Iran and Iraq. Their followers clashed with Hülegü's men, then fled back to the Golden Horde. At around the same time Hülegü led his army to meet a Golden Horde force that had ridden south, through the Darband Pass, into Shirvan. The war that followed is poorly recorded. In the first clash Hülegü's advance force was defeated, though the invaders withdrew. The next major battle was fought on 14th November, well to the north of the Caucasus mountains near present-day Kuba. This time Hülegü's army was victorious. Hülegü, at the head of his main army, took Darband by storm and routed the Golden Horde in a third battle. Yet his triumph was short-lived. Hülegü's son and successor Abaqa was sent in pursuit of the defeated foe, capturing their well-stocked camp on the far bank of the frozen Terek river.

There they feasted for three days until, without warning, Berke himself appeared at the head of an enormous force. A terrible winter battle was fought on 13th January 1263, after which Abaqa's army fled back across the Terek. The ice gave way, throwing thousands of men into the freezing river, though Abaqa himself escaped and Berke returned to his own territory. During this war both sides slaughtered the opposition's merchants wherever they could be found, thus bringing trade to a virtual standstill – much to the advantage of Mamluk Egypt, which controlled the only other existing trade route between Europe and the Far East.

Neither side could achieve outright victory and such was the personal hostility that now existed between Berke and Hülegü that the war dragged on for several years. The Golden Horde, despite its conversion to Islam, remained nomadic and stood as a bastion of traditional Mongol values in the west. Hülegü's Il-Khanate, though it converted to Islam

Other finds from Tsarevskoe Gorodishche and nearby Golden Horde settlements are decorative tiles in typical Islamic style, one including an Arabic inscription.

Gold sword-quillon, Iran 13th–14th centuries. This magnificent piece of sword furniture would probably have gone on a straight-bladed weapon and is in an Islamic tradition that goes back far earlier than the Mongol conquest. Such weapons were clearly still used through, and beyond, the Il-Khan period (St. Louis Art Museum).

only at a later date, was already becoming an ordinary Middle Eastern state just as Kublai's China was becoming culturally absorbed by the civilization that it had conquered. In fact the struggle between Il-Khans and the Golden Horde persisted even after the deaths of Hülegü in 1265 and of Berke in 1266, finally being brought to a close by Hülegü's successor Abaqa.

The Il-Khan Empire

Although the quarrel with Berke was the most pressing problem facing Hülegü, he also consolidated Mongol control over Iran, Iraq, Anatolia and the lands north-east of the Euphrates that formed the Mongol frontier with Mamluk Syria. The Saljuqs of Rum were now resigned to their status as vassals. The Mamluks of Egypt occasionally tried to replace Mongol control with their own but these efforts failed and, paradoxically, the Saljuqs of Rum entered a golden age as far as their art and architecture were concerned. This may have been an unconscious effort to maintain their Turkish and Islamic identity in the face of pagan Mongol domination. The Turkish language was, for the first time in the Middle East, given official recognition and it also began to be used for serious literary purposes.

The Armenian Kingdom of Cilicia was much more enthusiastic in its loyalty to the Mongol Il-Khans. It also suffered at the hands of various Mamluk invasions as a result of this ill-founded alliance. True, the Armenians had regained some territory previously lost to the Saljuqs and they earned great wealth through trade because their Cilician port of Ayas was the Mongols' best outlet onto the Mediterranean. But as Il-Khan power declined the Mongols gave the Armenians less and less real support against Mamluk raids and encroachment by nomadic Turcomans from central Anatolia. At the same time, there was a steady migration of Armenians away from their ancestral homeland, many trading and settling as far away as Kiev and Ruthenia in south-western Russia.

In 1261 the courageous old Atabeg of Mosul, Badr al Din Lu'lu, died at the age of ninety-six. His son made contact with the Mamluks but was betrayed to Hülegü by his own wife, who had been brought up in the Mongol Court. Despite a heroic defence, and attempts by the Mamluks to relieve the city, Mosul fell once again to the Mongols after a year-long siege. The inhabitants were massacred and Lu'lu's son put to death, on Hülegü's personal orders, in a particularly obscene manner. Mosul was then annexed, as was the semi-autonomous vassal principality of Fars in southern Iran following a rebellion in 1264. Kirman in the far south-east was effectively taken over when Hülegü forced the last heiress of its autonomous dynasty to marry his son and heir, Abaqa.

120

Despite this rounding out of their conquests, the Mongols themselves largely remained in the north of Iran, where wide grasslands and a cooler mountain climate were better suited to their style of life.

Hülegü's Army

The army that Hülegü led into Iran in 1256 was a typical Mongol force of the fully developed kind. Like all Mongol armies, it was believed by its

A few surviving early 14th century manuscripts show scenes from the court of the Mongol Il-Khans. The attendant soldiers mostly have feathered hats and are armed with maces and swords while the court ladies wear exactly the same tall headdresses as are shown in Chinese art of the Mongol period (Topkapi Museum, Ms. Haz. 2153 f. 148v, Istanbul).

121

foes to be of quite staggering size. The whole question of the real or imagined size of Mongol armies continues to exercise the minds of historians. Nor is there yet much agreement on the subject. Some still take the figures offered by medieval historians at face value, while others dismiss them out of hand. A new group of specialists studies available pasture and the current livestock populations of various regions in an attempt to work out how many men and animals could have lived off the land during a campaign, as the Mongols clearly did.

A higher percentage of the Mongol male population took part in warfare than in most medieval societies. Genghis Khan and his successors may also have developed a system of political organization and military discipline that enabled them to make fuller use of nomad manpower than their predecessors had achieved. Mongol tribal armies seem, for example, to have been much larger than those of the similarly steppe-nomadic Saljuq Turks. The Ottomans are said to have summoned at most one-fifth of nomads from their camps. But the Mongols were able to enlist between two hundred thousand and three hundred thousand Mongol and Turkish males from the ages of fourteen to sixty who were on the Il-Khan military register by the year 1300. Marco Polo, describing Hülegü's army on campaign in 1261, said that it 'mustered quite 300,000 horsemen.' The historian al Juvayni also described the Il-Khan army as a militia, stating that it was:

A peasantry in the dress of an army, of which in time of need all, from small to great, from those of high rank to those of low estate, are swordsmen, archers or spearmen.

Nevertheless, Mongols were still only the élite of the Il-Khan armies, the bulk of which were drawn from nomadic Turkish tribes and from the forces of vassal rulers. Even in the early days, most of Hülegü's troops appear to have been Kipchak Turks recruited from largely pagan tribes inhabiting steppes north of the Aral and Caspian seas. These Kipchaks provided soldiers for so many medieval armies, from Russia, the Balkan states and Byzantine Empire to Georgia and the Muslim Middle East, that they might fairly be called the Gurkhas of the Middle Ages. Many of the Mamluk Sultans were of Kipchak origin though they, of course, first arrived in Egypt as military slaves.

The huge numbers listed on Il-Khan military registers excluded vassal troops, so that the potential size of Il-Khan armies was staggering. The numbers were increased still further under Khan Ghazan, but a clear distinction must be drawn between available military manpower and the numbers actually sent on any particular campaign. In addition to Mongols, Turks and vassals, the Il-Khans employed a few Western mercenaries. The Mongols had an obvious respect for European military prowess, despite having defeated a number of Western armies. A few armoured knights may have been recruited, but greater interest was shown in European crossbowmen, whom the Mongols, like all lightly

armoured horse-archers, greatly feared Genoese crossbow-armed marines are even said to have been enlisted by Hülegü's grandson Arghun.

The military organization of Il-Khan Iran was also fully within Mongol traditions, though older Islamic patterns soon re-emerged. The main operational unit remained the *tümen* of theoretically 10,000 men. In Iran the term *tümen* also seems to have referred to a district that provided 10,000 men or, in areas not settled by Mongols, that provided 10,000 local troops or the taxes to maintain them. In the early days Mongol troops received no pay, as service in the army was regarded as a natural duty. Indeed the soldiers themselves not only paid a *qübchür* to maintain impoverished comrades but were also liable for taxes to maintain the government communications service. Meanwhile the soldiers themselves lived off their own flocks, some trade and any plunder they won in time of war.

The system was, however, breaking down by the reign of Khan Ghazan and troops close to the capital started to get provisions, collected as a form of taxation from subject peoples. But graft and corruption meant that even this system failed to work properly and had to be supplemented by cash payments. Gradually, therefore, Il-Khan military organization came to resemble the sophisticated systems of earlier Islamic armies. Early in the fourteenth century Ghazan also introduced a system of *iqta*'s or military fiefs, particularly along the routes habitually used by armies on campaign and in the vital regions of summer or winter pasture. The *iqta*' system was, of course, also of earlier Islamic origin. Unlike the European knight's fief, however, the *iqta*' remained the Khan's property, held by a soldier only as long as the government

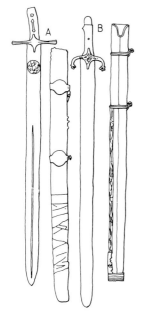

Middle Eastern swords of the Mongol period: (left) late 13th-early 14th century Iran, the inlaid decoration on the blade is later (Topkapi Palace Museum, Istanbul); (right) sword attributed to an unnamed Abbasid Caliph, 13th century Iraq (Topkapi Palace Museum, Istanbul);

wished him to. Nevertheless a warrior, be he Mongol, Mamluk or any other kind of *iqta'* holder, could live off the rents of such a fief while concentrating on military training or war. *Iqta's* were also allocated to indigenous Iranian infantry, in particular those concerned with static frontier defence. Such evidence shows just how the old Mongol militia-army was turning into a Middle Eastern professional force. Local Iranian troops were, however, still organized in hundreds and thousands along classic Mongol lines.

Though north-western Iran contained large areas of grassy steppe, the Il-Khan state consisted largely of deserts, bleak mountains and irrigated agricultural zones. A lack of pasture on which to keep the vast horse-herds needed by traditional Mongol forces inevitably had its effect on the structure of Il-Khan armies. The cavalry that invaded Syria had, for example, fewer spare mounts than the followers of Genghis Khan had taken on campaign. This in turn influenced Il-Khan battle tactics, though their Mamluk foes were still rarely able to catch the Mongols despite the Mamluks' possession of finer horses. By Ghazan's time the Il-Khan state was even reduced to requisitioning animals from the peasantry.

Compared to medieval European armies, that of the Il-Khans had a much more unified and reliable command structure. Officers were appointed by the Khan, not simply by hereditary or feudal right, and this made Il-Khan armies easier to command. But even the efficient communications systems developed by the Mongols had their limitations and the realities of battlefield control also placed limits on the size of the Khan's armies. Training seems to have become more structured and organized than in earlier Mongol forces, though the great annual hunt or *nerge* still played a vital rôle. These hunts could be massive, with a circle of warriors many miles across taking up to three months to contract around the trapped animals before killing them. Such exercises improved not only cavalry skills, archery and discipline, but also a commander's control over large numbers of men.

In battle Il-Khan troops used all the old Mongol tactics. These included trapping foes upon a hilltop then cutting them down with showers of arrows as if they were animals in a *nerge* hunt, or repeatedly charging a less manoeuvrable foe, shooting volleys of arrows at each turn. Reference to the use of large numbers of baggage camels, fifes and drums does, however, suggest local Islamic military influence. An increased use of infantry must also have altered traditional Mongol tactics, as would the habit, developed only after Hülegü's death, of carrying fodder and other supplies instead of relying solely on pasture along an army's line of march.

Available descriptions of major battles only hint at such changes but it seems possible that the Il-Khan army now employed various traditional Iranian tactics, in addition to the Mongol ones inherited from their forebears. Among the idealized battle formations described by the early-thirteenth-century Muslim scholar Fakhr al Din Mubarakshah was the Crescent array credited to ancient Persian kings. This was certainly used by the Saracens against the Crusaders and by the Mamluk army of Egypt. In it a continuous crescent-shaped formation of cavalry faced the enemy, with the horns of the crescent thrust well forward. Behind this, on the right, stood the ruler, his household and treasury. On the left stood the second-in-command or *wazir* with the armoury. Massed behind the left horn of the crescent was additional cavalry with spare horses and flocks. Similarly massed behind the right horn were 'prison guards' (perhaps élite infantry). To the rear came the baggage train and hospital protected by further infantry, while behind them all came the rearguard.

Relatively little is known about cavalry training exercises in Mongol Iran but something can be gathered by studying the *furisiyya* training games of Mamluk Egypt. Some of these exercises were of Mongol origin while others may have been known in Il-Khan Iran. The *Qabaq* game was certainly Turco–Mongol. Here a target, originally an empty gourd, was mounted on top of a pole and a horse-archer would loose arrows at it, either from a standstill or, for fancy shooting, while riding by. Although such an exercise improved an archer's accuracy and dexterity, the *Qabaq* was not real war training. The target was unlike anything normally met in battle and there was no cooperation between units during the game. The second most well-known Mamluk archery training exercise was the *Qiqaj*, though it is unclear how popular it was in Il-Khan areas. This was real battle training in which a horse-archer had to shoot downwards at a target on the ground as he rode past. In battle most shooting was, in fact, at ground level either at enemy infantry or at rival horsemen.

An Il-Khan army on the march must have been an impressive sight. Al Juvayni described Hülegü's force as it approached the Assassin castles as:

> . . . a mountain of iron. The hills which had held their heads so high and had such strong hearts now lay trampled with broken necks under the hooves of horses and camels. And from the din of the braying of those camels and the noise of pipe and kettle-drum the ears of the world were deafened, and from the neighing of the horses and the flashing of the lances the hearts and eyes of the enemy were blinded

To add to such confusion, dust and noise, later Mongol armies sometimes took great flocks of sheep and goats with them – up to thirty per soldier – to provide meat. Then there were the men's families, which sometimes also went on campaign. It must have taken great logistical planning to deal with such an army, particularly as available pasture had to be close to an army's line of march. Even in friendly territory messengers had to be sent well ahead of the troops to prepare stores of food and drink. They also had to requisition land for grazing and hold boats in readiness at river crossings. Engineers would accompany the messengers to repair bridges, clear roads of thorns and boulders and, if

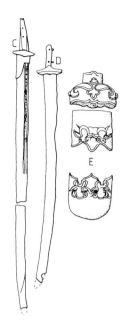

A sabre in Mongol Central Asian style with an Armenian inscription found in the northern Urals, Russia (left), thirteenth century and now in the Archaeological Institute Academy of Sciences, Leningrad; a sabre from Kazakstan, 13th–14th century (ex-Pletnyeva); solid bronze matrices for beating out the quillons and scabbard mounts of a straight sword (right), evidence of mass-produced weapons in 12th–14th century Iran and now in the Metropolitan Museum, New York.

necessary, to widen passes. These messengers maintained communications between the widely separated divisions of the army as it marched, as well as carrying messages from the ruler to his vassals or to the Great Khan in Mongolia. Much the same system of requisitioning local supplies and horses also applied when an army besieged a castle or city.

However efficient this supply system, an Il-Khan army still had to move on when the local pastures were used up. Mongol ponies lived off grass, not fodder or grain, and their numbers would in any case have been far too great for fodder to be carried by the army. Several Mongol invasions of Syria prove this point. Although northern Syria does have broad steppe lands, these can support only a limited number of animals and they dry out virtually to nothing in high summer and early autumn. One additional reason that encouraged Hülegü to withdraw from Syria after hearing of Möngke's death in 1260 was simply that the grazing was used up. The Mamluks also knew of the Mongols' dependence on pasture and they regularly burnt off the grass ahead of an invading Il-Khan force. Meanwhile Mamluk war horses used horseshoes, which Mongol ponies apparently still did not, and as early as 1244 there is mention of Syria's hard stoney ground hurting the feet of Mongol ponies. The reasons for Hülegü and his successors' failure against the Mamluks were clearly much more complex than has generally been realized.

Arms and Armour

Arms and armour were captured in large quantities during the initial conquest in Iran, while local rulers were expected to offer military equipment as a form of tribute as early as 1253. Despite serving new masters, Iranian armourers do not seem to have changed their styles to suit Mongol tastes until the very late thirteenth century. Then, however, new features did start to appear, such as thigh-length lamellar cuirasses, greaves for the lower legs and differently shaped helmets. Government armaments officers had bought arms from private armourers since the days of Abaqa and perhaps even Hülegü, but by Ghazan's time the state had set up its own supply arsenals. Azerbayjan, as the site of the Il-Khan capital, now became an important arms-manufacturing centre. The demand for military supplies could affect everyone in the land as, for example, when the owners of particularly straight trees found these being felled for spear shafts. Tailors were also given enormous government orders for what must have been largely standardized uniforms.

The warriors of later Il-Khan Iran still appeared very Mongol to their foes, however. They continued to use small round shields of spiral cane construction, hung large box-like quivers from their belts and had a

habit of sliding their light lances beneath their saddle girths while using other weapons. In Iran mail armour, including fabric-covered and padded forms, declined in popularity, while lamellar was more extensively used. Horse armour which, contrary to popular opinion, had never fallen out of favour in the medieval Middle East now changed as the old padded or quilted forms were replaced by lamellar horse armours of generally hardened-leather construction. Meanwhile Mongol and Il-Khan arms had an influence on those of the rest of the Muslim and Byzantine Middle East. It is even possible that the much later European *zischägge* 'lobster-tailed' helmet, so characteristic of the English Civil War period, could be traced back not only to the Ottoman *chichak* but to an even earlier Mongol prototype. Il-Khan Iran also played an important part in the spread of Chinese gunpowder technology, although Muslims also made an essential contribution to the development of real firearms through their discovery and use of saltpetre.

One aspect of archery in Il-Khan Iran that remains unclear is the use of the archer's thumb-ring. This device protected the thumb when loosing a very powerful composite bow. It has been suggested that the small studs on the outside of such rings acted as a kind of backsight when the bowstring was pulled against an archer's cheek, but in general thumb-rings do not appear to have been widely used in warfare. Most references concern hunting and one even mentions a thumb-ring being used by a Mongol youth hunting with a stone-throwing bow near Isfahan in the mid-thirteenth century.

Despite their shortage of pasture and mounts, Il-Khan cavalry still

One of the most beautiful buildings remaining from the time of the last Abbasid Caliphs is the Mustansir Madrasah, an Islamic religious college built in 1233. It stood very close to the Caliph's enclosure or palace area and later became a customs building. Today its magnificent decorative brickwork survives as testimony of the superb architecture of the city sacked by Hülegü.

went on campaign with spare ponies. These were relatively small animals unsuitable for a heavy fully-armoured trooper. References to Mongols using leather-loop stirrups rather than stirrups of iron or bronze also indicate that only a minority wore heavy armour. Nor were the bows of the average Mongol warrior likely to have been particularly good, as Mongol tribesmen still made most of their own equipment. In fact, compared to their professional Mamluk foes, the bulk of Il-Khan cavalry, outside an élite of heavily armoured and better mounted troopers, would have appeared a ragged and lightly armed bunch.

Hülegü's Battles

Maymun-Diz

The fortress of Maymun-Diz consisted of a great spur of rock rising almost vertically from the valley. Although there were some fortifications on the summit these faced down into the valley, with little concern being shown for the bleak mountains to the rear. Much of the face of the precipice was covered by masonry cemented together with plaster and gravel. This was pierced by arches and openings that led into a series of galleries and cave-like defensive positions linked by a main staircase. Overlooking these defences and within the range of the new siege engines used by Hülegü, was another higher hill.

After a series of protracted negotiations Hülegü suddenly decided to strike. His troops made a remarkable forced march over the Taliqan mountains and burst into the valley of Maymun-Diz so unexpectedly that they almost caught the garrison napping. On 8th November 1256, having failed to take the fortress by surprise, Hülegü set up his imperial parasol on a hilltop facing the cave-fortress from the north. The invading Mongols had brought with them the most up-to-date siege machines and many references were made to the function of Chinese engineers. The moral effect of one particular engine operated by Chinese specialists certainly succeeded in shortening the siege of Maymun-Diz. This *kaman-i-gav* or 'ox's bow' appears to have been a large crossbow, mounted on a frame and shooting bolts dipped into burning pitch that could reach right into the cave-like galleries of the Assassin castle. It must have been very like the *ziyar*, a late-twelfth-century Islamic frame-mounted crossbow that shot fire grenades, among other projectiles. The *kaman-i-gav* was, however, even more powerful, being credited with a range of 2500 paces – more than two kilometres!

However, the invention of much more powerful counterweight stone-throwing trebuchets probably had greater influence on this siege, as they did in so many late-twelfth- and thirteenth-century sieges. These weapons were invented in the Middle East and are clearly illustrated in a

Lu'lu, the aged governor of Mosul, gave a pair of splendid ear-rings to Hülegü, thus fulfilling a promise to his men that he would himself take the fearsome Mongol invader 'by the ears'.

number of Il-Khan manuscripts. It was probably to make the beam-slings of these powerful mangonels that Hülegü's pioneers cut down the Isma'ilis' own groves of pine trees. The historian al Juvayni, who witnessed the siege, wrote with grim satisfaction that those who planted these trees had no idea what crops they would one day produce. Teams of the fittest men in Hülegü's army were then distributed at quarter-of-a-kilometre intervals from the valley to the hilltop. The weapons' heavy poles and frames were then hauled to the summit in a classic example of Mongol military organization.

Once the bombardment began the garrison found that they had no answer to Hülegü's siege engines, which soon smashed the defenders' machines. The bombardment was kept up for three days and on the fourth the Mongols made an assault, but this was driven back. It was at this point that the fearsome *kaman-i-gav* was brought into play, probably against the main staircase to stop communication between the various galleries. The Isma'ili Grand Master then appears to have lost his nerve and sent a messge claiming that he had intended to surrender all along, but had been prevented by his own men, who had threatened to assassinate him. Hülegü's only reply was to advise the Grand Master to keep his head down while he erected more mangonels around the entire castle perimeter. Then followed a savage bombardment in which, according to al Juvayni, the surviving defenders:

. . . crept in their flight like mice into a hole or fled like lizards into crannies in the rock. Some were left wounded and some lifeless and all that day they struggled feebly and stirred themselves like mere women.

The Grand Master had obviously been hoping that winter snows would force the Mongols to retreat, but no snow came and old men of a hundred years said that they could not remember such a mild winter.

On 18th November the astronomer Nasir al Din Tusi, who had been held a virtual prisoner in Maymun-Diz, came down with an offer of surrender. The next day the Grand Master himself emerged. On the 20th the Grand Master's family were brought down and the Mongol troops set about demolishing the extraordinary cave-fortress of Maymun-Diz.

One aspect that has puzzled archaeologists and military historians to this day was why the neighbouring Assassin garrison at Alamut made no effort to raid the besieging Mongols and thus take pressure off their comrades in Maymun-Diz. The topography would clearly have enabled them to do so, but they did not.

Baghdad

Hülegü's most notable victories were all in siege warfare and the most dramatic of them all was the capture and devastation of Baghdad. The assault had long been planned. Mongol troops already had experience of campaigning in Iraq and had met the Abbasic Caliph's army on previous occasions, though not always successfully.

After conquering Iran, Hülegü indulged his interest in astrology by having the famous Persian mathematician Nasir al Din Tusi build an astronomical observatory.

The great city of Baghdad was now but a shadow of its former glory. Yet it was still immense by medieval standards. The Round City built for the Caliph al Mansur on the west bank of the Tigris had crumbled into ruin. The once extensive commercial suburbs on this side of the river had also shrunk into a series of separate quarters divided by fields, gardens and wasteland. Some were inhabited by Shi'a Muslims who felt little love for the Caliph, while others were populated by more loyal Sunni Muslims. The newer parts of Baghdad on the east bank were, however, in better repair and had even been given a stout defensive wall with four main gates, towers and a deep ditch filled with water from the Tigris. This had been built in the time of the Caliph al Mustazhir around 1100, but had been regularly repaired since. Within this eastern half of Baghdad stood the Palace area containing royal apartments, government buildings, various large religious structures, colleges, libraries and parks, all separated from the rest of the eastern city by another defensive wall. The main Christian quarter appears to have been on the east bank, slightly to the north of the walled city and within a now ruined wall built by the Caliph al Musta'in during the ninth century.

The city, and the small state that the Caliphs had managed to re-establish since the decline of the Saljuqs, had a small army of professional, slave-recruited *mamluk* soldiers, plus auxiliaries from the Arab tribes of southern Iraq. To this could be added a citizen militia of dubious reliability and very little training.

Hülegü and his army left Hamadan in November 1257, sacking the city of Kermanshah on their way down to the Tigris plain. Hülegü's finest general, Kit-Buqa, had already taken the left wing down through Luristan towards Baghdad while a third army under Baiju marched south from Mosul. A council of war was next held at the so-called Zagrian Gates, where the mountains of Iran meet the vast plain of Iraq. Threats and counterthreats flowed between Hülegü and the Caliph while the Mongols drew up their final invasion plan. This done, Hülegü set up camp on the banks of the Hulwan river while Baiju led his men back across the Tigris to attack Baghdad from the rear.

On 16th January 1258 Baiju's men crossed the river and an officer named Suqunchaq was sent forward with an advance force as far as Harbiyya. When the Caliph's Chancellor, Aibeg, heard of this threat from the rear he led the Caliph's army across to the west bank of the Tigris and attacked Suqunchaq near Anbar, about fifty kilometres north of Baghdad. The Mongols were at first driven back until rallied by Baiju himself. The Caliph's army was lured into marshy terrain where it was trapped when the Mongols opened a dyke. There the Caliph's men were cut to pieces, only their commander and a few troops escaping back to Baghdad, while other survivors fled south into the desert.

Hülegü's armies now converged upon Baghdad; Baiju seizing the western suburbs and Kit-Buqa the south-western, while Hülegü en-

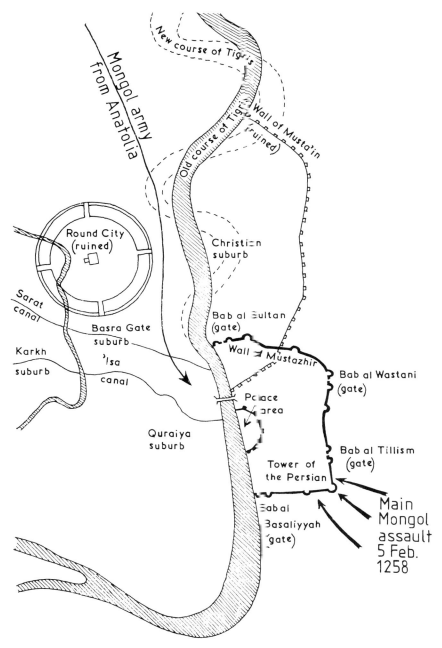

Within the map:

New course of Tigris

Mongol army from Anatolia

Old course of Tigris

Wall of Musta'in (ruined)

Round City (ruined)

Christian suburb

Sarat canal

Basra Gate suburb

Bab al Sultan (gate)

Karkh suburb

'Isa canal

Wall of Mustazhir

Bab al Wastani (gate)

Palace area

Quraiya suburb

Bab al Tillism (gate)

Tower of the Persian

Main Mongol assault 5 Feb. 1258

Bab al Basaliyyah (gate)

camped before the strongly defended walls of the eastern city. As was
now normal Mongol practice, a palisade and a ditch were built around
the entire besieged eastern city from river bank to river bank. Between
the palisade and the walls of Baghdad Hülegü set up his eagle standard,
described by the Persian historian Wassaf as the 'bird of good fortune'
from whose head 'fury and the fire of fight burst forth.' Here his
engineers also erected their stone-throwing engines and battering rams.

Hülegü's siege and capture of Baghdad, 1258.

131

Inside the city, streets were barricaded and the gates sealed shut while the remaining professional *mamluks* manned the walls, along with ordinary citizens who had been issued with whatever weapons were available.

The Mongols even used the bricks of long abandoned suburbs to build siege towers close to Baghdad's wall. From the summits of these the attackers could shoot stones, incendiary grenades and arrows right into the heart of the city. Towards the end of January the Caliph sent his *wazir* or Chief Minister and the Nestorian Patriarch to try and negotiate, but Hülegü refused them an audience.

On January 29th the Mongol bombardment began in earnest and by 4 February a breach had been opened in the south-eastern corner of the defences, near the Burj al 'Ajami or Persian Tower. This appears to have been a key position, perhaps an almost self-contained bastion, for its fall enabled the Mongols to spread along the walls to right and left. On the 5th the Mongols attacked again and by dawn next day they controlled a stretch of defensive wall from the Persian Tower to the neighbouring Bab al Tillism (also known as the Racecourse Gate). Baghdad lay at their mercy. The Chancellor Aibeg tried to escape down river but was captured, as was the commander-in-chief of the Caliph's army, Sulayman-Shah. Both were almost immediately executed.

The Caliph attempted to negotiate but his *wazir*, who was almost certainly in treacherous correspondence with Hülegü, advised unconditional surrender. On 10th February the Caliph came out of the city and gave himself up. Hülegü received him with apparent kindness and asked that the army of Baghdad lay down their arms. When instructed to do so by the Caliph, they emerged from the city walls only to be divided into groups and butchered once they were clear of the buildings. Before they entered the city the Mongols tore down large sections of the wall and filled the moat. This done, they swept into Baghdad on 13th February, beginning an orgy of massacre, looting, fire and rape that went on for seven days. As the historian Wassaf described it:

They swept through the city like hungry falcons attacking a flight of doves, or like raging wolves attacking sheep, with loose reins and shameless faces, murdering and spreading fear. . . . Beds and cushions made of gold and encrusted with jewels were cut to pieces with knives and torn to shreds. Those hidden behind the veils of the great harem were dragged . . . through the streets and alleys, each of them becoming a plaything in the hands of a Tatar monster.

The Final Days

Hülegü held his last *quriltai* near Tabriz in July 1264. It was an impressive gathering, attended by the Kings of Georgia and Armenia and by the Crusader Prince of Antioch. The Il-Khan's borders now

stretched from the Amu Darya river to within 250 kilometres of Istanbul. Hülegü was even negotiating with the Byzantines for the hand of a Greek princess, Maria, the illegitimate daughter of the Emperor Michael Palaeologos. Just over six months later, however, the Destroyer of the Assassins and Conqueror of Baghdad was dead.

The first Il-Khan was buried near his assembled loot on the island fortress of Shahu Tala in Lake Urmia. Towards the end of his life Hülegü had shown great savagery but also a respect for civilization and, in particular, Islamic culture. At his death, however, some of the most primitive aspects of Mongol tribal tradition once again rose to the surface. Several of the most beautiful young women at Court were buried with the old conqueror, this being the last recorded example of human sacrifice at the funeral of a prince of Genghis Khan's line. These sacrifices also make Hülegü's claim to have been a follower of the Buddha ring hollow. He was, in fact, probably a traditional Mongol shamanist with a superficial interest in Buddhism.

Later that summer Hülegü's devoted Christian wife, Doquz-khatun, also died. As a fervent Nestorian, the Khatun had been both protector and patron of the eastern Christians throughout Hülegü's reign. She helped all sects, but made no secret of her dislike of Islam. Small wonder, then, that the loss of this lady and even of her terrifying husband was mourned by Christians across much of the Middle East. Kirakos of Ganja, the Armenian chronicler, described them as having been 'another Constantine, another Helen'. The historian Bar Hebraeus, who had recently been elected head of the Jacobite Syriac Church, bemoaned their loss in fulsome phrases:

In 1265 Hülegü, the King of Kings, departed from this world. The wisdom of this man, and his greatness of soul, and his wonderful actions are incomparable. And in the days of summer Doquz-khatun, the believing queen, departed and great sorrow came to all the Christians throughout the world because of the departure of these two great lights who made the Christian religion triumphant.

Even the Muslim Persian chronicler al Juvayn wrote that Hülegü 'united

The art of early 14th century Mongol Iran includes an amazing variety of styles, from the old arts of the previous Arab and Saljuq periods to Central Asian and Chinese influence. Among the finest examples of such Il-Khan art are two copies of a World History by the Il-Khan scholar Rashid al Din. Made in north-western Iran 1306–14, they are in almost exactly the same style and show Mongol, Turkish, Arab and other warriors in great detail. This miniature – showing Defeat of Qasdar rebels by Mahmud ibn Sebuktegin, *illustrates what was at the time a relatively recent historical event and both armies are dressed in Mongol style. Most of the wariors wear full lamellar armour though one on each side has fabric-covered or soft armour. On the ground between the forces is an abandoned war drum. This is the copy in Edinburgh University (Ms. 20).*

133

in his person all the graces of kingly beneficence and all the wonder of royal kindness'. The eastern Christians had good reason to bewail Hülegü's death for, although the Il-Khans would continue to show them favour for a while, things would never be the same again. The ruling dynasty would become Muslim towards the end of the thirteenth century and would thereafter rapidly decline in power. After the death of Hülegü's great-great-grandson Abu Sa'id in 1335 the Mongol Il-Khanate would degenerate into chaos whereas its rival, the Golden Horde, would last in one form or another until its absorption by the Russian Empire in 1502.

The Il-Khan Achievement

When the Mongols conquered Iran and Iraq they took over an area where people were identified primarily by their religion, not by language, race or land of birth. Islam was the dominant religion, while other 'Peoples of the Book', such as Christians, Jews and Zoroastrians, had previously been given complete freedom of religion. Yet Islam had been the faith of the rulers and of the élite since the seventh century. Unlike the Chinese, the Muslims generally had no experience of being ruled by non-believers, while Islam itself was intended to be a superior faith superseding all previous Divine Revelations. To be conquered by non-Muslims was bad enough, but the Mongols were not even recognized 'People of the Book'. Most of them were not even Buddhists but were shamanists, followers of tribal cults, which made them no more than pagans in Muslim eyes.

These pagans, plus their Buddhist and Christian followers, ruled much of the Muslim Middle East with an iron hand. Nevertheless their alien culture, particularly that of the Uighurs, flourished in Iran for several generations, while central Asian and Chinese fashion had a strong influence on Court costume and the military élite. Mongol personal habits were also very different to those of the conquered Iranians. Though not necessarily as filthy as sometimes described, the Mongols certainly did not profess the same concern for personal cleanliness as did the Muslims. The Mongol fear of witchcraft and sorcery was proverbial. They also shocked the Muslims by their continued use of pagan fire rituals, including purification by fire at funerals. On the other hand the Mongols' belief in magical rain stones to control the weather, which they had learned from the pre-Islamic Turks, survived even after they themselves became Muslim.

Although Hülegü remained essentially shamanist, he was a nominal adherent of Buddhism and considered himself a devotee of the Boddhisattva Maitreya. Buddhism was, in fact, the most important 'civilized' religion among the first Il-Khans. Buddhist monks came from

134

China, Tibet and Uighur Central Asia. They erected pagodas decorated with paintings and statues, the so-called ṣagan temples that Hülegü built near Maragha probably being Buddhist All these structures were later obliterated without trace, but archaeologists have recently discovered that a series of man-made caves near Maragha were originally Buddhist temples. As such they are the only known relics of this extraordinary period in Iranian religious history. How far the Buddhist art in such temples influenced Islamic painting remains unclear, but artists did come to Iran from China while many aspects of Chinese and Central Asian art can be seen in later Il–Khan manuscripts Hülegü's grandson Arghun took his Buddhist faith more seriously and brought both Buddhist priests and men skilled in yoga mysticism from India. It is even possible that Buddhist yogis and the half-Buddhist half-shamanist *bakhshi* ascetics in the Il–Khan Court influenced the development of certain later forms of Islamic Sufi mysticism. This in turn influenced aspects of modern Iranian Shi'a Islam.

Christians and Jews could also be found in the Il–Khan Court. Some achieved power and wealth as doctors, government ministers and scholars. In fact the greatest Il–Khan historian, Rashid al Din, is said to have been of Jewish origin. The Christians were at times even more influential. Hülegü's chief wife, Doquz-khatun, was a Nestorian Christian as was at least one of his other wives. Doquz-khatun remained a champion and protector of the Christian community throughout her life and Hülegü consulted her on many matters. She had churches built throughout the land while she herself prayed in a church-shaped tent that was carried wherever the nomadic Il–Khan Court travelled. Abaqa, Hülegü's immediate successor, gave this tent-church to Doquz-khatun's niece, a concubine of Hülegü, who continued her aunt's religious mission.

Hülegü himself showed great favour to the Christians, as did the next Il–Khans Abaqa and Arghun. This was often to the detriment of the Muslim majority and further fuelled the resentment that would eventually do so much damage to eastern Christianity. Meanwhile, however,

A similar style of art is found in other copies of the World History *made in Il-Khan Tabriz. This picture of Pharoah's army in the Red Sea was made in 1314 and shows full lamellar armour. Some of the warriors have mail aventails hanging from their helmets while others are protected by circular ear defences.*

135

the Christians of Iran, Iraq, the Jazira and eastern Anatolia flourished. The Nestorians, who had contacts and co-religionists across the entire Mongol world empire, enjoyed particularly high status. In 1281 the Nestorian church fathers even elected a Chinese monk named Markus as their new Patriarch, largely as a political move to please their Mongol rulers. This humble man, who knew little Syriac and no Arabic, had come on pilgrimage to the Middle East, hoping to visit Jerusalem. His way had been blocked by a war between the Il-Khans and Mamluks and instead he found himself suddenly raised to the head of his church as Patriarch Mar Yahballaha III.

For centuries the Nestorians had got on with the dominant Muslims better than did most Christian sects, largely because their view of Christ almost as a divinely-inspired man rather than as God was close to the Islamic view. Yet the Nestorians could not escape Muslim wrath, even before the Il-Khans converted to Islam. Anti-Christian riots were recorded in Baghdad as early as 1263. When Khan Ghazan made Islam the official religion of the Il-Khan Empire in 1295 this unleashed the pent-up fury of the Muslims and there were several pogroms. Even the now-aged Nestorian Patriarch Mar Yahballaha III was hung up by his feet and beaten before Ghazan could restore order. Other persecutions followed, though the Christian sects survived even in Iran where old Mar Yahballaha III continued to lead his shrunken flock until 1317. Further west, in the Artuqid vassal state in what is now south-eastern Turkey, Christianity flourished for several more centuries. Even today the Jacobite Patriarch has his little palace in Mardin, while the twin monasteries of Derzafaran and Mar Gabriel remain centres of Syriac learning and ancient church music.

Some Mongols had converted to Islam before Hülegü arrived in Iran. Körgüz (George), the Uighur governor of Khurasan was among the first, and his sympathy for the conquered peoples led to a start being made in the rehabilitation of devastated north-eastern Iran. Hülegü's son Tëgüdur Ahmad turned Muslim soon after he became Il-Khan in 1282, but his Mongol followers were not ready for such a move, which led to civil war. Tëgüdur was deserted by his army, deposed and executed. Not until Ghazan came to the throne and publicly proclaimed his Muslim faith in 1295 did Islam become the official religion of the Il-Khan Empire. All the minority faiths then felt the Muslim backlash but it was Buddhism that suffered most. Ghazan denounced the worship of Buddhist idols, which were dragged through the streets in mockery. Temples were destroyed and statues placed beneath the doorsteps of mosques so that worshippers stepped on them as they went to pray. Buddhist lamas and monks had either to become Muslim or return to India, Kashmir or Tibet. Many died in outbursts of popular anger while even some churches and synagogues were ransacked.

Ghazan's declaration did not, however, mean that all the Mongols in

Iran immediately converted to Islam. Even Öljeitü, who ruled as Il-Khan from 1304, had been in turn a Buddhist, a Christian, a shamanist and a Sunni Muslim before finally settling on Shi'a Islam. Conversion to Islam was, for most Mongols, a superficial matter. After listening to a tedious and lengthy religious debate one of Öljeitü's generals lost patience and demanded a return to the *yasaq* and *yusun*, laws and customs, of Genghis Khan. Yet the die had been cast and the gradual assimilation of the Mongols into Islamic Iran became inevitable. Though they remained largely nomadic, the Mongol military élite developed closer relations with the settled population, just as previous Turkish conquerors had done. Some Mongols even settled down as cultivators or landowners. By 1300 Mongol society in Il-Khan Iran was changing irreversibly and before long lost its identity entirely.

Well before the official conversion to Islam, Khan Abaqa chose Tabriz as the Il-Khan's permanent capital and his government gradually began adopting traditional Middle Eastern systems of administration. Mongol and Chinese devices, such as inscribed metal rods or plaques carried as official insignia, continued to be used in Iran but, until Ghazan's adoption of Islam, Il-Khan rule boiled down to little more than ruthless exploitation.

In Hülegü's time, the Court did not cost much to maintain and it largely lived off booty, the taxes of a few private estates and its own animal herds, plus gifts from those seeking favour. Under Abaqa and Arghun small allowances were set aside for the ruling family, but a large part of the state revenues was siphoned off by corrupt officials before reaching the Khan's treasury. The introduction of Chinese-style paper money was a total failure. It was intended to replace a now-forbidden precious-metal currency, which would theoretically, revert to the government. The printed-paper money was, however, refused by the merchant classes and commerce came to a dead stop. Woodblock printing had, of course, been known in the Muslim world for centuries. The Il-Khans still did not trust local administrators and relied on foreign or non-Muslim bureaucrats wherever possible. Nor, until Ghazan's reign, was much effort made to rebuild the shattered civil service that had served previous rulers.

There were, however, sound military reasons behind Ghazan's attempt to improve administration. The old Mongol methods of raising money could not support an army tied down in frontier defences or in military encampments across the empire. Tribute in milk and meat was no longer adequate and large amounts of money were now needed to buy supplies. Ghazan recognized this and his reforms concentrated on the tax-paying peasantry. Nevertheless Ghazan still had to justify such reforms to his own Mongol followers on the grounds that, rather than being soft on the Iranians, he was merely ensuring that they could continue supporting the conquerors.

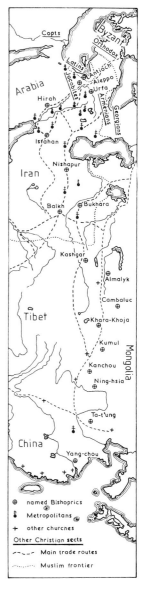

named Bishoprics
Metropolitans
other churches
Other Christian sects
Main trade routes
Muslim frontier

Tax gatherers and government messengers were always greatly feared. Many peasants fled from their farms to the towns while in the cities people would seal up their doors and windows, only entering their houses via the roof or through secret underground passages. This was not only to keep out tax inspectors but also the hordes of state messengers who could billet themselves on anyone at any time. The Khan, the princes, the princesses, courtiers, army officers down to the rank of leader of one hundred, even royal panther keepers and superintendents of the imperial kitchens were entitled to use the Mongol messenger services for matters great or small. Eventually these messengers became a veritable plague and government suffered because there were sometimes not enough horses in the postal way-stations when a really important message had to get through. Enterprising highwaymen began posing as messengers, stealing their official insignia and demanding the horses and provisions of passing merchants in the government's name. The Il-Khan's own gendarmerie, recruited to patrol the roads, preyed upon travellers, while certain bandits won the support of local people by robbing only rich travellers or government agents. Such bandits often had spies in the main trading towns who would inform them if a wealthy caravan was about to set out. Pliant merchants would then sell goods that the bandits had stolen. One wonders, in fact, whether many tales of Ali Baba and other heroes of the *Arabian Nights* were not accurate accounts of life in Il-Khan Iran.

Despite the carnage of the original Mongol conquest and the chaos that remained widespread under Il-Khan rule, Hülegü and his successors did try to revive the cities of Iran and Iraq. Even in 1255, during his first march across Khurasan, Hülegü allowed his secretary, the historian al Juvayni, to rebuild the shattered town of Khabushan (modern Quchan). Al Juvayni later became governor of Baghdad, southern Iraq and Khuzistan in south-western Iran. There he was credited with restoring a whole series of mosques and Islamic religious colleges. The Il-Khan period also saw the reappearance of massive buildings as expressions of political power. Monumental imperial cities had rarely been seen in Iran since pre-Islamic times as they ran counter to the democratic spirit of Islam. Nevertheless this new architecture of power survived the fall of the Il-Khans to remain characteristic of Iranian building until modern times.

Outside the cities, however, there was a steady increase in nomadism and a decline in settled agriculture despite the Khans' efforts to protect the peasantry. This reflected the fact that military power now rested entirely upon those tribes who continued to provide the bulk of Iranian soldiers until the twentieth century. Despite the introduction of *iqta'* fiefs, the pre-Mongol military structure in which a professional army was maintained by taxing a prosperous and well-administered agriculture never returned. Iranian agriculture had itself been dealt an almost fatal blow by the Mongol conquest and it never recovered, despite the efforts of men like al Juvayni. The situation in Iraq was just as bad. Irrigation and agricultural settlement in Abbasid Iraq had been particularly intense and Hülegü's invasion contributed to an acute decline, partly by killing off many inhabitants and partly by allowing river-fed irrigation to be neglected. Al Juvayni did re-establish a hundred and fifty villages and had a canal dug from Anbar to Najaf and Kufa at a cost of 10000 gold dinars. But stories about southern Iraq achieving a prosperity greater even than that under the Caliphs were poetic exaggerations.

Parts of Iraq did recover a little from the Mongol devastations, but northern and north-eastern Syria and neighbouring parts of Turkey had no such hope. They became once again a battlefield between two mighty and warlike states, the Il-Khans and the Mamluks. This had been the area's fate before the coming of Islam, when Romans, Byzantines and their various Persian foes struggled for domination of the Middle East. Indeed recent studies have shown that the area around the so-called Dead Cities of northern Syria was not abandoned after the Arab conquest, as was once thought. In fact both sides of the Euphrates had supported large agricultural populations until Ayyubid times, but now all this was lost. Even today north-eastern Syria forms a kind of frontier zone where only the toughest care to settle and reclaim the land.

In Anatolia there was a similar revival of nomadism, with the Turcomen tribes benefiting from Mongol imperial rule. This was also seen further south, in the Artuqid vassal region around Mardin. Hülegü's invasion of the Middle East, like that of Genghis Khan before him, remained a catastrophe. The only area to reap any benefit was Egypt which, under the oppressive but remarkably cultured Mamluks, survived as the last centre of old Arab-Islamic civilization.

The Il-Khan period was more productive in terms of science and art. This was partly due to closer links with China but also because some Il-Khan rulers, Hülegü included, were themselves interested in such matters. One of the first things that Hülegü did after the sack of Baghdad was authorize Nasir al Din Tusi to construct his famous observatory near Maragha.

Nasir al Din Tusi was not the only scientist at Hülegü's Court, but he was the best known and his extraordinary life reflected the chaos, violence and opportunities of his time. Born in the town of Tus around the year 1200, he soon found himself held against his will in the Isma'ili castle of Alamut. There, in the service of the Assassin Grand Master, he continued his mathematical and astronomical studies. When Alamut fell to the Mongols, Tusi entered the service of Hülegü and, by reassuring that superstitious conqueror that nothing supernatural would happen if he conquered Baghdad, earned a reputation as a reliable prophet.

The remains of the hilltop observatory built to his design can still be seen. As far as Hülegü was concerned this observatory was to help make

Carved bone plaques of the 13th–14th centuries. Most would have been used to decorate quivers or bowcases. They are among the finest pieces of Mongol art and come from the Volga region of the Golden Horde.

astrological predictions, but Nasir al Din Tusi and his colleagues were also able to use it for serious scientific research. This was, in fact, the world's first real astronomical observatory in terms of design, the instruments it contained and its staff. The complex was large, with several imposing buildings and a well stocked library. The instruments were designed by a mathematician and astronomer from Damascus named Mu'ayyid al Din al 'Urdi and they included a mural quadrant, a sphere of the heavens showing all known stars, devices to chart the movement of the sun and planets and a special quadrant that could simultaneously measure the angles of two stars from the horizon.

Tusi's own work covered minerology and precious stones, philosophy, religious ethics, theories of government finance, translations of the Greek scientific classics and medicine. Shortly before he died, Nasir al Din Tusi operated on a septic hunting wound for the Il-Khan Abaqa, a wound that none of the Khan's other physicians dared open. On another occasion he saved the life of the historian al Juvayni, who was under sentence of death, by playing upon Hülegü's superstitions. Though Tusi never broke away from the old earth-centred view of the universe, he did improve Ptolemy's explanation by inventing what became known as the Tusi Couple, which restored uniform planetary motion around the earth. The Tusi Couple dealt with the mathematical relationship between small and large circles when the smaller was rolling around inside the circumference of the larger. It was, in fact, the insoluble problems posed by an earth-centred view of the universe that led Tusi to his most original ideas, which were in the field of mathematics. He could even be credited with establishing trigonometry as an independent branch of pure mathematics while the work done at this Maragha observatory also did much to establish the separate identity of computational mathematics.

Among Nasir al Din Tusi's colleagues at Maragha was at least one Chinese astronomer named Fu Meng-chi. Chinese doctors are also recorded at the Court of Ghazan in Tabriz. Tusi himself died in 1274 and was buried in the famous Shi'a shrine at Kadimain, north of Baghdad. He had lived, according to the historian Rashid al Din, for seventy-seven years, seven months and seven days. Nasir al Din Tusi's son then took over the observatory where important work was carried on, among the most interesting developments being Qutb al Din Shirazi's first scientifically correct explanation of the rainbow. Such work was continued in Damascus, Samarqand and Istanbul well into the sixteenth century. By then, however, the torch of astronomical learning had passed to Europe, to men like the Dane Tycho Brahe whose instruments often showed a remarkable, but as yet unexplained, similarity to those previously used at Maragha, Samarqand and Istanbul.

The Il Khan Dynasty of Iran

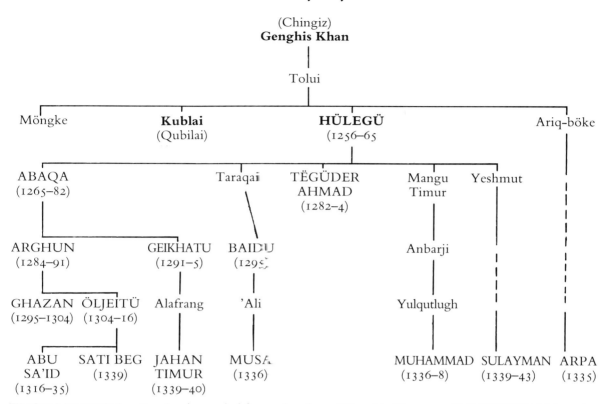

(Chingiz)
Genghis Khan

Tolui

| Möngke | **Kublai**
(Qubilai) | **HÜLEGÜ**
(1256–65 | | Ariq-böke |

ABAQA (1265–82)   Taraqai   TÉGÜDER AHMAD (1282–4)   Mangu Timur   Yeshmut

ARGHUN (1284–91)   GEIKHATU (1291–5)   BAIDU (1295)   Anbarji

GHAZAN (1295–1304)   ÖLJEITÜ (1304–16)   Alafrang   'Ali   Yulqutlugh

ABU SA'ID (1316–35)   SATI BEG (1339)   JAHAN TIMUR (1339–40)   MUSA (1336)   MUHAMMAD (1336–8)   SULAYMAN (1339–43)   ARPA (1335)

TUGHA TIMUR (1338–51) – descended from a brother of Genghis Khan – and NUSHIRWAN (1344) – of doubtful descent – were also set up as puppet Khans by rival military emirs.

Bibliography

Boyle, J.A. (ed.) *The Cambridge History of Iran*, Vol. 5, *The Saljuq and Mongol Periods* Cambridge, 1968.

Boyle, J.A. (trans.) *The History of the World Conqueror by 'Ala-ad-Din 'Ata-Malik Juvaini* Manchester, 1958.

Boyle, J.A. *The Mongol World Empire* 1206–1370 (London, 1977).

Cahen, C. 'The Mongols and the Near East' in *A History of the Crusades*, pp. 715–32 Vol. II, (ed. Setton, K.M.) Madison 1969, .

Grousset, R. (trans. Walford, N.) *The Empire of the Steppes: A History of Central Asia* New Brunswick, 1970.

McEwen, E. 'Persian Archery Texts: Chapter Eleven of Fakhr-i Mudabbir's Adab al Harb (Early Thirteenth Century)' *The Islamic Quarterly* XVIII/3–4, pp.76–99, 1974.

Morgan, D.O. *The Mongols* London, 1986.

Morgan, D.O. 'The Mongol Armies in Persia' *Der Islam* LVI/1, pp.81–96, 1979.

Morgan, D.O. 'The Mongols in Syria, 1260–1300' in *Crusade and Settlement* (ed. Edbury, P.W.) Cardiff, pp. 231–5, 1985.

Richard, J. 'The Mongols and the Franks' *Journal of Asian History* III, 1969, pp. 45–57; reprinted in Richard, J. *Orient et Occident au moyen age: contacts et relations (XIIe–XVe s.)* London, 1976.

Saunders, J.J. *Muslims and Mongols: Essays on Medieval Asia* Christchurch, NZ, 1977.

Shreve Simpson, M. *The Illustration of an Epic: The Earliest 'Shahnama' Manuscripts* New York, 1979.

Smith, J.M. 'Ayn Jalut: Mamluk Success or Mongol Failure?' *Harvard Journal of Asiatic Studies* XLIV/2, pp. 307–45, 1984.

Smith, J.M. 'Mongol manpower and Persian population' *Journal of the Economic and Social History of the Orient* XVIII/3, pp. 271–99, 1975.

Spuler, B. *Die Mongolen in Iran* Berlin, 1968.

Spuler, B. *History of the Mongols* London, 1972.

Thorau, P. 'The Battle of Ayn Jalut: A Re-examination' in *Crusade and Settlement.* (ed. Edbury, P.W.) Cardiff, pp. 236–41, 1985.

TAMERLANE
THE SCOURGE OF GOD

Said to represent Tamerlane, Timur-i-Lenk himself, this miniature may have been made around 1380 and certainly shows a prince wearing cloth-covered lamellar armour, rigid vambraces below his elbows, perhaps greaves over his shins and a fluted helmet with multiple plumes (ex. F.R. Martin Coll.).

Portrait head of Timur made by the Soviet scholar M.M. Gerasimov. This sculpture is very accurate as it is based upon the skull found in Timur's grave. By closely studying such skulls and then working out the exact position of muscles, eyes, skin, hair and so on, Gerasimov pioneered the reconstruction of the portrait heads of long dead people.

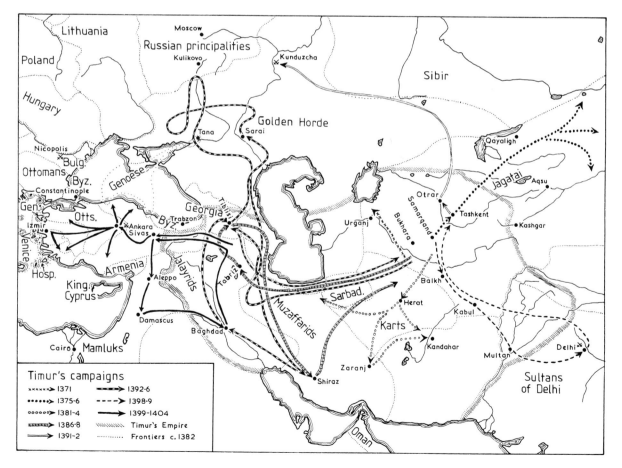

For Tamburlaine, the Scourge of God, must die.
Tamburlaine the Great 2.IV.iii.249
(Marlowe)

Legend of Cruelty

Timur-i Lenk, better known in Europe as Tamerlane, supposedly a descendent of Genghis Khan, was in the direct line of the great Mongol conquerors. He overran large areas of Russia, Iran, India and central Asia and was prevented only by his death from undertaking the conquest of China. His campaigns, though, were marked by savage massacres and by cruelties that exceeded in number and in viciousness those committed by his predecessors. As a result, although he was in some ways a man of considerable culture, his name has gone down in history and legend as a synonym for cruelty.

Not entirely because of his atrocities, he became a legend in his own lifetime. His deeds caught and held the imagination of Islamic and other Middle Eastern chroniclers. The *Zafarnama*, a sycophantic account of Timur's military exploits by Sharif al Din 'Ali Yazdi, was probably written before he died. The savagely vindictive *Aja'ibi'l Maqdur*, by Ahmad ibn Arabshah, was penned after its author fled to Ottoman territory, where he served as a secretary to Sultan Muhammad I. Many later Muslim writers recorded Tamerlane's deeds, favourably or otherwise, and his story was well known in Europe, too, by the early sixteenth century. At this time Europe was threatened by the advancing Ottoman Turks and so the exploits of a hero who had not only defeated them in battle but had captured their Sultan was bound to receive a sympathetic hearing. Yet Europeans also knew about Tamerlane's many massacres and his blood-curdling reputation, all of which were woven into Christopher Marlowe's play, *Tamburlaine the Great*, written and performed before 1587. Marlowe puts the following condemnation of Timur's cruelty into the mouth of the 'Soldan of Egypt':

Merciless villain, peasant, ignorant
Of lawful arms or martial discipline!
Pillage and murder are his usual trades:
The slave usurps the glorious name of war.

(1.IV.i)

Elsewhere, Tamburlaine glories in the brutal reality of Persian politics:

> *For he shall wear the crown of Persia*
> *Whose head hath deepest scars, whose breast most wounds,*
> *Which, being wroth, sends lightning from his eyes,*
> *And in the furrows of his frowning brows*
> *Harbours revenge, war, death and cruelty;*
> *For in a field whose superficies*
> *Is covered with a liquid purple veil*
> *And sprinkled with the brains of slaughtered men,*
> *My royal chair of state shall be advanced;*
> *And he that means to place himself therein*
> *Must armed wade up to the chin in blood.*
>
> (2 I.iii)

Marlowe was not the only European dramatist to write a play about Timur. Another Englishman, Nicholas Rowe, whose play was first performed at Drury Lane theatre in 1702, turned him into a philosophic, thoughtful prince but the early-seventeenth-century Spanish writer Luis Velez de Guevera and the late-seventeenth-century French playwright Nicolas Pradon had portrayed him, more truthfully, as a ruthless conqueror.

The reality, of course, was rather more complex.

Timur the Man

We have a much better idea about Timur's personal appearance than we do of most other leading medieval figures. Detailed descriptions survive from the pens of both friendly and unfavourable biographers, and the Spaniard Clavijo also described him. Then there is the work done by Soviet archaeologist M. Gerasimov, who reconstructed the conqueror's features from the skeleton, including remains of a chestnut moustache, found in Timur's tomb. Though lame, Timur was tall for a Turco–Mongol and was powerfully built. In old age his eyesight failed and he also had to be carried, though he could ride almost until the end.

Modern psychologists have also have a field day with Timur-i Lenk. Though by both medieval Islamic and modern standards Timur was a monster of cruelty, he was undoubtedly very intelligent. Illiterate, though by no means ignorant, he spoke three languages, loved listening to history but not poetry, admired artists and craftsmen and had a passion for sumptuously decorated tents. He was also one of the best chess players of his day. He played not only the standard game similar to that played today, but other versions that have fallen out of fashion, including the 'greater game', played on a board ten squares by eleven and with additional pieces, such as two camels, two giraffes, two sentries, two siege engines, and a prime minister. Other forms of chess enjoyed by Timur-i Lenk were those on a round board and on a long board.

146

Timur's appetite for food, drink and women was enormous, though in this he remained fully within pre-Islamic Turkish and Mongol tradition. He had four wives, as permitted by Islam, but many more concubines. Timur's wives, as often seen in Turkish rather than Arab or Iranian Islam, enjoyed high status, relative social freedom and considerable political influence.

Despite the superficial sophistication of Timur's court he himself remained a nomad at heart, despising the *Tajiks* or Iranianized peasants and their feudal leaders. His personality was a mixture of strange contradictions. He was responsible for the slaughter of perhaps hundreds of thousands of innocent men, women and children, but he scrupulously respected religious buildings and delighted in theological debate. Though he assumed an air of considerable piety, Timur-i Lenk seems basically to have cared only for the good opinion of his soldiers, who in turn adored him. He showed great personal courage in battle, often sharing the dangers of front-line combat. Whereas Genghis Khan and his sons also indulged in massacres, these were usually carried out dispassionately and with a coldly calculated purpose – to terrorize their foes into submission. Timur's massacres were more frequent, more obviously sadistic and often served no apparent purpose. Yet Clavijo could still report that Timur was admired for his justice!

While a mortal enemy like Ahmad Arabshah could describe Timur as a mad dog, he also admitted that he:

> did not love jest or falsehood. Nor did wit or sport please him while truth, though troublesome to him, did please him. He was not downcast by adversity nor joyful in prosperity. . . . He was spirited and brave, inspiring awe and obedience.

The sycophantic author of the *Zafarnama* (Book of Victory), Sharif al

Two sections from a large manuscript picture of a typical Mongol hunting expedition. This Timurid illustration was made around 1460 and shows a line of horsemen making a ring around the trapped animals, a trumpeter signalling the killing to begin, a selected few horse-archers shooting at the prey and a man on foot taking away a slain animal (ex-Imperial Lib., Leningrad).

Din 'Ali Yazdi, enthused about Timur's 'generous personality which manifested the boundless grace of God.' A European historian, Gibbon, could declare, somewhat primly, that 'perhaps we shall conclude that the Mogul Emperor was rather the scourge than the benefactor of mankind.' A more recent historian, the Frenchman René Grousset, concluded that Timur was dominated by 'long-term machiavellianism, sustained by hypocrisy identified with reasons of state'. Though a brilliant general and a strategist who knew when to retreat as well as when to advance, Timur was also much less of a statesman than Genghis Khan, despite the fact that he grew up in a highly civilized Islamic environment whereas his greater predecessor spent his formative years among primitive Mongol tribes.

Timur's Inheritance

Asia at the time of Timur's birth in 1336 had changed considerably since the days of Genghis Khan, yet the relationship between the nomadic peoples of the steppes and their settled neighbours had not. They still lived in a symbiotic relationship, each relying to some degree on the other, and would continue to do so for several more centuries. Only the emergence of modern technologically based empires would alter that. In the meantime the cultures of central Asia continued to reflect those of the more civilized lands to the south. Nomadic peoples remained fully aware of what was happening among their richer neighbours and the 'barbarian terrors' that periodically erupted out of central Asia were, as always, largely in response to events within the urbanized, agricultural regions.

The quillons of a sabre, carved from a single piece of jade, probably from Samarqand, 15th century. Timur's troops took care to carry as much jade as they could home from their campaigns into what is now Chinese Central Asia (Met. Museum, inv. 1902.01.18.765, New York).

The reasons that caused nomad empires to crumble so fast also remained the same. Almost everywhere the nomads' need for vast horse-herds, which could only be raised on steppe grasslands, clashed with their need for iron, which was largely obtained from the forested mountains. Added to the basic contradiction between the needs of nomads and farmers was the imperial need to foster trade. This meant protecting merchants and setting up garrisoned strongpoints. The preservation of nomad military skills demanded that the tribesmen be dispersed across vast areas, not concentrated in forts or cities. All these factors rapidly weakened the empires set up by nomad rulers and Timur-i-Lenk is typical. Timur's empire was, however, unusual because it was rooted not in the steppes themselves but in the borderland between the steppes and settled worlds, in Transoxania, which lies between the ancient civilized land of Iran and the wide plains of what is now Soviet central Asia.

The Il-Khan state established by Hülegü in Iran had fallen apart in the mid-fourteenth century and the other great Islamic empires further

148

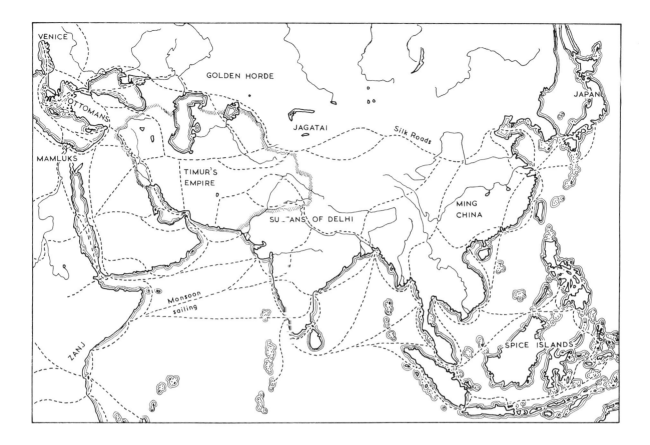

south were also in a state of confusion. Muslim northern India was fragmented and even the powerful Mamluk empire of Egypt and Syria was going through a period of instability. Paradoxically, perhaps, Transoxania was flourishing. It still formed part of the sprawling Jagatai Khanate, the Mongol successor-state that occupied the centre of what had been Genghis Khan's world empire. Transoxania was, however, the only part of the Jagatai state where a Mongol élite had become largely urbanized. Under Kebek, fourteenth ruler of the Jagatai dynasty, Samarqand and Bukhara had revived. Trade prospered with the unification of the *kebeki* coinage, the ancestor of the modern Russian *kopek*. Meanwhile other Mongol tribes had returned to their traditional way of life after the break-up of the Mongol Empire and on some parts of the Eurasian steppe, particularly in what is now the Ukraine, a strange mixture of nomadic pastoralism and semi-settled agriculture had developed. Those Mongols and nomad Turks who had been converted to Islam continued to use the old legal code of Genghis Khan and their Muslim faith was often only skin-deep. The chaos and civil wars that tore the Jagatai Khanate apart in the mid-fourteenth century also caused the almost

The routes trade of Asia in th 14th–15th centuries covered huge distances by both land and sea long before European explorers rounded Africa on their way to India. Timur's Empire, though not as big as that carved out by Genghis Khan, was strategically placed across the land routes from China to Europe and also those by sea from India through the Persian Gulf. Such a location ensured great wealth from tolls and taxes.

149

complete destruction of the Nestorian Christian communities that had earlier been so important.

At the same time Muslim Transoxania, with its great cities and fertile river valleys, was increasingly separate from the other half of the Jagatai state where, to the north-east in an area known as Mughulistan (Mongol territory), people remained both nomadic and largely pagan. The citizens of Samarqand and Bukhara referred to their neighbours in Mughulistan simply as *jete* or 'robbers' and such mistrust would help Timur's rise to power in wealthy Transoxania. Power in the Jagatai state now lay in the hands of a largely Turkish military élite while the Mongol ruling family were little more than figureheads. In 1360 the Jagatai attempted to reassert control but they could not prevent Transoxania, though rich, from declining into anarchy as various clans seized this or that town, oasis or valley. In the great trading cities another force, that of the *sarbadars*, struggled to maintain security and keep marauding tribesmen at bay. These *sarbadars* formed a militia of craftsmen, merchants and teachers who saw themselves as Muslim fighters defending Islam from Mongol oppression.

Similar chaos could be seen in Iran, which had also broken up into a series of small states. Unlike Transoxania, however, the economy of Iran had not revived and the damage wrought by Genghis Khan and Hülegü remained largely unrepaired. Further to the west two Turcoman tribal states, those of the Aq Qoyunlu (White Sheep) and Qara Qoyunlu (Black Sheep), ruled eastern Anatolia and Armenia, competing with each other and with the rising power of the Ottoman Turks. Meanwhile Kurds and Armenians competed for land in this same area in a bitter struggle that would continue into the twentieth century. Even the Armenians and Georgians, both of whom were Christians, mistrusted each other. While the still independent Georgians were even expanding from their lush Caucasus valleys before Timur arrived on the scene, the Armenians were no longer masters of their ancestral homeland. Ever increasing numbers now migrated to other countries, particularly north of the Black Sea.

The whole area, along with Europe and China, had also recently witnessed a terror worse even than the Mongols – the Black Death and the recurrent plagues that followed. Europe, Asia and Africa had entered what some historians have called The Golden Age of Bacteria. Almost entire populations had been slaughtered, though the effects did vary from one area to another. The total loss of human life is, of course, impossible to calculate but modern research in those areas where records survive, as well as archaeological study of settlement patterns, show that, in some regions, up to a third of the inhabitants died – which is roughly what medieval chroniclers themselves believed. The western Mongol Khanate of the Golden Horde appears to have been particularly badly hit, at least as far as its military potential was concerned. Perhaps

this was because, in such a nomadic society, the loss of a third of all males meant the loss of a third of the army. In settled areas of the Middle East, where armies were often smaller professional forces, the ranks could be filled with slaves or volunteers eager for the privileges that went with a military career. This would all have its effect on Timur's forthcoming career of conquest.

Muslim reaction to the catastrophic Black Death also appears to have been very different from what was seen in Europe. Whereas Christian Europeans tended to see the Black Death as divine punishment for their sins and thus turned to religious hysteria, the Flagellant movement and the persecution of Jewish minorities, the typical Middle Eastern reaction was a turning inwards, back to the security of family and tribe. Instead of mass hysteria there seems to have been an increasing use of birth control which was sanctioned by Islam but not by the Christian church. As life got harder, children were seen as an added burden. The medieval Arab attitude towards love and sex was already summed up in the saying: 'Love is kissing and the touching of hands – Going beyond that is asking for a child.' As a result the population of the Middle East never fully recovered from the effect of the plagues. A vicious spiral was created, linking drastic population reduction to economic decline and contracting agriculture. This, then, was the world into which Timur-i-Lenk was born in the late fourteenth century.

A battle between Turks and Iranians shown in a Shahnamah *manuscript made around 1370, probably in Tabriz. The victorious Iranians on the left wear full lamellar armour and have mail aventails hung from their helmets. The fleeing Turks have scale-lined coats-of-plates to protect their chests and backs (Topkapi Lib., Ms. Haz. 2153, f. 102a, Istanbul).*

The Young Timur

Timur was born on 11th April 1336 in Kish (modern Shahr-i Sabz) a small town on the edge of the mountains just south of Samarqand. Snow-fed streams made the valleys fertile and the forested lower slopes were rich in game. The bleak Pamirs rose to the east, while to the west lay the semi–desert steppes. Timur's family, the Barlas clan, dominated the area. As Turks or Turcified Mongols they were members of the Jagatai Khanate's military élite and, although their fame was only local, they were not as obscure or barbaric as some later writers would suggest. Timur's name, meaning 'iron', was a common one. Legends would eventually be attached to his birth, saying that he came into the world clutching a clot of blood and that burning coals leapt from the fire as he was born. In fact Timur's early life appears to have been unremarkable. His uncle, Hajji Barlas, shared leadership of the clan with Timur's father and was among those who tried to drive out the Jagatai in 1358. Two years later Hajji Barlas was himself forced into exile, an event which may have given the young Timur a lesson in political and military realities.

As a youth Timur learned all the skills of traditional Turco–Mongol life – horsemanship, hunting, archery and survival in a harsh climate. Yet he never learned to read or write, despite being brought up in an area that had been Muslim for six centuries. The records are silent about these early years, though largely apocryphal stories suggest that he gathered a small band of followers and operated as a bandit. In 1360 Timur was recognized as lord of Kish by the Jagatai after they drove out his uncle, but Timur's loyalties were now to himself alone. He attacked his uncle when the latter tried to make a comeback and a year later attached himself to the Jagatai viceroy of Transoxania. When Hajji Barlas was assassinated in neighbouring Khurasan Timur tracked down and punished the murderers, though in reality they had freed him from a dangerous rival. Soon the ambitious young Turk abandoned the Jagatai in favour of Mir Hussain, the rebel ruler of Balkh, and together they fought to drive the Jagatai from Transoxania.

Often defeated, but never abandoning the struggle, Timur is said once to have been reduced to a single loyal follower. The story goes that, having had his horse shot from under him, Timur took that of his wife and left her to hide near a waterhole. On another occasion Timur and his tiny band were pursued to the banks of the flooded Amu Darya river. Ordering his men to hold their horse bridles, Timur told them to cross at once. 'Anyone who does not meet at the agreed place on the other side will know that he has had it!' he cried as he leapt into the flood. A further tale tells how Timur and his band raided the strongly fortified town of Nakhshab by scrambling through a water channel beneath the walls. They captured the governor, grabbed the contents of his armoury and treasury but then found that the alarm had been raised. Trapped within

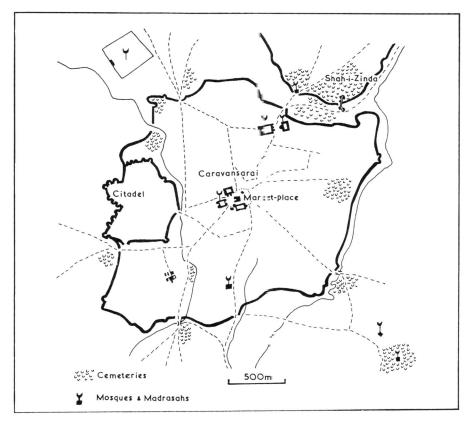

Cemeteries

Mosques & Madrasahs

500m

Citadel

Caravansarai

Market-place

Shah-i-Zinda

the city, Timur's men were in despair, but he told them to stick together and charge straight for the main gate. Against all odds they not only broke out but took their booty into the mountains, seized a small castle and held it as their lair despite all that the Jagatai could do.

It was around this time that Timur got the wound that earned him the name of Timur-i Lenk, 'Timur the Lame'. In fact Timur sustained two serious arrow wounds in his right arm and right leg. He lost the use of his elbow and his hip seized up, leaving his right leg not only rigid but shorter than the left. This suggests that he had been struck by the very broad-bladed arrows found in many Mongol and Turkish graves. The wounds were confirmed when Soviet archaeologists opened Timur's tomb in 1941 and found, too, that he had another wound in his right hand. Many years later Timur met the man who had shot him, a tribal chief from Sistan, and ordered him to be riddled with arrows. Unlike Genghis Khan, Timur-i Lenk felt little respect for a man who had bested him in combat. Indeed biographers such as Ibn Arabshah state that these crippling wounds turned Timur into a vengeful monster. Whatever the truth about Timur's psychological condition he remained a brilliant war leader who continued to increase his following of adventurers. Timur's generosity to his men was also renowned, though perhaps calculated.

153

Liberation of Transoxania

In 1364, Timur and Mir Hussain finally drove the Jagatai Mongols out of Transoxania. Politically astute and utterly ruthless, Timur now attracted ever more supporters among those who looked for firm leadership at a time of confusion and bloodshed. While other leaders built their power either on the nomadic tribes or the almost feudal rural aristocracy, Timur managed to win the support of both. He also won the backing of urban merchants by keeping the trade routes relatively safe. Timur's very public piety, whether or not it was rooted in genuine religious conviction, even earned him the support of the Muslim religious leadership. Whatever his contemporaries said about Timur's morality, none ever questioned his cunning!

The Jagatai Khans were, however, not willing to let Transoxania fall without a fight and in 1365 they defeated Timur and Mir Hussain in the Battle of the Mire. Here the two allies were virtually washed away in a torrential downpour that turned the battlefield into a sea of mud – a catastrophe that cost Timur and Mir Hussain thousands of troops. Interestingly enough their defeat was attributed to the Jagatai's use of shamanistic rain stones, those magical totems that were believed to give control over the elements. Despite the fact that Timur and his successors considered themselves pious Muslims, a Timurid army was still using rain stones as late as 1451.

Timur and Mir Hussain had suffered a major setback, but the *sarbadar* militia of Samarqand defeated the Jagatai attempt to re-establish control over Transoxania. Yet by successfully driving off the Jagatai the *sarbadars* also threatened the traditional dominance of the Turkish military and feudal élite – including Mir Hussain and Timur, who turned upon the *sarbadar* leaders and had them executed for 'insolence'. Timur, however, interceded on behalf of one popular *sarbadar* and so managed to present himself as a champion of the people in contrast to the oppressive Mir Hussain.

One thing, however, Timur lacked and that was political respectability. Central Asia still lay under the shadow of Genghis Khan's memory. His world empire had long passed but as yet no one could claim the right to rule unless he was either a member of the Golden Family of the Great Khan's descendants or was in some way linked to this Chingisid clan. Timur solved the problem in three ways. He and Mir Hussain found a minor member of the Golden Family named Kabil-shah and set him up as titular ruler of all the territory they now held. In public the two Turks offered Kabil-shah all the respect due to a Chingisid ruler, but in reality they allowed him nothing more. Even after Timur conquered a huge empire he continued to claim that he was merely a sultan and that everything he did was on behalf of the legitimate but powerless khan. Timur further maintained that he was trying to reconstruct Genghis Khan's true empire, along with the claim to be his great-great-grandson.

After liberating Transoxania from the Jagatai, the real heirs of Genghis Khan, Timur and Mir Hussain quarrelled. Their puppet khan sided with Mir Hussain but such was Timur's need for a Chingisid figurehead that he forgave the man and continued to give him meaningless honours. First, however, Timur had to defeat his rival and for a while things did not go his way. Forced out of Transoxania, he was deserted by most of his followers and for several years was reduced to fighting a guerrilla campaign full of the most extraordinary adventures, treachery and reversals of fortune. Yet these minor battles, raids and sieges showed Timur to be an extraordinary military leader as well as a strategic and tactical genius.

In 1370, after a long fight, Timur suddenly appeared before the gates of Mir Hussain's capital of Balkh. The city was taken and Timur publicly made peace with his rival but had him murdered shortly after. In an awful forewarning of future conquests Timur also put a large part of the population of Balkh to the sword. Among Mir Hussain's wives Timur found a princess of the Chingisid line Saray Mulk Khanum. By promptly marrying her Timur found another way of giving himself political legitimacy, for he now became a son-in-law of the last Jagatai Khan of Transoxania. Surprisingly, perhaps, Timur and his new bride got on well. Saray Mulk became chief wife and, though she bore him no surviving children, she did act as one of the conqueror's closest advisers. Later, in an effort to confirm his still dubious right to rule, Timur invented a clearly mythical genealogy that claimed that both he and the honoured Genghis Khan were descended from Alan-goa, a maiden who had been ravished by a moonbeam in ancient central Asian legend.

Apart from cultivating the support of orthodox Muslim religious leaders, Timur had a close relationship with Nur Sayyid Baraka, a mystic and sage whom he found at Balkh. This pious old man, a native of Mecca in Arabia, gave Timur a large flag and a huge drum, symbols of royalty in the Muslim east, and forecast his future of conquest and glory. Sayyid Baraka remained Timur's spiritual guide and they were eventually buried together in Timur-i Lenk's great mausoleum at Samarkand.

Timur's greatness lay in the future, of course. For the present he had to confirm his control over Transoxania. Timur already had the support of nomad tribes, the feudal aristocracy and the religious establishment, while the *sarbadars* had been crushed. A great *quriltai*, or gathering of local leaders, was organized, at which Timur was recognized as successor to the Jagatai Khans of Transoxania. The country was, of course, still under the titular rule of the puppet khan, Kabil-shah, but, as Timur's hostile biographer Ibn Arabshah so eloquently put it, 'the khan was in his bondage like a centipede in mud.' Meanwhile Timur adopted the title of *Sahib Qiran*, 'Lord of the Favourable Planetary Conjunction'.

Some of the most beautiful and detailed manuscripts in Islamic art were made even as Timur's troops ravaged the Middle East. This book of poems, the Khawaju Kirmani, was painted in Baghdad in 1396. Here two warriors recognize each other after a combat. The man on the right probably has standard lamellar armour but the victor appears to wear a new form of mail-and-plate armour which may even have been invented in Iraq in the late 14th century (British Lib., Ms. Add. 18113, London).

155

Early Conquests

Timur now turned upon Khwarazm, a fertile zone watered by the lower reaches of the Amu Darya and lying on the southern shore of the Aral Sea. The first attack came in 1371 but although Timur annexed the area to Transoxania, Khwarazmian resistance was not crushed for another eight years. Timur's efforts in 1375–7 to drive the Jagatai Khans out of their remaining territory north-west of the Tien Shan mountains were more dramatic and more successful. These campaigns were also interesting from a purely military point of view, for here Timur was fighting an elusive nomadic foe in exceptionally difficult terrain. The confrontation in what had been known as Semirecye, between Lake Balkhash and the vast Tien Shan mountains, was a reversal of those wars fought in the same area by Genghis Khan. Now the Muslims of Transoxania were on the offensive, the Mongols in retreat. This time, however, both sides employed essentially the same Mongol tactics that Genghis had used a century and a half earlier.

But, instead of recreating Genghis Khan's empire, Timur merely smashed Mongol power in eastern Turkestan, just as the Ming Chinese nationalist revival had overthrown Kublai Khan's successors in China itself. The struggle did not, however, end there – as late as 1390 Timur's troops were still campaigning deep in the Altai Mountains of Mongolia, where they amused themselves by burning Timur's name into the tree trunks. Unlike Genghis Khan, Timur also built a chain of forts along his new eastern frontier, for he had no wish to conquer the wilds of east-central Asia. His interests lay south and west, within the rich but weak and divided world of Islam.

Timur-i Lenk's territory now stretched from Lake Balkhash to the frontiers of Iran and Afghanistan. From this base he set out, at the age of forty, on a career of conquest that would astonish and terrify half the known world. Even so Timur could not ignore the steppes, for another threat soon faced him from the north-west. This was Toqtamish, Khan of the Golden Horde. The Golden Horde, like the Il-Khanate in Iran, was one of the successors to Genghis Khan's world empire. It had endured longer but, by the mid-fourteenth century, was split into the Golden and White Hordes and was fast slipping into anarchy. In 1378 Timur had helped Toqtamish, a rebel member of the ruling family, to seize control of the White Horde. Timur seems to have been flattered that a member of Genghis Khan's Golden Family should have sought his support, but two years later Toqtamish also took over the Golden Horde, thus reuniting one of the most powerful Mongol states. He went on to re-establish Mongol suzerainty over the restive Russian vassal principalities. Timur, it seemed, had unwittingly created a rival on his northern frontier. Meanwhile, however, he himself started reuniting what had been Mongol imperial territory within the Muslim world.

He began in 1381 by attacking Ghiyath al Din of the Kart dynasty, whose capital was at Herat in what is now Afghanistan. The Karts had themselves recently annexed Nishapur, but Ghiyath al Din's army surrendered to Timur almost without a fight. Tough mountain men from the province of Ghur formed Herat's garrison, but the population insisted on opening their gates and Ghiyath was banished. A year later Herat rose in revolt, but this was savagely crushed. The walls were razed and a large part of the population massacred, their heads being piled into towers. This was the first example of the 'minarets', as the chroniclers ironically described them, that were to mark Timur-i Lenk's blood-stained passage across the Middle East.

At around this time Timur met another of those half-crazed holy men who were becoming a feature of a devastated, plague-ridden and de-moralized Muslim world. This strange individual, Baba Sangu, apparently threw some chunks of raw meat at Timur, who interpreted the gesture as a prophesy of victory. In 1382 Timur suffered a personal tragedy with the deaths of Dilshad-agha, one of his favourite wives, and of Qutluq Turkhan-agha, his beloved elder sister. Whether these losses contributed to his growing savagery is unknown. Certainly Timur's tactics in the irrigated province of Sistan showed him to be nothing less than a monster. This region was invaded in 1383, after Timur had devastated Sabzawar, one of the chief centres of the warlike Ghurs. Here, in an additional refinement of cruelty, two thousand people are said to have been laid in wet plaster and built into a briefly living tower. Sistan

A battle-scene from one of the so-called Red Ground Shahnamahs made in southern Iran around 1300. Though their style is primitive, these manuscripts include many details of mid-14th century Iranian or Mongol arms and armour. Here every soldier wears lamellar defences, some shown made of large pieces suggesting hardened leather construction, others with narrower pieces indicating iron or bronze. Such armour appears to have been worn throughout most of the eastern Islamic world (Topkapi Saray Lib., Ms. Haz. 1479, Istanbul).

suffered the now usual massacre, while its elaborate irrigation dams, canals and regulators were methodically demolished. The area returned to the desert from which centuries of labour by hard-working Muslim peasants and enlightened rulers had raised it. The devastation begun by Genghis Khan was complete and Sistan remains a desert to this day; a land still dotted with the crumbling and totally abandoned ruins of once-flourishing towns. Timur went on to rampage across western Afghanistan, seizing Kandahar and devastating Mazandaran, leaving yet more massacres in his wake.

Timur's army was a permanent force in an almost constant state of mobilization and in 1355–6 it was the turn of western Iran, Iraq and Georgia to feel its fury. Tabriz, capital of the Jalayrid dynasty, fell and the Jalayrid ruler, Ahmad ibn Uwais, retreated to Baghdad. Early the following year Timur sent his troops to raid mountainous Luristan on the border between Iran and Iraq. Here, instead of building towers of skulls, people were slaughtered simply by being pushed over cliffs. In the summer of 1386 Timur's army turned against the Christian kingdom of Georgia. Their attack was irresistible, Timur himself taking part in the final assault on the Georgian capital of Tbilisi. The Georgian king, Bagrat, was captured, dragged off in chains and persuaded to convert to Islam. On being released he gave Timur a mail hauberk said to have been made by the biblical King David himself and returned to Georgia to repair the damage.

Timur's army rested on the grassy steppes of Azerbayjan, where Timur is said to have met the Shi'ite spiritual leader of the Safavi sect and to have tried to poison him. The attempt failed because the Safavi leader sweated out the poison while taking part in a trance-like religious dance of a kind still performed by Muslim mystics in many parts of the Middle East. This story was, however, probably a legend spread by the Safavi dynasty, which took over Iran after the collapse of Timurid power a century later.

More real was Timur's attack on the Qara Qoyunlu, who then ruled eastern Anatolia. The Qara Qoyunlu, who were warlike and still nomadic Turcomans, beat off the first raids until Timur himself seized their capital of Van in the summer of 1387. Huge numbers of Armenian inhabitants were again bound and thrown from the surrounding cliffs but here, as an Armenian chronicler tells us, a few survived because their fall was broken by the piled corpses of those who went before. Such massacres were repeated across southern Iran in 1387 where, at Shiraz, Timur came close to killing Hafiz, one of the greatest Persian poets. The bloodthirsty conqueror had apparently taken exception to a verse which said:

> *If that unkindly maid of Shiraz would give me love,*
> *I'd give Bukhara for the mole upon her cheek, or Samarqand.*

Hafiz was dragged before Timur, who raged:

With blows of my bright sword I have conquered most of the world and devastated thousands of towns and countries to beautify my cities of Samarqand and Bukhara. And you, miserable wretch, would sell them both for the mole on a Turkish girl's cheek!

Hafiz bowed low and replied:

Alas, Sire, it is because of such extravagance that I have fallen on evil days.

Fortunately Timur showed an unexpected sense of humour and, instead of killing the poet, showered him with gifts.

Though it was painted at around the same time as the so-called Red-Ground Shah-namas, the Demotte Shahnamah is a far finer work of art. Made for the Il-Khan court at Tabriz it shows the costume, arms, armour and horse harness used in Iran shortly before Timur's conquests (Mus. of Fine Art, inv. 30.105, Boston).

Toqtamish and the Golden Horde

Rivalry between Timur and Toqtamish of the Golden Horde now led to the inevitable clash. Fighting broke out in 1387 and false rumours of a defeat led to risings against Timur in various areas. After dealing with these rebels with his usual savagery, Timur decided to crush Toqtamish once and for all. First, however, another great *quriltai* was held in which Timur justified his proposed attack on a true descendant of the revered

159

Genghis Khan. It also gave Timur a chance to reorganize and restore the efficiency of his army, which had perhaps grown lax following years of victory. Timur knew that the campaign lying ahead would be the greatest challenge his troops had yet faced.

On 19th January 1391, when the steppes were still in the grip of winter, Timur and an army of perhaps two hundred thousand men set off from Tashkent. As fast as he advanced northward, Toqtamish retreated before him, drawing the invaders ever deeper into the steppes. These were classic Mongol tactics, but Toqtamish and the Golden Horde now faced an army that was itself within the Mongol-steppe tradition of warfare. Moreover it was an army led by the greatest general of his age and one that was armed, equipped and logistically supported by the technological expertise of the Muslim world. Even so, Timur's men grew weary and desperately hungry as they crossed the appropriately named Starving Steppe.

In April Timur reached the Ulugh-Dag mountains, halfway across modern Soviet Kazakhstan. There he had an inscribed pillar erected, a monument that was rediscovered in the 1930s and can now be seen in Leningrad's Hermitage Museum. Still Toqtamish fell back, and to maintain morale Timur ordered a great hunt, which brought in much needed meat, a feast and a full-scale military review. Eventually the army reached the forests of Siberia, a cold land of mists and swamps. Broad rivers were forded using brushwood and tree trunks. Though the enemy's tracks had been found there was no sign of his army, so Timur's men could not relax their guard. Discipline was extremely strict and careful precautions were taken against ambushes, which might be expected as part of the strategy Toqtamish was using. The invaders had now come so far north that there was no real night during the summer months, so the men were excused normal midnight prayers by their *imams*.

If Toqtamish had continued to retreat he might finally have worn down Timur's almost exhausted army. However, he did not. Perhaps there was nowhere else for Toqtamish to go. Perhaps his men were themselves tired of retreating, or perhaps he thought that Timur was ripe for destruction. Whatever the reason, Toqtamish made a stand near Kunduzcha, close to where the Kama river meets the mighty Volga less than a thousand kilometres east of Moscow. The battle that followed resulted in total victory for Timur, but rather than trying to rule the Golden Horde directly Timur divided this vast region between various princes of the Chingisid Golden Family. He thus hoped to foster civil war and ensure that the Golden Horde never again rivalled his own power, but in this he failed. Toqtamish had survived the battle of Kunduzcha and, within a short while, reasserted his authority to such an extent that he was able to defeat rebellious Russian princes and reimpose his suzerainty.

As a child, Tamerlane (Timur) is said to have organized his friends into armies. The same stories are told of many conquerors, including Napoleon.

The Five-year War

Unlike Genghis Khan, Timur-i Lenk often had to reconquer territory from rebels who rose against his rule as soon as his army was occupied elsewhere. From 1392 for five years, on and off, Timur was thus engaged in Iran, though this extraordinary campaign also took him back to Anatolia and once more into battle against the Golden Horde. The first victims of the Five Year War were the people of the mountainous and sub-tropical province of Mazandaran along the southern coast of the Caspian Sea. After seizing Astarbad, Timur's army not only had to hack its way through dense forests and across swamps but to fight a novel form of naval warfare. Boats, towed along the Uzboy channel, which then linked the Amu Darya river to the Caspian Sea, were filled with pitch and sent against the harbours and sea walls of the coastal towns. Shi'ite Muslims who had long inhabited this region were persecuted, particularly those of the communistic Hurufi sect, whose founder, Fadl of Astarbad, was put to death in Timur's reign. The remaining Isma'ili Assassins of the area were also hunted down.

Next it was the turn of southern Iran, whose ruling Muzaffarid dynasty had been unwise enough to throw off their enforced allegiance to Timur. The lord of Shiraz, Shah Mansur, faced Timur's host with only three thousand men, two-thirds of whom fled before the battle began. Nevertheless Shah Mansur led such an impetuous charge that he was able to wound Timur himself on the neck and shoulder before being cut down by Timur's son, Shah Rukh. This time the bloodthirsty conqueror showed even less mercy than usual, the Muzaffarids being exterminated in 1393.

From southern Iran Timur's army, likened to 'ants and locusts covering the whole countryside, plundering and ravaging', moved into Iraq. Ahmad ibn Uwais, the Jalayrid ruler of Baghdad, refused to face this appalling swarm and fled to Egypt, but the castle of al Naja, where Ibn Uwais had secured both his treasure and his family high in the mountains of Luristan, continued to resist. So successful was its defiance that Timur abandoned hope of capturing the fortress and instead built his own small castle nearby as an observation point. Fully twelve years were to pass before al Naja finally succumbed, in the year that Timur himself died. After three months of feasting, plundering and massacre, Timur left Baghdad early in 1394 and moved up the Tigris towards Anatolia, pausing only to besiege and sack the towering citadel of Tikrit. The garrison was, of course, massacred, their skulls being piled up into 'minarets', while the shattered walls of Tikrit were left as a reminder of Timur's power.

In the forbidding uplands of eastern Anatolia, a region that even today has a wider selection of ferocious wild animals than any other part of western Asia or Europe, Timur once more came up against the grim and

Among the tricks used by Timur as a young commander was having his men trail branches from their saddles, to raise enough dust for a much larger army.

remarkably successful resistance of the Qara Qoyunlu. These fierce Turcoman nomads never really accepted Timur's domination and they also held a series of virtually inaccessible castles. Timur's army did, however, capture the city of Mardin, where the defeated garrison was unexpectedly spared because the conqueror had received news of the birth of a grandson – Ulughbeg, the future 'astronomer king' of Samarqand. Van was taken, for the second time, before Timur's host again moved north into Christian Georgia.

This time Timur did little more than pass through on his way to settle final accounts with Toqtamish, who was once more threatening Timur's northern frontier. Timur marched through the Darband Gates, a narrow pass between the Caspian Sea and the Caucasus mountains. On 15th April 1395 the armies of Timur and Toqtamish met near the river Terek, a strategic point where so many battles had been fought. Timur himself took part until, as the *Zafarnama* put it, 'his arrows were all spent, his spear broken, but his sword he still brandished'. This time Timur's victory was complete. The shattered remnants of Toqtamish's army and of his Russian vassals were pursued as far as Yelets, not far from the Principality of Moscow. There Timur turned back not, as the terrified Muscovites believed, because of the miraculous intervention of the Virgin Mary and still less through fear of Moscow's military might, but because he had no interest in conquering the poor and backward Russian principalities. His eyes were already set on China. Meanwhile he turned south, sacked the European trading post of Tana at the mouth of the river Don and then headed for Sarai, capital of the Golden Horde.

The destruction of Tana (modern Azov) was hardly more than an excursion for Timur, yet it was a carefully calculated one that betrayed considerable understanding of international trade and its economic implications. Less is known about the organization and defence of Tana than about those of Kaffa on the Crimean coast to the south, but all these trading posts were held by the Genoese. They were the lynch-pins of the immensely rich trade routes across the steppes to China, for it was from them that Genoese, Venetian and other ships took the exports of the Orient to Europe. It was also from them that Russian and Turkish slaves were exported to Egypt, to be trained as professional warriors, the original *mamluks* upon whom the power of the Mamluk Sultanate was built. The destruction of Tana did not cut these trade routes but it did them terrible damage. Thereafter most of the trade between China and Europe used a more southerly route through Timur's own empire, with all the profit from tolls and taxes which that entailed.

Timur's subsequent sack of Sarai and Astrakhan on the river Volga dealt a death blow to the northern steppe route. The people of Astrakhan tried to defend themselves by building walls of ice-blocks cut from the frozen Volga, but it was to no avail. Sarai fell even more quickly and archaeological evidence suggests that the actual attack, in the winter of

1395–6, came unexpectedly. In the bazaars clothes were found ready for sale, the inkwells of the scribes still with the remains of ink. Bread, fruit, nuts and an extraordinary selection of everyday items lay scorched by the fire that destroyed the city. Skeletons were found scattered, without heads, hands or feet. Though the puppet khan whom Timur placed at the head of the Golden Horde defeated the fast expanding Lithuanian empire in 1399, and although Toqtamish kept up a bitter struggle until he died one year after Timur-i Lenk, the power of the Golden Horde was broken at last, thus making way for the rise of Russia.

The Jalayrid rulers of Baghdad, who bore the brunt of Timur's invasion of Iraq, were also great patrons of the arts. Under their rule the old pre-Mongol styles had a comeback but the costumes and weapons shown in such manuscripts are still Turco-Mongol. The allegorical figure in this copy of Qazwini's encyclopedia wears a typical Turkish coat and carries a curved sabre from his belt (Freer Gallery of Art, inv. 54.46v, Washington).

The Later Conquests

For two years it appeared that Timur-i Lenk, the now aged conqueror, was at last settling down to enjoy the spoils of victory. From 1396 to 1398 he spent most of his time in his favourite city of Samarkand, feasting and building those architectural monuments whose beauty still stands in stark contrast to their builder's bloodthirsty life. Timur had gathered in Samarkand not only the plundered wealth of western Asia but also crowds of skilful artists, scholars, engineers and craftsmen dragged from every corner of his empire. Timur's capital was in fact, erected on a new site. The ruins of old Samarkand still stand, as a mound of accumulated debris surmounted by the *Shah-i Zinda,* an array of elegant religious buildings dating from the Timurid period. Some way away Timur's own tomb would soon rise not only as a resting place for the conqueror and his spiritual mentor Nur Sayyid Baraka, but as an expression of raw political power.

These quiet years were, however, an illusion. Timur had by no means retired from the battlefield. In fact he was planning to invade one of the richest parts of the Muslim world, the Delhi Sultanate of northern India. Though Timur proclaimed his intention of punishing the Muslim rulers of Delhi for their excessive toleration of Hindus, in reality he was lured by loot and the fact that, like so many of his once-powerful neighbours, the Delhi Sultanate was in decline. Another *quriltai* was held, which predictably sanctioned Timur's 'crusade'. The first to fall victim to this new assault were the *Siyah-push,* the 'black-robed' pagans of Kafiristan (Land of Unbelievers). They had resisted repeated Muslim invasions since the eighth century and still survive in one of the wildest parts of Afghanistan. Neither Alexander the Great nor the modern Soviet army ever managed to subdue their ice-bound peaks overlooking the road between Kabul and Peshawar. So precipitous was the terrain that Timur's army managed to get only two cavalry horses over the mountains alive. Nevertheless, the wild Kafirs were conquered, huge numbers being slaughtered, while forts and garrisons were left to keep open Timur's invasion route.

Timur's defeat of the Delhi Sultanate appears to have been much easier and involved even greater carnage. By the time his army took up position on a ridge some ten kilometres north of Delhi it had already captured up to a hundred thousand prisoners. They included both Muslims and Hindus, since the Delhi Sultans happily employed both in their army. The bulk of the Delhi army was, however, intact and still greatly outnumbered Timur's troops. Predictably, perhaps, Timur ordered all prisoners to be killed so as to release his troops for combat. On 12th December 1398 the Muslims had their throats cut while the Hindus, victims of what Timur had claimed to be a holy war, were either flayed alive or burned.

The battle that followed again ended in overwhelming victory and Delhi was taken. At first the inhabitants were promised their safety but, after suffering the arrogance and looting of Timur's soldiery, someone was foolish enough to strike back. As a result Delhi was left a city of the dead, marked by the usual towers of severed heads. Timur made no effort to administer the conquered territories. Instead he and his army marched home, laden with booty, leaving northern India rent by civil war between Timur's nominee and the previous Sultan of Delhi.

Timur's warlike energy amazed even his contemporaries, for hardly had he returned from India than he was preparing for war against his western foes. The Jalayrid ruler Ahmad ibn Uwais had retaken Baghdad but, of Timur's western enemies, the Ottomans and Mamluks were more powerful. Timur's grasp of strategy was such that he might even have had a broad and remarkably modern plan in this wide-ranging campaign. The military historian Lt. Gen. Sir John Glubb suggests that Timur first invaded eastern Anatolia to frighten the Ottoman Sultan Bayazit, then rapidly turned south to deal with the Jalayrids and Mamluks before these could threaten his rear and flank. Thereupon Timur returned to settle accounts with the Ottomans. It was by any standards an amazing expedition, which took Timur's army back and forth across half the Middle East, winning victories at every turn.

In the winter of 1399–1400, Timur again struck at Christian Georgia, laying much of the country waste and leaving a garrison in the capital of Tbilisi. Timur would return again in the summer of 1402 and, on his victorious way home from Anatolia, a year after that. During these campaigns the Georgians relied on their virtually inaccessible mountain-top castles but against an army such as Timur's this was not always effective. A story tells how one of Timur's young officers, a leader of one hundred men named Bir Muhammad Qumbar, captured such a fortress almost single-handed after a rival had been honoured by Timur for slaying a giant-like Georgian champion. Bir Muhammad put on his heaviest armour, then hid near the castle drawbridge. There he stayed all day until, as dusk fell, he saw the Georgian gate-guards return inside the castle and start to raise its drawbridge. Bir Muhammad then broke from his hiding place, cut the bridge ropes with his sword and pinned down the guards with his bow. Though the garrison showered him with stones and arrows he refused to budge. Meanwhile the rest of Timur's besieging troops saw that the Georgians could not close their gate and charged up the mountainside, bursting into the castle as Bir Muhammad finally collapsed with no less than eighteen wounds. Later he recovered, having been attended by Timur-i Lenk's own doctors, and was promoted to command a thousand men.

In August 1400 Timur marched against Sivas in the heart of Anatolia, a city that had only recently been incorporated into the Ottoman Empire. Prisoners were forced to work as pioneers, undermining the walls and erecting earth platforms from which Timur's siege machines could hurl

The mysterious perhaps early Timurid miniatures in the Fatih Albums *contain a picture of a parade, probably a marriage celebration, which includes these interesting foot-soldiers. One looks like an Indian, the other a Middle Easterner. Both are armed with axes and curved daggers but the larger figure also carries a slightly curved sabre over his left shoulder, a bow in his right arm, a shield on his back and a quiver from his belt (Topkapi Lib., Ms. Haz. 2153, ff. 3v–4r, Istanbul).*

rocks and fire-pots into the town. The garrison, largely consisting of Armenian *sipahi* feudal cavalry, put up a stout resistance but eventually had to capitulate. They were buried alive in the city's moat, although the Muslim inhabitants were spared. One Armenian chronicler, Thomas of Medzoph, maintained that a choir of children came out of the city singing in hope of softening the conqueror's heart, but that Timur ordered his horsemen to ride them down. Certainly, Timur-i Lenk's treatment of Christians in eastern Anatolia was particularly savage and probably accounted for the loyalty these communities developed for the mild rule of the Ottomans.

Thousands of Armenian captives were also transported to Iran and central Asia, where their descendants survived for many generations. Captured Turks, including those from the warlike Qara Qoyunlu, were sent east to be held ready for Timur's proposed invasion of China. Meanwhile the Qara Qoyunlu continued to resist. Their indomitable ruler, Qara Yusuf, was several times driven into exile but always returned. The second main Turcoman tribe in this area, the Aq Qoyunlu, came to terms with Timur and even sent troops to help him fight the Ottomans.

First, however, Timur had to deal with his southern flank. Though the Mamluks had refused an offer of alliance with the Ottoman Sultan Bayazit they also refused to accept Timur's suzereinty. Such, in fact, was the political confusion in Cairo that the Mamluks were unable to organize a defence until Timur actually invaded their territory. The frontier city of Malatya fell in September 1400 as did a number of north Syrian castles, though not without a fight. In one siege, at Bahasna, the defenders hurled a stone right into Timur's tent, but the only result was that no quarter was shown to the brave garrison. In October Timur's army reached the great city of Aleppo and on the 30th the Mamluk garrison marched out to give battle. The struggle was brief and one-sided, with Timur using war elephants captured in India. Among the defeated Mamluks was a young Syrian who fought on though he had received over thirty sabre cuts to his head and other wounds in his body. Found later among the dead and dying he was brought before Timur who, according to the Mamluk historian Ibn Taghri Birdi, 'marvelled extremely at his bravery and endurance and, it is said, ordered that he be given medical treatment.' Aleppo was not so fortunate. The city was taken by assault and the usual massacre and piling of severed heads followed, while Timur engaged in a theological debate with some of the city's terrified religious leaders.

Timur next marched south. Hama was sacked and its people slaughtered. Damascus was bypassed and Timur's men came face to face with the main Mamluk army at Qatrana, near the foothills of Mount Hermon. There the two forces remained until 8th January 1401, when the Mamluks suddenly withdrew on hearing of a threatened *coup d'état* in

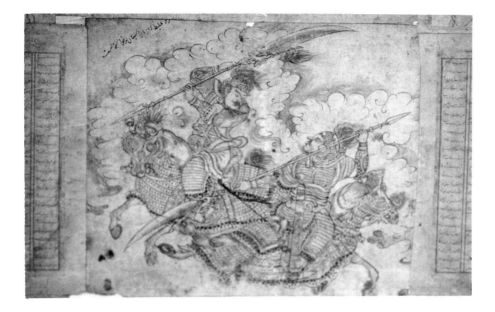

Cairo. Damascus was left virtually defenceless, its garrison having been decimated in a previous unsuccessful sortie. The city surrendered, but the governor decided to resist in the citadel. When, after a bitter month-long siege the citadel finally fell it was found to have been defended by hardly more than forty Mamluk warriors. The survivors were enslaved. Damascus itself had already been sacked while its inhabitants suffered some of the cruellest tortures yet recorded even in Timur's sadistic career. Others were enslaved and sent off to central Asia. Among them was a twelve-year old boy named Ahmad ibn Arabshah who was later to write a savage biography of the man who had enslaved him. Infants under five were simply left behind to die as their mothers were hauled off into captivity.

The Mamluk Sultan, not surprisingly, offered tribute in hope of getting Timur to leave and once again the conqueror made no real effort to retain the land he had overrun but instead led his army off to Iraq, while Syria collapsed into chaos. On the way east Timur ravaged the little Artuqid emirate of Mardin, whose long-lived dynasty had survived since before the First Crusades and would outlast Timur by four years. Among the inhabitants of Mardin was a strange sect known as *Arevortis* or *Areworik*, who believed that Christ was the Sun. They were probably descended from Armenians who had refused to convert to Christianity back in the fifth century and they had earlier appeared in Middle Eastern military history as renowned cavalry, usually serving in Muslim armies. Now, however, they were virtually wiped out by Timur.

Under the Jalayrids Baghdad had to some extent recovered from Mongol devastation. It had already fallen once to Timur, but his second

Included among the Fatih Album mysteries are some drawings in a remarkably Chinese style, though with Persian inscriptions. They almost certainly show eastern Mongol warriors or Chinese horsemen under strong Mongol influence. Timur's Central Asian Jagatai foes are likely to have included such troops, riding armoured horses, wearing lamellar armour but wielding long hafted Chinese staff weapons with huge blades (Topkapi Lib., Ms. Haz. 2153, f.87r, Istanbul).

assault in 1401 finally spelled the end of this once-splendid city. By 1437 the Egyptian historian Al Maqrizi recorded that Baghdad could hardly be called a city at all. The interesting tactic used by Timur in this second siege alone sets the fall of Baghdad apart from so many other conquests and massacres. The attack took place in the stifling Iraqi midsummer. Soldiers, it was said, roasted in their armour and birds fell dead from the sky. After six weeks of hellish hunger and exhaustion Timur chose the intolerable heat of noon to make a general assault knowing, for sure, that the 'guards' who lined the city walls were mostly helmets propped up on spear shafts. No quarter was given and the dead were too numerous for Timur's military aides to count. They did, however, record that a tree of pure gold, decorated with precious stones, was recovered from a boat, full of the late governor's treasure, sunk in the nearby Euphrates. This tree was later seen in Samarkand by the Spanish ambassador Clavijo.

Now Timur turned to face his most powerful foe, the Ottoman Sultan Bayazit. Both men were successful conquerors. Bayazit had crushed a European Crusade at Nicopolis in 1396 and his army enjoyed the same record of success as did Timur's. Not surprisingly the two warriors were wary of each other. They had been rivals in central Anatolia for many years and at first limited themselves to an exchange of flowery threats. Timur also appears to have hoped for an anti-Ottoman alliance with various Christian powers and in the winter of 1401–2 he tried to draw in local Christian rulers but they, recalling Timur's all too recent massacres, demurred. The Byzantines of Trabzon were already Timur's vassals, but they simply could not supply the twenty galleys he now demanded. The Byzantines of Istanbul and the Genoese of Pera (the modern Galata suburb of Istanbul) may have promised naval support against Bayazit but nothing came of it. Meanwhile both sides prepared for war. Timur's first action was to sieze Erzinjan, where he demolished the Armenian Cathedral of St. Sergius. From there his army moved to Sivas, where it held a full-scale military review that showed just how modern and sophisticated its organization and uniforms had become. Such reviews not only checked an army's equipment and readiness but also boosted morale before a coming battle.

Timur now completely outmanoeuvered Bayazit, despite the latter's formidable military reputation. Whereas Timur's army was still a highly mobile Turco-Mongol force primarily consisting of cavalry, the Ottoman army already included a large number of infantry. These no longer served merely as siege troops or skirmishers but had a central military rôle. Yet it was Bayazit's men who were obliged to do most of the marching while Timur besieged Ankara. On 20th July 1402, tired and thirsty, the Ottomans were thrown into what has been described as one of the first 'modern' battles in Middle Eastern history. It was hard fought and long but by the end of the day Timur had won and Bayazit was his prisoner.

The shattered Ottoman army fled westward, many of the survivors being ferried across the Dardanelles to Europe in Genoese and Venetian ships. Meanwhile Genoa thought the time ripe for an alliance with Timur, though the Venetians kept the conqueror at arm's length. The defeat and subsequent death of Sultan Bayazit threw the Ottomans into turmoil, but their Empire was already as much a Balkan-European state as an Anatolian-Asian one. They not only survived but recovered to reconquer modern Turkey, half the Middle East, North Africa and Europe to the gates of Vienna. In the short term, however, Timur's invasion strengthened the nomadic Turcoman element in Anatolia against that of the peasants and towns, a factor that would eventually help the Ottomans revive their fortunes.

After the battle of Ankara, Timur ravaged right up to the Aegean Sea, using the citadel of Kütahya as his base. Down on the coast the city of Izmir had been in European Crusader hands since 1344, though the westerners never took the citadel or surrounding territory. Many different people had contributed to this extraordinary Christian outpost, including Venetians, Genoese, the remaining Crusader principalities in Greece and Cyprus, a French army under the Dauphin of Vienne and, above all, the Order of Hospitallers based at Rhodes. The garrison now consisted of two hundred knights and their followers under the Spaniard Inigo d'Alfaro.

Timur demanded that they surrender and either accept Islam or pay tribute but D'Alfaro refused and on 2nd December 1402 the siege began. Izmir harbour was partially blocked by causeways built out into the sea and Timur's engineers also constructed huge mobile wooden towers manned by up to two hundred soldiers. These were wheeled against the walls, which Timur's sappers meanwhile undermined. After less than

The vast but ruined fortress of Kutahya in western Turkey. Here Timur set up his head-quarters after defeating the Ottomans at the battle of Ankara. Once again the walls and towers largely date from the Byzantine period.

fifteen days the city fell, the population being massacred while the surviving defenders fled to the neighbouring island of Chios. On his long way back east Timur again ravaged Georgia, spent the winter of 1403–4 in the pastures of Azerbayjan and, in the following spring, led his army home to Samarqand, there to plan the invasion of China. He was now sixty-eight years old.

It was at this time that an embassy arrived from the far west of the Christian world, from the Kingdom of Castile, bearing gifts and led by Ruy Gonzalez de Clavijo. Timur himself had little interest in Europe but during his reign, and those of his successors, contacts between Europe and Central Asia were revived. Timur did, however, admire some of the gifts that Clavijo brought, particularly the decorated fine fabrics.

In 1395 an embassy had also reached Samarqand from the Ming Emperor of China, with a message that referred to Timur as a vassal. Deeply insulted, Timur decided on war. Now, with all his other neighbours defeated if not actually conquered, Timur felt the time had come both to revive the Mongol domination of China and to take the banners of Islam into this, the most populous part of Asia. With hindsight the whole concept might appear fantastic, but China had succumbed to Mongol–Turkic armies before and there were already substantial Muslim minorities within the Chinese Empire.

As usual Timur summoned a *quriltai*. Next he gathered his armies and laid on a series of sumptuous feasts on the plain of Kani-Gol. These included not only mountains of food and lakes of highly alcoholic drink but entertainment – music, masquerades, martial displays, clowning and, astonishing to modern observers of the Muslim scene, displays by pretty girls dressed as various animals or posing in camel litters. Ambassadors brought gifts from half of Europe and Asia while some of Timur's grandchildren were married during the celebrations. After nuptials performed according to strict Muslim rite, there was an almost pagan Turkish party in which the drunken old conqueror joined in the dancing and, according to Ibn Arabshah; 'tottered amongst them because of his age and lameness'.

A reconstruction of a late 14th century Mongol armour of a type used by both the Golden Horde and Timur's armies. It was made by Dr. Michael Gorelik of Moscow ('Battle of Kulikovo Field' Museum, Kulikovo, USSR).

Even as this bacchanal was under way, preparations for the conquest of China continued. Eastern frontier forts were strengthened and provisioned, as were the proposed stopping places along the invasion route. The formidable army that set out in December 1404 was very mixed, including Mongols, Turks from Central Asia and Anatolia, Iranians and Afghans. It was later said to be carrying enough supplies for seven years, though this was almost certainly an exaggeration. Ahead lay five and a half thousand kilometres of desert, steppe and cultivated land on the road to Peking. Meanwhile the winter was bitterly cold and, after crossing the frozen Syr Darya, the army found its way blocked by snow two-spearshafts deep beyond Utrar. Here, three hundred kilometres north of Samarkand, Timur-i Lenk's strength finally gave out. He fell ill and, on

18th February 1405, died. Ahmad ibn Arabshah must have summed up the feelings of many when he wrote:

Then they brought forth garments of hair from Hell and drew forth his soul like a spit from a soaked fleece and he was carried to the cursing and punishment of God, remaining in torment and God's infernal punishment.

Timur's family and followers took a more optimistic view, of course. The invasion of China was called off and the old conqueror's body was taken back to Samarkand where it was buried four days later in an octagonal mausoleum in which Timur's grandson Muhammad Sultan already lay. A steel coffin was later made by a craftsman from Shiraz, to which Timur's corpse was transferred. The beautiful tile-covered Gur Emir tomb complex still stands in the city.

Timur's grave lies within the beautiful tile covered Gur-Emir mausoleum. Here the conqueror lies humbly at the feet of a saint who offered Timur religious advice throughout his bloodthirsty career, both being buried within a building whose delicate decoration belies the carnage that Timur brought upon the Middle East (Novosti Press).

Timur's Army

Clavijo stated that Timur's army was always with him and certainly, while this might not have been strictly true, the army was a semi-permanent force of professionals. Naturally it changed over the years as Timur's power and empire grew. In the early days Timur's followers were recruited almost entirely from nomadic Turkish and Mongol horse-archers and such men continued to form the basis of Timur's power throughout his reign. Though it was largely of nomad origin, this did not prevent the army from becoming highly organized, superbly equipped and, at least in later years, uniformed along remarkably modern lines.

Elite units, including Timur's own guards, were drawn from forty tribes of Jagatai Mongol rather than Turkish origin. An officer corps of *aymak* was also recruited from the same source. Each tribe provided an agreed number of men according to its size. Among them were men who had not even superficially converted to Islam so that the army of the 'pious' Timur-i Lenk shocked Middle Eastern observers by including pagans, probably shamanists, within its ranks. Foreigners were later enlisted, including the remnants of defeated foes as well as more exotic recruits such as the Bavarian squire Schiltberger, who was first captured by the Ottomans at Nicopolis and then by Timur at Ankara and served his last master faithfully before escaping back to central Europe. The army that invaded Anatolia in Timur's last great campaign was particularly mixed, including men from Central Asia, Transoxania, India and Iran, not to mention east-Anatolian allies.

Organization was based upon the system developed by Genghis Khan, even including the messengers who played such an important part in Mongol warfare. Timur also had a highly developed postal system based on carrier pigeons. There had, however, been changes over the previous century. Troops from settled areas now played a more important part and the sophisticated traditions of Islamic administration, engineering and fortification had been added to the old Mongol military traditions. Most military terms remained Mongol though ranks ranged from the Arab term *amir* or senior officer, through the Turkish *ming bashi* (chief of a thousand), *yuz bashi* (chief of one hundred) and *on bashi* (chief of ten). Other officers were given the Persian title of *sardar* while an army or horde was called an *ordu*, a corps a *fauj*, a small unit a *goshun* and an auxiliary or lightly equipped raiding force a *harsha*. Support troops, such as infantry, engineers, pioneers and a regional gendarmerie police force were similarly structured.

One feature of Timur's army that never failed to impress foreigners, particularly Europeans, was its iron discipline. Ranks were said to form without a word of command, orders anticipated before a drum or trumpet was heard. Discipline during long and immensely difficult marches across hostile territory almost never broke down. One story shows the degree of unquestioning obedience seen in Timur's army. During a long march the conqueror saw a soldier who had fallen asleep in the saddle. Muttering, presumably to himself, that the man should lose his head, Timur was amazed to find the unfortunate soldier's head being presented to him by an officer. Thereupon the bloodthirsty conqueror gave thanks to God for having such men under his command!

Orders in camp and on the battlefield were transmitted by a tall bronze drum, the beating of which was understood by all soldiers. Various forms of flag were also used for silent command, even when giving precise orders for pillage and the distribution of booty. Though Timur's soldiers now received regular pay and pensions from state revenues, Timur also recognized the value of conspicuous generosity in maintaining loyalty, as he wrote in the 'Institutions' in which he left advice for his successors:

To encourage my officers and my soldiers I have not hoarded gold or jewels for myself. I admit my men to my table and in return they give me their lives in battle. I give generously and share in their sufferings, thus I am assured of their loyalty. . . .

Money as well as additional weapons were distributed before a battle and afterwards those who had distinguished themselves were rewarded with promotion or by being named as *tarkhans*. This distinction exempted a soldier from tax, entitled him to keep all the booty he won on future campaigns, and made him liable for prosecution only after the ninth time he committed a crime. He also enjoyed access to the royal audience without prior permission. *Tarkhans* formed a kind of Order of Chivalry that their descendants inherited for seven generations. The widows of men who died while performing deeds of distinction similarly received those favours that their husbands would otherwise have enjoyed.

It is, perhaps, surprising to read that single combat between the champions of opposing armies was still common, even in such a highly disciplined force. Even Timur and his descendants occasionally fought such duels. Commanders who betrayed cowardice or lack of resolution were humiliated by having their beards shaved and their faces painted with women's make-up and being forced to run barefoot through the streets. Efforts were also made to recruit defeated foes but only if they had been loyal to their previous leaders – which must have reduced such a pool of recruits considerably, given Timur's tendency to massacre! As Timur again made clear in his 'Institutions':

The enemy soldier who is loyal to his master has my friendship. When he passes beneath my banner I reward his merits and his fidelity and have confidence in him. But the soldier who, at the moment of action, fails in his duty and deserts his general, him I regard as the most execrable of men. . . .

Other details of Timur's military system include the Three Circles emblem which appeared on his seals, coins, palaces and perhaps some banners. Women were also recorded as taking part in certain battles – an ancient Turkish but somewhat un-Islamic practice – and they certainly donned armour to defend a camp or at least fool a foe while their menfolk

This miniature in the Fatih Albums *of* Iskander and the Wolves *was probably painted in Shiraz in the early 15th century. Here the ancient Greek hero Alexander the Great is shown as a Persian champion wearing the decorated lamellar armour, rigid arm vambraces and domed helmet of the typical Timurid cavalier (Topkapi Lib., Ms. Haz. 2153, f.73v, Istanbul).*

made a sudden raid upon the unsuspecting enemy. In addition to the normal Islamic battle cries, Timur's men shouted in Turkish *surun!* (charge!) as they attacked.

The army's peacetime organization was almost as sophisticated as in time of war. The nobility were expected to look after military horse-herds and presumably to increase them. If necessary, animals would also be requisitioned from the populace. Islamic armies had been subject to regular muster and review ever since the days of the first Caliphs. This system continued under Timur and provided an opportunity to check the men's fitness, fighting skills, equipment and organization. A number of such reviews were recorded in detail. Troops were expected to bring food for a year's campaigning, a bow, a quiver with thirty arrows and a shield. There should be a spare horse for every two men, a tent for every ten plus two spades, a pick-axe, scythe, awl, axe, one hundred needles, rope or perhaps a lasso, an animal hide and a cooking pot.

At the review held deep inside Golden Horde territory in 1391 the élite troops were described as riding caparisoned and probably armoured horses, being armoured from head to foot and carrying spear, sword, dagger, mace, javelin, and shield – though it is unlikely that all men carried all such weapons. This army was drawn up in ranks with left and right flanks, centre and advance guard. Each unit had its banners and horse-tail standards. As Timur rode along the lines, each commanding officer would leap from his mount, kneel before his sovereign and then lead Timur's horse by the bridle to inspect the men. The whole review lasted two days and ended with a roll on the great kettle-drums and a roar of battle cries. Similar details are recorded for the great review held outside Sivas in Anatolia in 1402, though here we read of units being dressed all in red, yellow, white or some other colour, with matching shields, saddles, quivers, belts, pennons and banners.

As in Genghis Khan's time, great hunts were organized not only to supply meat for the winter but to refine the men's cavalry skills and tactical coordination. Apart from the usual forms of military training, wrestling had now become a highly structured sport and seems to have been virtually identical to that still practiced in Turkey and Iran.

On the march Timur himself rode behind the advance guard and ahead of the bulk of cavalry. Next came the infantry, now an important if still not very highly regarded part of the army, and behind them the baggage train with supplies and Timur's own family. Last of all came the families of the nomad cavalry, which almost always accompanied the army on major campaigns, plus herds of animals.

Turkish and Mongol tents could, of course, be dismantled but some of the larger and more splendid were carried intact on huge wagons, simply being lifted to the ground for the night. Timurid military camps were, in fact, like mobile towns, complete with elaborate pavilions for the nobility and stalls, markets and craft areas with armourers, saddlers

and farriers. There were even mobile wooden bath-houses complete with hot water, heating systems and attendants. Such a feature was a new idea reflecting the Turks' conversion to Islam. The camps themselves were also highly structured, being laid out with streets and quarters according to rigid rules.

Tactics were developments of those seen in earlier Mongol times. Changes since Genghis Khan's day included much more sophisticated siege craft as well as engineering, while the wagons that accompanied an army were still used to erect remarkably effective field fortifications. In an emergency these wagons could be drawn up around a threatened ruler and his bodyguard. Pointed calthrops were often scattered ahead of an army when it adopted a defensive position, while on the march engineers not only cleared wide roads through forested areas but constructed fords across even the broadest Siberian rivers and marshes by using felled tree trunks, matting made from branches or felt tent material.

Timur's use of war elephants was also new, at least for Mongols and Turks. Clavijo described these beasts as having their tusks cut short with relatively small iron blades attached. In battle, he said, the elephant advanced in a series of jumps like a wild bear, striking upwards with his tusks each time. On the animal's back was a wooden castle into which soldiers climbed or dismounted using ropes attached to the side. Clavijo made no mention of elephant armour, which seems to have been a later

The most impressive surviving citadel from Timurid time, the Herat citadel mostly consists of grim brick towers, walls and gateways. One tower is, however, finely decorated with blue and turquoise tiles in the same style as many Timurid palaces, mosques or tombs. A fragment of tiled inscription can just be seen to the left of this tower, perhaps indicating that such inscriptions once ran around the tops of many of the Citadel's walls (photo Geza Fehervari).

175

development in India, perhaps in response to the appearance of firearms.

In purely tactical terms Timur was renowned for his ability to alter his plans in response to changing circumstances even in the middle of a battle, a fact that is a tribute to his army's communications, training and discipline. He was also a master of deception, once feigning sickness by vomiting animal's blood in the presence of foreign envoys and thus lulling his neighbours into a false sense of security. On another occasion he used the old trick of lighting numerous fires on hills around his camp to convince enemy scouts that his army was stronger than it was. Much earlier in his career he had similarly tricked a foe in daytime by fastening trailing branches to his men's saddles, thus raising dust enough for a much larger force.

Timur's intelligence services were both admired and feared. Regular reports arrived from neighbouring states, supplied by spies and informers who ranged from members of the enemy's military élite to travelling dervishes, sailors and prostitutes. He even knew the price of food in an enemy's markets, the condition of his roads, the names and loyalty of his supporters, as well as possessing a huge store of maps and charts. Internal security was maintained by police agents known as *kurtchi* and penalties for sedition were very harsh.

Timur spent his military career attacking his neighbours and so had little use for fortifications. Yet he did construct and repair castles, particularly along his exposed north-eastern frontier. Very little is known about these defences. Documentary sources merely say that Timur kept his fortifications in good repair, fully garrisoned and properly provisioned. We also know that existing feudal élites were often permitted to retain such static military positions. In conquered Armenia there was, for example, record of an Armenian lady holding a castle as chatelaine in Timur's name. The most impressive surviving fortification from the Timurid period is the citadel of Herat in Afghanistan. Having been destroyed both by the Mongols and by Timur himself, it was rebuilt by Timur's more peaceable son Shah Rukh. Seven thousand workers raised the new walls and one at least of the citadel's corner towers was decorated with colour-glazed bricks. Such glazed decoration served a useful function by making the citadel, the seat of secular power, stand out from the surrounding dusty brown buildings. It also enabled it to compete architecturally with the only other decorated structures, the mosques and seats of religious authority.

Arms, Armour and Equipment

The age of Timur and his successors was one of considerable change in arms and armour, in the Middle East just as in Europe. Timur himself

Even after the Mongols converted to Islam, Mongol women had a much more public rôle in Mongol society than was seen in most other parts of the Middle East.

took captured armourers, along with other kinds of craftsmen, back to central Asia. Those seized in Damascus are merely the best known and an armourers' quarter soon sprang up in the grounds of Timur's Gok-Saray 'Blue Palace' in Samarkand. Although the city never became a major arms-producing centre it did carry on a tradition of Transoxanian weapons manufacture dating back beyond the Islamic conquest. Bridles, horse harness and saddles were also made in the same quarter, along with decorative fabrics for military and ceremonial use, all of which activity has been confirmed by Russian archaeologists. According to Clavijo, Timur-i Lenk took a personal interest in such activity and he described one of the conqueror's visits to the arsenal in the Citadel. Clavijo also draws some interesting parallels between Timurid and early fifteenth century Spanish military equipment:

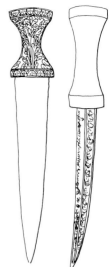

Early 15th century Iranian daggers. One (left) has a gilded chased iron grip and was found in East Prussia, probably having got there during the Mongol invasion of 1410 (Osterode Museum, East Germany). The other has a plain grip but highly decorated slightly curved blade (Historisches Museum, Dresden).

. . . he [Timur] caused to be brought before him for inspection the arms and armour that those workmen, his captives, had completed since the time when he set forth and last had been present. Among the rest, they brought to show him three thousand new suits of scale armour [what in Europe would be called a coat-of-plates, brigandine or jack] which is the sort stitched on a backing of red cloth. To our thinking this appeared very well wrought, except that the plates are not thick enough, and they do not here know how properly to temper the steel. At the same time an immense number of helmets were exhibited, and these each with its suit of armour were that day many of them given as presents by his Highness, being distributed among the lords and nobles there in attendance. These helmets of theirs are made round and high, some turning back to a point, while in front a piece comes down to guard the face and nose, which is a plate two fingers broad reaching the level of the chin below. This piece can be raised or lowered at will and it serves to ward off a side stroke by a sword. These suits of armour are composed very much as in the custom with us in Spain [where armour was at that time generally lighter than elsewhere in western Europe], but they wear a long skirt made of a material separate from that which is scale-armoured and this comes down so as to appear below as might be with us a jerkin.

(based upon Guy le Strange's translation of *Clavijo, Embassy to Tamerlane 1403–1406*, London, 1928)

Though firearms were coming into use elsewhere in the Muslim Middle East and may even have been used against Timur by his Ottoman or Mamluk foes, there is no clear evidence that Timur had guns or cannon. The Mongol ruler Hülegü had earlier set up a form of military chemical laboratory in Maragha in north-western Iran. Highly effective but non-explosive incendiary devices were, of course, used in siege warfare as they had been for centuries. References to sophisticated stone and fire weapons being used against Urganj in 1379 might refer to gunpowder, while the 'loud throwing engines' used by Timur against the Indians in 1398 could mean primitive cannon or the largest type of stone-throwing mangonels.

In terms of ceremonial and military costume, the reign of Timur and his successors saw a decline in Mongol and Far Eastern (essentially Chinese) fashions and a reversion to Turkish and Iranian styles. Timur himself is said to have designed a special fur cap for his soldiers so that

The battle of Ankara pitted the two greatest conquerors of the age against each other. Yet it was Timur who won, capturing the Ottoman Turkish Sultan Bayazit after a bitter struggle.

they should be recognized at a distance. Some have regarded this as a form of *kalpak*, similar to those lambskin hats worn by officers of the Ottoman army during the First World War.

Timur's Battles

Kunduzcha

After its incredible march across the western Asian steppes to what is now the Tatar ASSR (part of the Russian Soviet Federal Socialist Republic of the USSR), Timur's army finally came face to face with the Mongol Golden Horde led by Toqtamish. Battle probably became inevitable because Toqtamish's men had been pursued beyond the open steppe into an area of forests and meadows on the edge of Siberia, close to terrain that would become increasingly unsuitable for their open style of warfare. Toqtamish now also had the broad Volga and Kama rivers at his back, effectively blocking further retreat.

Timur's careful use of scouts, plus the firm discipline maintained in camp and on the march, ensured that the Golden Horde had been unable to lure him into ambushes. A few prisoners had been taken along the way but not until he reached the Samara river, flowing down from the Ural mountains, did Timur pick up definite news of Toqtamish and his army. From then on Timur's troops marched in battle formation. No one was allowed to leave his unit, no fires were lit at night and no drums or cymbals used during the day. More prisoners were brought in and Timur realized that the enemy was now close at hand. He formed his men into a left wing, right wing and centre, every soldier to be ready with his shield and fully armed against surprise attack. Fortified camps were built at each night's stopping place, surrounded by observation posts, ditches and ramparts. Extra weapons were distributed from an armoury that formed part of the baggage train and Timur held a final council of war with his senior officers. The terrain was now marshy, misty and depressing for an army largely recruited in Transoxania. One of Timur's scouting parties was also severely mauled by the enemy, but Timur maintained morale by personally leading a counter-raid.

In the middle of June 1391 the weather at last cleared and the scouting parties of both armies made firm contact. On 18th June Timur changed the traditional battle formation in which his army had been marching and added vanguards to both his left and right flanks as well as a van and rear guard to his centre, which, however, remained the largest division of the army. The left van was commanded by the Emirs Berdi Beg and Khudaydad Hussain, the left flank by Umar Shaykh, the centre van by Sultan Mahmud Khan and Emir Sulayman Shah, the centre by Prince Muhammad Sultan, the right van by the Emir Hajji Sayf al Din and the right flank by Prince Miranshah. Timur himself commanded the rearguard and a reserve of élite guards units well behind the centre. Infantry and cavalry units appear to have been stationed close to each other in every section of the army.

The Mongol warriors of the Golden Horde were more numerous than Timur's men and Toqtamish adopted the normal three large divisions of right, left and centre spread in an enormous crescent in full view of Timur's troops. Some of the Golden Horde's chief men had, however, been suborned by Timur, even including Toqtamish's own standard bearer. The leader of the Aktagh Turks also chose this moment to desert and lead his entire tribe to settle in the Balkans.

Though both wings of the Golden Horde outflanked Timur's army, it was Sayf al Din who attacked first, smashing through the left wing of Toqtamish's force. When the Golden Horde tried to use their superior numbers to surround Sayf al Din, he was supported by the bulk of the right flank, which virtually destroyed the Golden Horde's left. Both armies now advanced all along the line, but Toqtamish soon found his people being forced back in the centre as well as the left, so he concentrated all his efforts on the right. So ferocious was the Golden Horde assault on this part of the battlefield that Toqtamish charged right through Timur's troops, separating Timur's left flank from the rest of the army. At this critical point Timur did a very daring thing. He ordered his grandson Abu Bakr with the guards regiments to pitch Timur's tents, lay down carpets and start preparing a meal. This piece of bravado unnerved the enemy and may have convinced Timur's own men that retreat was out of the question so deep inside enemy territory. Timur himself now led the reserves against Toqtamish and it seems to have been around this time that Toqtamish's standard bearer dipped his banner, further undermining Golden Horde morale. Toqtamish turned and fled, pursued by seven out of every ten horsemen in Timur's army. By the time the two forces broke contact the ground was strewn with corpses, it was said, for two hundred miles. Caught between Timur and the rivers Volga and Kama, the Golden Horde warriors were forced to surrender in huge numbers, Toqtamish's harem and treasure all being seized.

Delhi

The army of the Sultanate of Delhi was unlike any other in the Muslim world and presented Timur with different military problems. Most of its men were Hindu rather than Muslim. Despite the recent setbacks suffered by the Sultanate its army remained enormous, supposedly fielding ten thousand cavalry, twenty thousand infantry and one hundred and twenty war elephants. Warriors in wooden castles upon these beasts were armed with javelins, incendiary devices, bows and, perhaps, crossbows – though these may have been simply ordinary composite

A mail shirt, probably dating from the 15th or 16th century. In the Middle East such armour would normally be worn with other forms of protection or beneath ordinary clothes (National Archaeological Museum, Mosul, Iraq).

bows fitted with arrow guides and firing deadly short darts. The Mongols had already suffered severely from such weapons in the thirteenth century. It is also possible that the men carrying incendiary devices were stationed around the elephants rather than in their castles.

The Delhi army was organized along Persian lines and included slave-recruited professionals comparable to the Egyptian *mamluks*, plus provincial regular forces, irregulars recruited for a single campaign and volunteers. The Muslims would have been armed and armoured in much the same way as those of Afghanistan or Iran, and most of their cavalry were armoured horse-archers. In addition to an extraordinary mixture of mercenaries from as far afield as Anatolia and the borders of China, there were many Hindu cavalry. These were often armed with two swords – an ordinary weapon and a perhaps longer sword whose scabbard was fastened to the saddle. The huge numbers of Hindu infantry were armed with spear and sword.

European military historians have generally assumed that war elephants were unreliable and as dangerous to their own side as to the foe, but this was not really true. They were not only useful against fixed defences, where they served as living battering rams, and as beasts of burden, but they often proved extremely effective in open warfare until the invention of gunpowder. In battle they normally advanced surrounded, or preceded, by a protective phalanx of infantry to ward off enemy horsemen. At the decisive moment they could charge at a speed of 25kph and they were virtually unstoppable once they got going. The fact that a general of Timur's stature considered war elephants worth using against Mamluks, Ottomans and western Europeans suggests that they were no mere playthings. Of course the terror they inspired among troops not accustomed to them also made war elephants a valuable military asset.

Timur obviously had good information about the threat from elephants for he bore them in mind when establishing a defensive position on a ridge near Delhi on 10th December 1398. Interestingly enough, the site he chose was the same as that occupied by British troops during the Indian Mutiny four and a half centuries later. Detached forces of élite cavalry were also posted beyond each flank. Ahead of Timur's line a ditch was dug and then hidden, presumably with brushwood. Behind this was a wooden palisade strengthened with large shields or mantlets. Captured water buffaloes were tied together and tethered ahead of the lines in the knowledge that only these animals were strong enough to upset the advancing elephants. As a final defence Timur's men scattered large, three-pointed calthrops 'of new design' in front of the army. This was done secretly at night to avoid alerting the foe. The calthrops were barbed so that they stuck in the elephants' feet.

Instead of remaining behind the walls of Delhi and forcing Timur to conduct an expensive siege, the soldiers of the Sultanate came out to give battle. The noise they made was shattering and Timur's men subsequently admitted to being unnerved. Yet the battle was hardly ever in doubt. As soon as the enemy approached, a herd of terrified camels and buffaloes with bundles of blazing oil-soaked straw and cotton tied to their backs were driven towards the Indian army, making a number of elephants recoil into their own lines. Timur's main cavalry force at first advanced against the Indians but then wheeled around, as if their horses had been terrified by the elephants. This was, in fact, a common occurrence when untrained horses first met war elephants, but in this instance it appears to have been a stratagem to draw the elephants away from their protective infantry.

As the elephants pursued Timur's horsemen they stumbled upon the calthrops, which must have been arranged with safe avenues through which the horsemen could withdraw. The detached cavalry of Timur's right flank suddenly charged, forcing back the horse and infantry of the Indian left. Ferocious Indian attacks on Timur's left were beaten back, despite the fact that the Hindu cavalry fought particularly hard in savage close combat. Even the troops of the Sultan of Delhi's centre found themselves attacked in the rear by a detached force of Timur's cavalry. With their assaults defeated on left, right and centre the Indian army began to withdraw, the retreat turning into a rout as Timur's troops harried them to the gates of Delhi.

Ankara

Although Timur's armies often included infantry, they were still dominated by horse-archers who fought in the old Turco–Mongol tradition of the steppes. At least a third of the Ottoman troops that Timur faced in 1402 were, however, infantry – either Ottoman Turks or Slav vassals from the Balkans. The rest were quasi-feudal *sipahi* regular cavalry and Tatar or Turcoman auxiliary horsemen. Timur's force may also have been one hundred and forty thousand strong, compared to Bayazit's Ottoman army of only eighty-five thousand.

Bayazit, having been strategically outmanoeuvered, had a long march behind him, whereas Timur's men were fresh from besieging the nearby city of Ankara. Both took up defensive positions before the battle, Timur establishing a camp fortified with a ditch, piled rocks and a palisade. He had also taken the precaution of poisoning the wells along Bayazit's line of march so that the Ottoman troops and their horses were probably very thirsty by the time battle was joined. Sultan Bayazit formed his army behind the small Kizilçaköy stream and along a low spur of hills that ran from the flank of Mount Mire. These hills were held by élite Janissary and other infantry with the *sipahi* cavalry from Anatolia on their right flank and the *sipahis* of Rumelia (the Balkan part of the Ottoman Empire) on their left. Much of the Ottoman infantry, in

Three swords of less usual form from the Timurid period. (left to right) : Turkish or Turcoman, 15th century (Topkapi Mus., Istanbul); two Persian, 15th century (Topkapi Mus., Istanbul).

The Zafarmanah *was an idealized account of Timur's life. Here, in a copy made in Shiraz around 1434, the bloodthirsty conqueror is shaded beneath an attendant's parasol and wears the tall cap with upturned front brim typical of the Timurid period (location unknown).*

particular the Serbian vassals, were clad in heavy mail hauberks and fought with axes.

Timur again divided his army into seven divisions, as at Kunduzcha eleven years earlier, but here they were arranged in a different manner. Shah Rukh led the left flank, Mir'Ali the vanguard, Timur himself the centre, with his guards forming a separate division slightly to the rear. Abu Bakr led the right flank, which, together with a right flank reserve took up positions on the far side of the small river Çubuk. The main reserve stood between Timur's guards and the citadel of Ankara, which was still held by an Ottoman garrison.

The sequence of events in the battle of Ankara is open to dispute. Bayazit may have made the first move, sending the cavalry on his left to attack Timur's right flank. Or it could have been Timur who took the initiative, attacking the Ottoman left. One thing is clear, however. The Rumelian *sipahis* on this wing were either repulsed or began to waver, many fleeing the field. Timur's other wing then outflanked the Ottoman right and attacked Serbian vassal contingents forming the second line of the Ottoman right. Here Timur's men were either forced back by the Serbs or retreated in order to draw the enemy after them. Whatever the reason, the Serbs pursued Timur's cavalry but lost their own cohesion and fell back beyond their original position.

At this point Bayazit's Tatar auxiliaries changed sides, presumably having arranged this with Timur. They suddenly attacked the Ottoman left wing, where the Rumelian *sipahis* were already wavering. An Ottoman reserve force under Mehmet Çelebi charged the Tatars in an effort to retrieve the situation but Bayazit's left still gave ground. Turcoman contingents from regions of Anatolia that had only recently come under Ottoman rule formed the bulk of Bayazit's cavalry on the right flank. They now deserted as well, though it is unclear whether such a betrayal had been arranged beforehand.

With their cavalry falling back on both wings, the Ottoman infantry in the centre found their flanks exposed. The battle was clearly lost and while the Ottoman reserves now retreated to safety with the heir to the Ottoman throne, the Serbian cavalry also withdrew in good order. Meanwhile Sultan Bayazit led his own infantry guards to join the Serbian infantry and cover his son's escape. Six squadrons of cavalry from the shattered Ottoman right were already making a stand on a nearby hill known as Catal Tepe so it was to here that Bayazit and the remainder of his army retired. Timur's forces made repeated attacks upon this hill, though all were beaten back. As night fell Bayazit broke eastwards with about three hundred cavalry but his horse fell and he was captured, to be bound and dragged before Timur, who was by now playing chess in his tent with his son Shah Rukh.

Later sources state that Bayazit was held captive in an iron-barred cage, but this is probably a legend that grew out of Ahmad Arabshah's poetic description of the Ottoman Sultan having 'fallen into the hunter's snare and been confined like a bird in a cage'. Bayazit does, however, seem to have attempted an escape and thereafter was chained by night, travelling by day in a wagon or litter surrounded by a stout grille. Christopher Marlowe took the story a stage further by having Bayazit use these same bars to end the misery of his defeat:

> Now, Bajazeth, abridge thy baneful days,
> And beat thy brains out of thy conquered head,
> Since other means are all forbidden me,
> That may be ministers of my decay.

(I.V.i.)

Late 14th-early 15th century Iranian helmet (Hermitage Museum, Leningrad).

A Fragile Achievement?

Timur rose to power in one of the borderlands between steppe and sown, between the nomadic and settled worlds. Thus his state had a foot in both and one of the most obvious characteristics of Timur's empire was, in fact, its mixed character. Though the army may have been primarily of nomadic origin it was by no means entirely so, while most other aspects of the state, its government, organization, art and culture, seem to have been dominated by Islamic-Iranian traditions.

Even in terms of law Timur-i Lenk relied upon two systems, the traditional *yasaq* of Genghis Khan and the religious *sharia* code of Islam. Though Timur had revived the use of the *sharia*, this might have been for the sake of appearances, for he is said to have personally preferred the old Mongol *yasaq*. The behaviour seen in Timur's largely nomadic but still sumptuous Court was again a strange mixture of Islamic and pagan Turco–Mongol traditions. Only Christians were permitted to drink wine but Timur's courtiers regularly got drunk on other, non-grape alcoholic drinks. Though a nomad at heart and wreaking appalling damage to the fragile irrigation-based agricultural systems of his enemies, Timur was said to have been very interested in farming.

Promotion by merit lay at the very heart of Timur's military system, but the basic character of his empire was deeply conservative and emphasized that people should remain in the station to which they were born. This is very clear in the 'Institutions' that Timur addressed 'To My Children, Happy Conquerors of Kingdoms; To My Descendants, Sublime Sovereigns of the World'. This divided society into twelve classes: religious figures held the highest rank, followed by various government officers, military leaders and scholars, with foreign travellers at the bottom of the pile. Government was divided into four sections, dealing with provincial administration, the army, foreign affairs and the ruler's household. The Empire itself was divided into large *vilayat* provinces and smaller *tumen* districts, again reflecting both Mongol and Iranian

A 15th century Persian helmet of a particularly tall form. It was captured and re-used by the Ottoman Turks (Royal Armouries, Tower of London).

tradition. Each area was headed by three senior officials or governors responsible for soldiers, civilians and abandoned property.

In spite of the apparent sophistication of such administration, Timur's empire failed to take root even during the conqueror's lifetime. Despite his own advice to carry out conquests as if playing chess, as he claimed he had himself done, Timur's military career shows that he had to reconquer rebel areas again and again. Genghis Khan and his immediate successors rarely had to invade a country more than once, while Timur-i Lenk was never able to consolidate his hold over much more than Transoxania and his empire fell apart as soon as he died. His son, Shah Rukh, managed to re-establish control over some provinces and may, in fact, have been a more successful state builder than his more famous father. Timur never incorporated eastern Turkestan into his empire and though he defeated all his foes in battle he never broke the power of his most serious rivals, the Mamluks of Egypt and Syria, the Ottomans of Anatolia and the Balkans, nor even the Aq Qoyunlu and Qara Qoyunlu of eastern Anatolia. All revived immediately after Timur left the scene; the Aq and Qara Qoyunlu going on to erect their own more firmly rooted states on the ruins of Timur's empire.

Though some of Timur's descendants were brilliant rulers, fine generals and famous patrons of the arts, they were never able to build on Timur's fragile foundations. Yet his dynasty hung on until the end of the fifteenth century, making cities like Herat, Samarkand and Bukhara major centres of late-medieval Islamic art and culture. The last of them, Babur, fled first to Afghanistan and then to India, there to establish a more lasting dynasty – the Moghuls.

The basic weakness of Timur's empire compared to that of Genghis Khan seems to have been its absence of cohesion, its mixed and frequently mutually hostile elements and its lack of recognized dynastic legitimacy. In fact Timur never abandoned the fiction that he was merely fighting on behalf of a puppet Khan of the Chingisid Golden Family. Over and above these inherent weaknesses the whole central Asian and Middle Eastern world was changing militarily and politically. Empires based upon the strength of steppe-nomadic tribes were becoming anachronisms. Timur's would, in most respects, be the last to have any major impact. The balance of power was shifting, perhaps for the first time since the domestication of the riding horse, away from the nomads and in favour of the settled, agricultural and urbanized states that bordered the steppes.

Though Timur's empire might be counted a failure, its effect on its neighbours was considerable. The fragile civilization of the Golden Horde was smashed with the destruction of Sarai and Astrakhan. The western steppes fragmented into a series of successor states, of whom the Crimean Tatars were the most enduring. By allying themselves with the Ottoman Empire south of the Black Sea, these Crimean Tatars main-

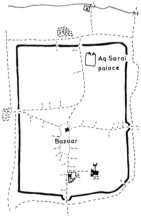

Shahr-i-Sabz (Kish) south of Samarkand, was Timur's birthplace and was the site of his enormous but now ruined Aq-Sarai palace. The little town also stood at an important trading crossroads and had a market (after G.A. Pugachenkova).

tained and even extended Turkish-Islamic power in the western steppes. In eastern Anatolia the Qara Qoyunlu went on to defeat Timur's sons and, to some degree, to pave the way for Ottoman expansion into eastern Iran and Iraq. The Christian kingdom of Georgia never recovered from Timur's depredations and fragmented into three or more separate states, which eventually fell under Muslim domination. Armenia had already lost its independence and now it became a battleground for other peoples' wars. Some local Armenian lords re-

The ruins of Timur's Aq-Sarai (White Palace) at Shari-Sabz, near Samarkand. Though now desolate, the monumental gateway still has much of the magnificent coloured tile decoration that made it one of the most magnificent buildings in Central Asia (Novosti Press).

185

tained a precarious semi-autonomous existence, while the head of the Armenian Church retreated from the old eastern Anatolian heartland to Etchmedzian, in what is now the modern Soviet Republic of Armenia. Muslim rule over northern India was severely shaken and the Sultanate of Delhi also fragmented, eventually enabling Timur's great-great-great-grandson Babur to build his own Mogul Empire on its ruins.

Two foot soldiers in one of a series of mysterious manuscript pages in the Fatih Albums. *As already noted, these strange miniatures are in a style that shows considerable Central Asian and even Chinese influence, but also includes elements from Armenia and other parts of the Middle East. Some scholars believe they were made in the very early Timurid period, perhaps during Timur's lifetime. The military styles they illustrate include both tall and low brimmed helmets, fabric-covered lamellar armour and a multitude of weapons from straight swords to pike-like infantry devices (Topkapi Lib., Ms. Haz. 2153, f.138v, Istanbul).*

The Timurid Dynasty of Transoxania

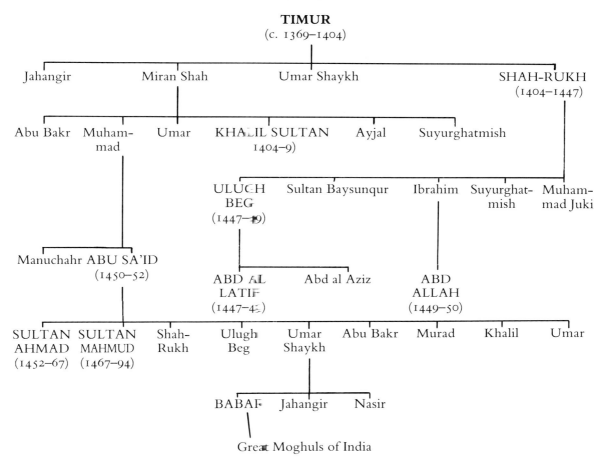

TIMUR
(c. 1369–1404)

- Jahangir
- Miran Shah
- Umar Shaykh
- SHAH-RUKH (1404–1447)

- Abu Bakr
- Muham-mad
- Umar
- KHALIL SULTAN 1404–9)
- Ayjal
- Suyurghatmish

- ULUGH BEG (1447–9)
- Sultan Baysunqur
- Ibrahim
- Suyurghat-mish
- Muham-mad Juki

- Manuchahr ABU SA'ID (1450–52)
- ABD AL LATIF (1447–4?)
- Abd al Aziz
- ABD ALLAH (1449–50)

- SULTAN AHMAD (1452–67)
- SULTAN MAHMUD (1467–94)
- Shah-Rukh
- Ulugh Beg
- Umar Shaykh
- Abu Bakr
- Murad
- Khalil
- Umar

- BABAR
- Jahangir
- Nasir

Great Moghuls of India

Bibliography

Alexandrescu-Dersca, M.M. *La Campagne de Timur en Anat-olie (1402)* (reprint) London, 1977.

Bouvat, L. *L'Empire Mongol (2ème phase)* Paris, 1927.

Brion, M. *Le Mémorial des Siècles: XIVe siècle, les hommes, Tamerlan* Paris, 1963.

Bruno, A. and Perbellini, G. 'La Fortezza di Herat in Afghanistan,' in *Architettura Fortificata, Atti del 1 Congresso Internazionale Piacenza-Bologna 18–21 Marzo 1976* Istituto Italiano dei Castelli, Rome, 1978.

Charmoy, F-B. *Expédition de Timoûr-i-Lenk (Tamerlan) Contre Toqtamiche* St. Petersburg 1835; (reprint) Amsterdam, 1975.

Clavijo (trans. Strange G. Le), *Clavijo, Embassy to Tamerlane (1403–1406)* London, 1928.

Gorelik, M.V. 'Oruzhie i Dospekh Russkikh i Mongolo-Tatarskikh voinob kontsa XIV v (Weapons and Armour of the Russians and Mongolo-Tatars of the late 14th century)' (in Russian) *Vestnik Akademi i Nawk SSSR* VIII, 1980, pp 102–3.

Hookham, H. *Tamburlaine the Conqueror* London, 1962.

Howarth, H.H. *History of the Mongols from the 9th to the 19th century. Part II, The so-called Tartars of Russia and Central Asia* London 1880; (reprint, no date) New York.

Lamb, H. *Tamerlane, The Earth Shaker* London, 1929.

Marlowe, C. (Cunningham, J.S. ed. & commentary), *Tamburlaine the Great* Manchester, 1981.

Minorsky, V. *The Turks, Iran and the Caucasus in the Middle Ages* London, 1978.

Morelli, G. 'Povero Bajazetto. Osservazioni su alcuni apetti dell'abbattimento tematico della "paura del turco" nell 'opera veneziana del Sei-Settecento' in *Venezia e i Turchi, scontri e confronti di due civiltà*, (Pirovano C. ed.) Milan, 1985.

Nève, F. Exposés des Guerres de Tamerlan et de Shah-Rokh, *Memoires couronnées . . . par l'Académie royale . . . de Belgique* XI, 1860.

Sanders, J.H. (trans. of Ahmad ibn Arabshah) *Tamerlane or Timur the Great Amir* London, 1936.

Schiltberger, J. (trans. Telfer, J.B.) *Travels and Bondage* London, 1879.

Chronology of Events

Other major events in world history shown in italics

1126	Nomadic Manchurian Chin conquer northern China; Chinese Sung rulers confined to south.
1162	Birth of Temüchin – Genghis Khan.
1171	*Saladin takes control of Egypt.*
1175	*Establishment of first Muslim Empire in India.*
1185	*Minamoto warlords supreme in Japan.*
1187	*Saladin defeats Crusader Kingdom of Jerusalem at battle of Hattin.*
1204	*Fourth Crusade captures Byzantine Constantinople.*
1204–6	Temüchin unites Mongol tribes.
1206	Temüchin becomes Great Khan of the Mongols; adopts name of Genghis Khan.
1211	Genghis Khan invades China.
1212	*Muslim power in Spain broken at battle of Las Navas de Tolosa.*
1215	Mongols capture Beijing (Peking).
1215	Birth of Kublai Khan
1215	*King John of England signs Magna Carta.*
1220–21	Genghis Khan invades Muslim Transoxania.
1221	Genghis Khan defeats last Khwarazmshah of Iran at battle of River Indus.
1222–4	Mongol army marches through southern Russia.
1227	Death of Genghis Khan.
1229	Ögatäi becomes Great Khan.
1234	Mongols overthrow Chin rulers of northern China.
1236–41	Mongol campaigns across eastern Europe.
1242	*Alexander Nevsky, leader of Novgorod, defeats Crusader Teutonic Knights at battle of Lake Peipus; subsequently made Grand Prince of Russia by Mongols.*
1243	Mongols defeat Saljuqs of Anatolia.
1246	Küyük becomes Great Khan.
1250	*Death of German Emperor Frederick II; collapse of Imperial authority in Germany and Italy.*
1251	Möngke becomes Great Khan.
1256	Hülegü becomes Mongol ruler of Iran.
1257–8	Mongol invasion of Vietnam.
1258	Hülegü conquers Baghdad; execution of last effective Abbasid Caliph.
1260	Hülegü conquers Syria.
1260	Mongols defeated by Mamluks at battle of Ayn Jalut.
1260	Kublai becomes Mongol Great Khan.
1261	*Byzantines recapture Constantinople from Crusader 'Latin Empire'.*
1264	Kublai Khan establishes Mongol Yüan dynasty of China.
1265	Death of Hülegü.
1273–4	Kublai Khan's first invasion of Japan.
1277	Mongol invasion of Burma.
1279	Kublai Khan conquers Sung rulers of southern China.
1281	Kublai Khan's second invasion of Japan.
1285–8	Mongol invasions of Vietnam.
1287	Second Mongol invasion of Burma.
1292–3	Mongol expeditions to Indonesia.
1294	Death of Kublai Khan.
1336	Birth of Timur-i-Lenk – Tamerlane the Great.
1337	*Start of Hundred Years War between France and England.*
1341	Approximate time of appearance of 'Black Death' plague in Asia.
1346–51	*'Black Death' ravages Middle East and Europe.*
1351	End of Mongol Il-Khan dynasty of Iran.
1358	*Ottoman Turks established in Europe.*
1369	Timur becomes effective ruler of Transoxania.
1370	Mongol rulers expelled from China.
1381	Timur conquers and destroys Herat.
1385	Timur captures Tabriz.
1387	Timur captures Isfahan and Shiraz.
1389	*Ottoman Turks defeat Serbians at battle of Kossovo*
1393	Timur occupies Baghdad.
1395–6	Timur's second campaign against Mongol Golden Horde in southern Russia.
1396	*Ottoman Turks defeat Crusaders at battle of Nicopolis.*
1398–9	Timur invades India.
1400–1	Timur's invasion of Mamluk Syria.
1402	Timur defeats Ottoman Turks at battle of Ankara.
1404	Death of Timur-i-Lenk.
1453	*Ottoman Turks capture Constantinople-Istanbul.*
1478	*Ivan III of Russia throws off Mongol suzereinty.*
1492	*Muslim Kingdom of Granada conquered by Spanish rulers. Columbus reaches Americas.*
1497–9	*Vasco da Gama sails from Europe to India and back.*
1500	Establishment of Safavid dynasty in Iran; effective end of Timurid dynasty in Afghanistan.
1634	Death of last nominal Mongol Great Khan.

Index

Page numbers in *italics* refer to illustrations.